My Bookstore

My Bookstore

Writers Celebrate Their
Favorite Places
to Browse, Read, *and* Shop

. . . .

Edited *by* Ronald Rice *and*
Booksellers Across America

Introduction *by* Richard Russo
Afterword *by* Emily St. John Mandel

Illustrations *by* Leif Parsons

BLACK DOG
& LEVENTHAL
PUBLISHERS
NEW YORK

Published by
Black Dog & Leventhal Publishers, Inc.
151 West 19th Street
New York, NY 10011

Distributed by
Workman Publishing Company
225 Varick Street
New York, NY 10014

Manufactured in the United States of America

Cover design by Nicole Caputo
Interior design by Cindy Belinfanti

Cover illustration by Leif Parsons

ISBN-13: 978-1-57912-910-1   5038 2380 12/12

h g f e d c b a

Library of Congress Cataloging-in-Publication Data available on file.

The editor and publisher wish to thank the booksellers and authors who have given their time, energy, and creative ideas to the making of this book. A special thank you also goes to Carl Lennertz, the American Booksellers Association, Regional Booksellers Associations, ABFFE, and the Association of American Publishers for their guidance and support.

Contents

Introduction

The first great bookstore in my life wasn't really even a bookstore. Alvord and Smith was located on North Main Street in Gloversville, New York, and if memory serves, they referred to themselves as stationers. I don't remember the place being air-conditioned, but it was always dark and cool inside, even on the most sweltering summer days. In addition to a very small selection of books, the store sold boxed stationery, diaries, journals, and high-end fountain and ballpoint-pen sets, as well as drafting and art supplies: brushes, rulers, compasses, slide rules, sketch pads, canvas, and tubes of paint. The shelves went up and up the walls, all the way to the high ceiling, and I remember wondering what was in the cardboard boxes so far beyond my reach. The same things that were on the shelves below? Other, undreamed-of wonders? Alvord and Smith was a store for people who—though I couldn't have articulated it at the time—had aspirations beyond life in a grungy mill town. It was never busy.

Because she worked all week, my mother and I ran our weekly errands on Saturday mornings, and Alvord and Smith was usually our first stop. There, I'd plop down on the floor in front of the bottom two shelves where the children's books were displayed: long, uniform phalanxes of the Hardy Boys and Nancy Drew mysteries as well as the lesser-known but, to my mind, far superior Ken Holt and Rick Brandt series. I can still remember the incomparable thrill of coming upon that elusive number eleven or seventeen in my favorite series, the one I'd been searching for for years, now magically there, where it hadn't been the week before, filling me with wonder at the way the world worked, how you had to wait to the point of almost unbearable longing for the good stuff in life. (It would take five decades and the emergence of Amazon.com, with its point-and-click, to vanquish that primal wonder.) Just as mysterious as the appearance of the books themselves was where the money to pay for them came from. My mother was forever reminding me that money didn't grow on trees, at least not on ours, and if I had my eye on some toy gun at Woolworth, she'd say that this was what my allowance, which I saved dutifully, was for. Otherwise, I'd have to wait for my birthday or Christmas. But if I was a dollar short for a book, she'd always find one in her purse (how? where?) so I wouldn't have to wait the extra week, during which time some other boy might buy it.

Coming out of Alvord and Smith, blinking in the bright sunlight, you could see all the way down Main Street, past the Four Corners, to South Main, where the gin mills and pool hall were. Outside these stood dusky, shiftless, idle men, flexing at the knees and whistling at the pretty women who passed by. Occasionally my father was among them. Much later, when I turned 18, legal drinking age in New York back then, I would join him in those same dives. Like the stationery store, they were cool and dark and mysterious, and for a while I preferred them, though I never really belonged. That's what I'd felt as a boy, sitting on the floor at Alvord and Smith, touching, lovingly, the spines of books: Here was a place I belonged.

Fast-forward twenty years. I'm now an assistant professor of English, married, with two small daughters, living in New Haven, Connecticut, teaching full-time and trying desperately to become a writer. My wife and I are nearly as poor as my mother and I had been back in Gloversville. We live in an apartment in a neighborhood where experience has taught me to put a sign in both the front and rear windows of our old beater, telling the neighborhood thieves the car is unlocked so they won't smash the windows. There is nothing of value inside, I write, the radio and speakers having been boosted long ago. But of course, that's a lie. A university professor, I forget books in the car all the time. Sometimes when I come out in the morning, it's clear that someone's been in the car, but the books are right where I left them. No takers.

Once a month or so, on a Saturday night, if we've managed to save up, my wife and I go down to Wooster Street and have an inexpensive—though expensive to us—meal in an Italian restaurant. On the way home we always stop at Atticus Bookstore, where, miraculously, the early-morning edition of the Sunday *Times* awaits us. How can this be? Tomorrow's newspaper, today. Atticus is a clean, well-lighted place, one of the first bookstores in the country to understand that books and good coffee go together. It's stretching our budget after splurging on a restaurant meal, but we buy coffees and find a tiny bistro table and take books down off nearby shelves to examine. Books. By this time I've published a few short stories, but nothing so grand as a book. From where we sit I can see the R's, the exact spot where my book will sit if I ever publish one. I may, one day, rub spines with Philip Roth. In a way, it's almost too much to contemplate. In another, well, I can't help feeling I belong here, just as I did on the floor of Alvord's in Gloversville.

Many people love good bookstores, but writers? We completely lose our heads over them. We tell each other stories about them. We form lifelong, irrational attachments to our favorites. We take every independent bookstore's failure personally. Surely there's something we might have done. We do not hate e-books purchased online—well, OK, some of us do—but we owe our careers, at least my generation of writers does, to the great independents, so many of them long gone now. Those that remain gamely continue to fight the good fight, even as customers increasingly use their stores as showrooms, their employees for their expertise, and their sales-tax dollars to fund their schools, but then go home and surrender to the online retailer's chilly embrace. They point and click, and in this simple act, without meaning to, undermine the future of the next generation of writers and the one after that. Because it's independent booksellers who always get the word out (as they did for me). With their help, if they're still around, great young writers you don't know about yet will take their place on shelves next to their heroes, from Margaret Atwood to Emile Zola, just as I have somehow managed to do. Without them, well, I shudder to think.

I'm an old fart, of course, more at home with paper and print than touch screens, and yes, I agree with those who argue that in the end it's more about the message of books than the medium of their delivery. A good book read on an electronic device is better than a bad one between hard covers. But to me, bookstores, like my first one, remain places of genuine wonder. They fill me with both pride and humility when I come upon my own books in them. Bookstores, like libraries, are the physical manifestation of the wide world's longest, best, most thrilling conversation. The people who work in them will tell you who's saying what. If you ask, they'll tell you what Richard Russo's up to in his new one, but more important, they'll put in your hand something you just *have* to read, by someone you've never heard of, someone just now entering the conversation, who wants to talk to you about things that matter.

If you haven't been in a good bookstore in a while, the book you now hold in your hand will welcome you, lovingly, home.

Richard Russo, 2012

Martha Ackmann

The Odyssey Bookshop
SOUTH HADLEY, MASSACHUSETTS

When I moved from Missouri to western Massachusetts in 1979, everyone I met had the same two recommendations: You have to try the carrot cake at Chanticleer's, and you have to open an account at the Odyssey Bookshop.

They were right. Chanticleer's carrot cake *was* delicious—just the right combination of sweet and spicy. I wish that unpretentious coffee shop was still around, but—like so many things—it dissolved into a procession of dull establishments whose names no one could remember.

But the Odyssey?

The Odyssey flourished.

Thank goodness.

The two-story white frame building is the heart and soul of South Hadley, Massachusetts, and a survivor to boot. Not only has the bookstore stood the test of time and marketplace, but it also persevered through two catastrophes that nearly killed it.

I came to western Massachusetts to study Emily Dickinson and attend graduate school in the region's lovely Pioneer Valley—home to Amherst, Smith, Hampshire, and Mount Holyoke colleges and the University of Massachusetts. I bought books at the Odyssey for my literature classes and found myself spending Saturday afternoons in the shop's lower level, sitting on the floor next to shelves of Victorian novels. Back then the Odyssey arranged its books by publisher—an eccentric system, but not unlike bookstores in the United Kingdom. Many of the books I was reading were published by Penguin—all in inexpensive editions with distinctive orange spines. As a marketing device, Penguin color-coded its editions: green for mystery, blue for biography, red for drama, orange for fiction. I loved the Odyssey's oddball organizing scheme. It made me feel like an insider when I cracked the code and descended into the lower level in pursuit of all those orange spines.

But nothing made a book lover feel more like an Odyssey insider than getting to know Romeo Grenier. Romeo, as everyone called him, was the bookshop's owner—a formal-looking gentleman who spoke in low, precise tones and wore a cravat. The book-organizing scheme was his idea and perhaps a nod to all things British. Romeo was an Anglophile through and through: He took tea at four o'clock and thought *Middlemarch* was the best book ever written. Some store patrons even mistakenly thought Romeo was British; he seemed so proper and—well—starched. But nothing could have been further from the truth.

Romeo came from a family of lumberjacks in the backwoods of Quebec. In 1923, he immigrated to the United States, settled in Holyoke, Massachusetts, and found a job cleaning out the cellar of a local pharmacist. Working for Simon Flynn was a stroke of luck. Over the years, Romeo moved up—literally from the cellar. He helped out in the store, learned the pharmacy trade, and studied for his license. He also took a liking to the boss's daughter. Ten days after Pearl Harbor, Betty Flynn and Romeo Grenier eloped and eventually bought Glesmann's pharmacy in nearby South Hadley. Romeo and Betty sold toothbrushes and shampoo and added a small shelf of books at the front of the store. Romeo couldn't help himself with the books; he already had a personal habit of buying a book a week. As Glessie's book space expanded, more shelves were added, and soon the copies of Thackeray overtook emery boards and Old Spice. Although a pharmacy by name, Glesmann's became the town's literary gathering place. Students and faculty from across the street at Mount Holyoke College congregated at the pharmacy's round table and booths for lively discussions about art, politics, and literature. The College community became so fond of Glessie's that at reunion time, students swung by as if to visit their favorite nook in the library. Romeo Grenier, one professor observed, "resolved to be the most cultivated apothecary since John Keats."

In 1963, the inevitable came to pass. The cough syrup lost and books won. At the urging of Mount Holyoke, Romeo opened the Odyssey Bookshop, a few doors down from Glesmann's. Students and faculty helped pack the pharmacy's stock of books and carry them down the sidewalk to the new shop. For two decades, Romeo, Betty, and the shop's dedicated and knowledgeable staff ran the Odyssey Bookshop, making it not only a popular bookstore but a tourist destination as well. Vacationers who stopped in nearby Amherst during foliage season or parents who visited children at the local colleges came by the Odyssey for a chat with Romeo. Customers loved it when staffers hand-selected books for them and explained why they thought the choice was a good fit. For a region that claimed Emily Dickinson, Robert Frost, and Richard Wilbur as locals, the Odyssey was the very embodiment of what residents valued: Literature was as important as breathing.

> *For a region that claimed Emily Dickinson, Robert Frost, and Richard Wilbur as locals, the Odyssey was the very embodiment of what residents valued: Literature was as important as breathing.*

That's why it hurt so badly when the unthinkable happened.

In 1985, Joan Grenier, Romeo and Betty's daughter, was in the final months of finishing her degree in history at the University of Massachusetts. With graduate school in mind, Joan sat in an auditorium that December morning with hundreds of other students poring over entrance exams. She was so concentrated on her work that she jumped when an exam official called her name at the end of the testing session. There was an urgent message. A friend, who didn't want Joan to drive home alone past the store, waited at the door. The Odyssey was on fire.

For the next months, Joan worked alongside her 75 year-old father to reopen the bookshop near the spot of the original Glesmann's. The College pitched in too. The theater department offered their set-design talents to decorate the store. Students and faculty filled out stock cards for incoming books. Grateful customers found themselves using the phrase "phoenix rising" to praise the Odyssey's remarkable recovery. But five months later, just as the tulip trees were beginning to bud around campus, a second fire consumed the store and the shops around it. Romeo didn't think he could go through the ordeal of salvaging and reopening another bookstore. Joan stepped in. "I probably didn't know what I was getting into," she admitted. Graduate school went out the window, and over the next year, Joan, the shell-shocked Odyssey staff, and the Mount Holyoke community once again worked to reopen the shop, this time in the hall of the nearby South Hadley Congregational Church. Months later, when a new shopping complex rose from the ashes of the second fire, the Odyssey was the first business to open its doors in the Village Commons opposite the college.

Joan took advantage of the unenviable clean slate before her. She expanded the retail space to nearly 4,000 square feet, organized author readings, instituted a First Editions Club, a Shakespeare Club, and a children's book club. The Odyssey became the spot not only for new books, but also for used and bargain books, and for unique gifts for bibliophiles. When social media became a powerful force in business, the Odyssey created a full-service website for customers to order physical books and e-books. Now the largest independent bookstore in western Massachusetts, the Odyssey hosts over 120 literary and cultural events a year, from Rachel Maddow to Alexander McCall Smith and Stephen King to Rosalynn Carter.

Betty Grenier died in 1989, and Romeo, the "most cultivated apothecary," followed a decade later in 1997. Romeo's portrait hangs prominently on the Odyssey's wall, along with photographs of Glessie's and the store's two fires—a reminder of the indomitable shop's past.

As for me, I finally read all those orange-spined Penguin novels and got up off the Odyssey floor. Like my friend, Joan, my career took a turn that I wasn't quite expecting. After years of teaching at that college across the street, I turned to writing narrative nonfiction books. There's nothing I love more than spending time in archives or traveling to a town where I've never been and interviewing someone I've never met before. When my first book was published, *The Mercury 13: The True Story of Thirteen Women and the Dream of Space Flight*, Joan called me with ideas for the book launch. I'll never forget the night of my first reading. C-Span *and* my entire softball team showed up, a reader presented me with a baseball cap from Sally Ride's inaugural flight, and Joan introduced me, making friendly jokes about our mutual age and my peripatetic career from Emily Dickinson scholar to space chronicler.

Later that evening, after the wine and those wonderful pastries that always seem to show up at Odyssey events, Joan helped us load the car for the trip back home. It was nearly ten o'clock, practically everyone was long gone, and the Odyssey—still all lit up—looked like a beacon against the dark New England mountains. When I looked back at the store, I couldn't help thinking about Romeo's beloved books crowding out the Old Spice, and I couldn't help feeling grateful for how this wonderful shop has enriched my life. As Joan grabbed a box of party supplies and carried them to the curb, she yelled back at the lone shopper still browsing the new fiction shelves. "Could you watch the store for a minute?" she asked. As the former grad student who loved sitting among the Odyssey shelves, I relished the joy in the customer's reply. "I'd be happy to," she said. "I've been waiting my whole life to be surrounded by books."

MARTHA ACKMANN is a journalist and author who writes about women who've changed America. Her books include *The Mercury 13* and *Curveball: The Remarkable Story of Toni Stone, First Woman to Play Professional Baseball in the Negro League*.

Isabel Allende

Book Passage, CORTE MADERA, CALIFORNIA

I am old-fashioned. I believe that one should have a personal doctor, a dentist, a hairdresser, and, of course, a trusted bookstore. I wouldn't think of buying books at random, without my bookseller's recommendation, no matter how good the reviews may be. Fortunately, when I immigrated to the United States twenty-five years ago—because I fell in lust with a guy whom I eventually forced into marriage—I ended up living in Marin County, California. Almost immediately, I found the perfect bookstore. However, to find the proper doctor, dentist, and hairdresser took some time. Book Passage, an independent bookstore in Corte Madera, is only ten minutes away from my home, and it rapidly became my refuge and the extension of my office. The owners, Elaine and Bill Petrocelli, welcomed me with open arms; not because I was a writer, but because I was a neighbor.

Since 1987 I've started the tours for each of my books at Book Passage, the favorite place for authors on tour because they get an enthusiastic audience and are treated like celebrities, even when they are not. I have had the opportunity to attend readings by great writers, politicians, scientists, stars, gurus, and many more whom I would never have met elsewhere. I have enjoyed fabulous meals at the Cooks with Books events organized by the store in classy restaurants. Due to the requirements of my job, I am a nomadic traveler. Before any journey I visit the store's great travel section, where I get maps and information, including, for example, where to buy beads in Morocco or where to get the best pasta in Florence.

Book Passage is much more than a store for me: It's the place where I meet friends, journalists, students, readers, and fellow writers; it's where I have my mailbox and an open account for me and my family to buy and to order all our books. As soon as my grandchildren learned to dial a phone they would call the store to order kids' books and then call again if they didn't get them the next day. For years, they were present every Sunday at story hour, and they were the first ones in line, wearing the appropriate outfits, for the fun midnight Harry Potter parties.

Willie Gordon, my husband (yes, the same guy I met a quarter of a century ago), retired as a lawyer and decided to become a writer. I couldn't believe that he intended to compete with me but he persisted. At Book Passage he attended the Annual Mystery Writers Conference and opted for crime novels as the most appropriate genre for him, not because he has a particularly mean streak, but because he knows a lot about law and forensics. He took writing classes and read the books suggested by the staff. To my dismay, Willie has written five novels in the last few years, translated into several languages. Nothing pleases Elaine Petrocelli so much as to see a student at her conferences return a couple of years later to teach as a published author. Willie is just one of many cases. Elaine is the first person to read Willie's manuscripts and review them. Bill helped Willie to publish in the States.

The buyer at Book Passage selects novels, audiobooks, and reader's copies for me. I don't even bother to choose my own reading material! She gave me *The Kite Runner* by Khaled Hosseini and *The Madonnas of Leningrad* by Debra Dean and *Cutting for Stone* by Abraham Verghese in manuscript, long before they were published. With the help of the store's knowledgeable staff I have researched sixteen books, including several historical novels and—go figure!—a treatise about aphrodisiacs. Before writing a trilogy for young adults I attended the store's Children's Writers Conference, and later, so that I could learn what kids really like to read, they organized a yearlong kids' book club.

This bookstore is the cultural soul of a large community. It's the place to take writing classes, learn languages, attend conferences, participate in book clubs and speakers' series, and, if you are a teenager, Twitter-talk (whatever that is). Elaine and Bill Petrocelli work with schools, community organizations, and restaurants, they do fund-raising for many causes, and they have a partnership with Dominican University so that students can receive credit for classes and conferences. Their clientele is so loyal that Amazon and the chains have not been able to put them out of business, and, let me tell you, they have tried.

The only place as comforting as a friendly bookstore is probably your grandmother's kitchen. The sight of shelves packed with books of all kinds, the smell of printed paper and coffee, and the secret rustle of the characters that live in the pages warm up any heart. I go to Book Passage to pass the time, to read, to gossip, and to lift my spirit. But I have also gone there to share my sorrow, as I did

> *The only place as comforting as a friendly bookstore is probably your grandmother's kitchen.*

when I was grieving for my daughter's death. At the store, amidst all those books, many of which were painful memoirs, I realized that I had to write Paula's story, as others had written about their broken hearts before me. During that terrible year of mourning I spent many hours at Book Passage writing by hand, sipping tea, and wiping my tears, supported by my friends at the store who kept me company while respecting my privacy.

Sometimes, when I have a fight with Willie, or when I feel particularly nostalgic, I fantasize about going back to live in Chile, but I know it will never happen—because my dog can't travel so far, and I am not willing to lose Book Passage.

ISABEL ALLENDE is the best-selling author of nine novels including *The House of the Spirits*, *Inés of My Soul*, *Portrait in Sepia*, and *Daughter of Fortune*.

Rick Atkinson

Politics & Prose Bookstore, WASHINGTON, D.C.

Sometimes in our lives habit becomes ritual, and ritual then becomes superstition. For me, such a transmutation began in October 1988, when I typed the last line to my first book, a group portrait of the U.S. Military Academy class of 1966. The final scene is set in the West Point cemetery, where so many of those killed in Vietnam are buried, and the book ends with the academy chaplain reflecting: *I loved these men. I loved these men with all my heart.*

Now what? I asked myself. What do authors do when they complete a manuscript? I pushed away from my writing desk, tugged on a pair of sneakers, and headed down Utah Street before turning right

11

on Nebraska Avenue to cross Connecticut Avenue. There in a drab retail building was a hole-in-the-wall shop that showed promise of becoming a neighborhood institution in Washington, D.C.—Politics & Prose Bookstore. This, I thought, is what writers should do when they finish writing: They should seek the company of other writers, at least through the books they have written. And what extraordinary new writings could be found at Politics & Prose that fall—Gabriel García Marquéz's *Love in the Time of Cholera*, Stephen W. Hawking's *A Brief History of Time*, Tom Wolfe's *The Bonfire of the Vanities*.

I would repeat that homely routine by trotting down to Politics & Prose upon finishing my second book in the fall of 1992. Then, fearful of jinxing myself by deviating from the ritual, I did it again, in 2000, and in 2003, and in 2006, and, most recently, on February 3, 2012. For me, a book feels incomplete without that capstone visit to the bookstore. Browsing among the shelves is the equivalent of typing *The End* on the last page, and less trite.

My family and I had moved into Washington's Chevy Chase neighborhood not long after Politics & Prose arrived. A remarkable woman named Carla Cohen opened the shop in the fall of 1984, selling the season's big books—Robert Ludlum's *The Aquitaine Progression* and an eponymously titled memoir by automobile executive Lee Iacocca—but also Barbara W. Tuchman's *The March of Folly*, Eudora Welty's *One Writer's Beginnings*, and a curious biography by local author Bob Woodward titled *Wired: The Short Life & Fast Times of John Belushi*. A Baltimore native who had worked as a city planner and a federal housing official, Carla was savvy, gregarious, and forceful, with avowed ambitions of running "the sort of bookstore in which I liked to spend time." Another local writer and store patron, Ron Suskind, later observed, "There are hundreds of writers who imagined Carla as their ideal reader. She is a tribal leader, like Abraham."

Carla had placed a newspaper ad for a store manager and instead found a business partner in Barbara Meade, who had returned to Washington after several years on the West Coast. Barbara knew books, and she knew retail. The two women, both voracious reading mothers soon to turn 50, complemented one another perfectly: the effusive, opinionated Cohen and the reserved, meticulous Meade. Barbara later described their collaboration: "I, the cat, walk unobtrusively into a room and sit quietly on the periphery, intently watching everything that is going on. Carla, the dog, joyfully bounds in and jumps on everyone." Among their few business disagreements was the name of the store, conceived by Carla as somehow emblematic of Washington. "I think that's a terrible mistake," Barbara told her, but the name stuck.

. . .

For the first few months, the staff consisted of the two owners and a part-time clerk. Within a year, a second sales associate was added, and by 1989 Politics & Prose had a half-dozen employees. That summer the store moved across the street to more spacious digs with a wider show window. A policeman tamed the traffic on Connecticut Avenue as neighbors mustered to carry 15,000 books from the old shop to the new. I was among them, hauling cartons of that season's big sellers: Salman Rushdie's *The Satanic Verses*, John Irving's *A Prayer for Owen Meany*, David Halberstam's *Summer of '49*, A. Scott Berg's *Goldwyn*, Simon Schama's *Citizens*. For many of us, the experience of lugging best sellers and backlist titles, obscure poetry anthologies and must-read classics that somehow we'd never read, embodied the store's slogan, printed on tote bags and T-shirts: "So many books, so little time."

In keeping with the owners' concept of a bookshop as both a community center and a tabernacle of ideas, Politics & Prose had been among the first stores in Washington to sponsor author events, nurturing personal and, usually, amiable conversations between writers and readers. The store had started with about five events each month, often using D.C. journalists and other hometown scribblers to draw a crowd; by 1989, that had doubled to ten a month. The store became, as *The New York Times* observed, "a virtually mandatory stop on the book tours of authors who write about politics." In truth, an affluent, educated clientele with catholic interests seemed keen to support all substantive genres, from literary fiction and poetry to narrative nonfiction and topical journalism. "Like the children of Lake Wobegon," the Politics and Prose staff liked to say, "all of our customers are above average."

> *"Like the children of Lake Wobegon," the Politics and Prose staff liked to say, "all of our customers are above average."*

Soon nearly every night of the calendar was booked with events, along with many afternoons. For each author given the podium at P&P—whether a Nobel laureate or a first-time local novelist—three or four others were necessarily turned away. For writers like me who have been lucky enough to speak at the bookstore repeatedly, the encounter with an inquisitive, mettlesome audience can be revelatory, deepening an author's understanding of his own work and giving new meaning to that old aphorism, "I write so I know what I think."

The store would expand again, spreading its wings and adding a coffee shop and a bigger children's section. Threats to the business came and went, including Crown Books and Borders. Other threats came and lingered: Barnes & Noble, Amazon.com, Costco pallets, the digital book. Several fine local competitors vanished, including the likes of Olsson's Books and Records. The existential struggle faced by independents around the country seemed ever more dire.

Still, knock wood, P&P continues to thrive by dint of a smart, enthusiastic staff and fiercely loyal customers. In the summer of 2010, Carla and Barbara, then both 74, announced an intent to sell the store after more than a quarter-century in business together, not least because Carla was sick; she died of cancer that October. Her surviving spouse, David Cohen, and her surviving partner, Barbara, could not have chosen better, more committed new owners, Bradley Graham and Lissa Muscatine, both old friends and colleagues of mine from our days as young reporters at *The Washington Post*.

Even as Brad and Lissa adapt to the new world of e-books and e-readers, Politics & Prose remains nothing less than the bricks-and-mortar incarnation of traits we cherish in Western civilization: learning, tolerance, diversity, civility, discourse, inquiry, lyricism. For those of us lucky enough to live down the street or around the corner, it's a port in the storm, a daydreaming hive, a bastion. How fortunate we are to be patrons, browsers, espresso sippers, guest speakers, neighbors. And when you finally finish that novel or memoir or meditation on the body politic, wander in for a little self-indulgent browsing. If you love words, it's the place to be.

RICK ATKINSON is the author of six books of narrative military history, including *The Long Gray Line*, *An Army at Dawn*, and *The Day of Battle*.

Wendell Berry

Carmichael's Bookstore, LOUISVILLE, KENTUCKY

I am hardly a materialist, but I am not an immaterialist either. The material, tangible presence of the things of this world is important to me, and I understand its worth increasingly as human experience becomes increasingly immaterial. A "text" existing only on a screen and in the mind is not, to me, a book. To me, it is not enough that a book is thought realized in language; it must also be language further realized in print on paper pages bound between covers. It is a material artifact, a thing made not only to be seen but also to be held and smelled, containing language that can be touched, and under-lined with an actual pencil, with margins that can be actually written on. And so a book, a real book, language incarnate, becomes a part of one's bodily life.

One's bodily life, furthermore, is necessarily local and economic. And so to the life embodied in books must be added the life of bookstores. One can order a book from some distant place and receive it by mail. I confess that I sometimes do that, and so I know by experience that to do so is to forsake one of the most decent and significant literary pleasures, and it is to subtract from the purchased book what may be one of the best parts of its own life. I still own books that have remained alive and dear in my thoughts since I was a boy, and a part of the life of each one is my memory of the bookstore where I bought it and of the bookseller who sold it to me.

> *I still own books that have remained alive and dear in my thoughts since I was a boy, and a part of the life of each one is my memory of the bookstore where I bought it and of the bookseller who sold it to me.*

Also, to order a book is to "buy a pig in a poke"—and so to submit oneself to the possibility of a bad deal. The book one receives may be so poorly made and so ugly as to be overpriced even as a bargain. If you are a book lover, if you care about the quality of books as made things, the value of your life is reduced by such a book.

And so when I am in Louisville, Kentucky, I like to visit Carmichael's Bookstore. Sometimes I go to buy a certain book. Sometimes I go with no purpose but to see what books may be there and to visit a little while with the people who work there. The place has the quietness, the friendliness, the smell, and the tangibility that a bookstore ought to have. It is a fair incarnation of the manifold life of books. To go there and find a book I didn't expect or didn't expect to want, to decide I want it, to buy it as a treasure to take home, to conduct the whole transaction in a passage of friendly conversation—that is in every way a pleasure. A part of my economic life thus becomes a part of my social life. For that I need actual people in an actual place in the actual world.

Long live tangibility! Long live slow communication!

WENDELL BERRY is the author of more than 50 works of fiction, nonfiction, and poetry and has been the recipient of numerous awards and honors, including the National Humanities Medal. Berry's latest works include *New Collected Poems* and *A Place in Time*, the newest addition to the Port William series since 2006.

Jeanne Birdsall

Broadside Bookshop, NORTHAMPTON, MASSACHUSETTS

E very writer needs her own personal bookstore. When our strug-
gles with sentences make us lonely and cranky, where better
to spread the gloom than a place dedicated to a product we may or
may not ever finish, especially if we keep leaving the house when
we should be working? Besides, reading is the best excuse for not
writing—thus we are always in dire need of books, lots and lots, piles
and more piles. There can never be too many books.

To get to my own bookstore, I walk down my street, cross two
parking lots, and slip around the corner. And there it is—Broadside
Bookshop, with a striped awning outside, and inside floor-to-ceiling

> *...reading is the best excuse for not writing—thus we are always in dire need of books, lots and lots, piles and more piles.*

shelves on every wall plus extra shelves placed enticingly here and there, full of books that pull at me like sirens on the rocks, if one can think of essay collections as sirens. Yes, I say, as long as they are written by the likes of E.B. White and Anne Fadiman. Or the mysteries across the aisle from the essays—these are certainly sirens, particularly the British ones. Reginald Hill! Sophie Hannah! Or the biographies cheek-to-cheek with the mysteries, or the NYRB Classics tucked in behind the essays, or the fiction section, naturally, because who isn't in thrall to fiction?

When I manage to survive all that, there is still the wild allure of Broadside's children's section. Copies of my own books are there to be admired—one never tires of that—or to console for lingering too long on the shelves, sad and unsold. On my more shameless days, I sit on the floor to sign my books, hoping that a curious child or its parent will ask if I'm the author and I can answer yes, I am, then bask in the sunlight of their amazed praise. Unless the praise isn't lavish enough or, worse, they confess to preferring Kate DiCamillo's books to mine, and then I wish I'd stayed home to watch old episodes of *Buffy the Vampire Slayer*.

The people who keep Broadside running smoothly are a brilliant and charming bunch, all of whom know a great deal about books, and just as much about handling the local writers who wander in too often. They do a lovely job of tolerating me and for that I adore them, especially...but no, I can't pick and choose. Let me say, however, that a certain employee—I'll call him Steve—once sang "Putting It Together" to me from behind the register, and for that I'll always be grateful. Thank you, Steve.

And thank you, Broadside Bookshop, for being my very own. Here's to books, forever and always. Amen.

JEANNE BIRDSALL writes for children. Her *New York Times* best-selling novels about the Penderwick family have collected many honors, including the National Book Award for Young People's Literature, and have been translated into 22 languages. She lives in Northampton, Massachusetts, and spends too much time at Broadside Bookshop, around the corner from her home.

Rick Bragg

The Alabama Booksmith, BIRMINGHAM, ALABAMA

First, before I proceed, this has to be said. There are no cats here, and I am so grateful for this I could just bust. No tabbies, no blue-eyed Himalayans or snooty Siamese or butt-naked Egyptians. I do not mind cats in the wider world and appreciate their contributions in rodent eradication, and have even tolerated them on my lap for long seconds at a time, because women love cats like peach ice cream. I just do not believe cat detritus and paper products are good things to have in proximity to each other, and anyone who has ever tried to read a *Cannery Row* or *Lonesome Dove* that smelled of a neglected litter box would agree with me, unless of course their wife was a cat person and then they would almost certainly lie about it like, well, a dog. The hard truth is books absorb cats, but there are no cats in the Alabama Booksmith in Homewood, Alabama, and that is almost enough, in a literary world lousy with people who think having a damn cat in the stacks or on the counter or lolling in the window is somehow quaint and almost by God *required*, to proclaim it a great bookstore, at least until someone lets in a calico. I do not think that will happen. Everybody who knows proprietor Jake Reiss knows he don't have no time for cats, and usually even for lunch. Now that I have that off my chest, we can move on....

. . .

He has the whole world pretty well fooled.

Listen to this description of Jake Reiss, from his local paper, *The Birmingham News*:

"Now, a big night for the proprietor...is going home to his Southside townhouse, popping a frozen Lean Cuisine in the microwave, pouring himself a glass of cabernet sauvignon and sitting down at the kitchen table to read one of the 200 or so books he will devour over the course of a year."

The fact is, while he would not want the whole world to know it, the man likes to shoot some dice.

Some men hunt. Some men fish. Some men buy million-dollar motor homes with horns that play

> *Jake Reiss is winning, because he is making a dollar by making good books and authors available to people who love to read and love the people who make it a pleasure, and because, late in his own life, he fell in love with books himself.*

the first bars of "Rammer-Jammer, Yellowhammer." Some men, though none I know, attend the opera. Jake Reiss, for relaxation, likes to feel them rattling bones, and let 'em go.

Who else but a gambler would turn his attentions from a lifetime success in the tailoring business and, in his fifties, without even shouting, "Come on, baby needs a new pair of shoes," open a *bookstore*? The odd thing is, he won.

He won, in this time of woe, in this age in which children seem mostly interested in playing games with their thumbs, when reading is a quaint notion from the dusty halls of antiquity, when public funding for libraries is being scraped to the white bone, Jake Reiss is winning, because he is making a dollar by making good books and authors available to people who love to read and love the people who make it a pleasure, and because, late in his own life, he fell in love with books himself. He really is a voracious reader—all kinds of good stories—and, in part because so many people said it couldn't be done, found a way to make the old-fashioned notion of it all, of books on paper, pay the light bill and a damn sight more. Maybe the reason I say Alabama Booksmith is my favorite is because Jake Reiss gives me hope that my craft will endure. I guess that is as good a reason as any, and more poignant than that stuff about cats.

Some people here in suburban Homewood, people with no gray in their hair and no concept of a world without smartphones, think Jake has always been in the book business, has always been a kind of free-spirited bibliophile with two inches of gray ponytail jutting from the back of his head, who sits surrounded by signed first editions of Pat Conroy and has Salman Rushdie on speed dial. But he used to be respectable. He used to run a tailoring house for some of the most influential people in the South, men who had to at least look respectable, CEOs and government men and high priests (football coaches). He made suits for Bob Hope, and for senators. He still likes to tell me, "I could build a suit that would even make you look good."

I guess the reason I have wasted so much time talking about the proprietor instead of his shop, his wares, is because Jake Reiss is the store. He does his own heavy lifting. He flings book cartons around like a young man. He hauls a thousand pounds at a time to readings and book events in his somewhat worn, magenta-colored Chevy van from the Reagan administration (the first one, before he and Nancy were regularly consulting the spirit world), always taking twice as many as any sane person would think he would need. But Jake is a gambler, and you never know when someone will need an extra 700 copies of a book in an auditorium that seats 215.

The bookstore itself, at the risk of hurting his delicate feelings, looks a little bit like the place in Piedmont, Alabama, where my mama used to go have her fortune told. Let us just say the Homewood Historic Commission will never come knocking at his door. Overhead, for Jake, is the moon and stars above. He has prospered in the book business for more than two decades, moving from a place in the somewhat tonier Highland Avenue section of Birmingham to this current location, this unassuming (a kinder word) wood-frame building off the highway that is a little tricky to find even on your third trip here. It is a throwback to an older time, or at least that is how it first appears. The ceiling is low, even on a short man, and the floor gives a bit. The shelves are made of honest wood and go floor to ceiling with history, the classics, poetry, mystery.

I feel at home here, and I am honored that my books are on these shelves, but as I sat down to describe why I liked the place, I found myself not with a list of things it is but things that it is not. It does not have comfy chairs, or cozy reading areas, but nor do I have to try and think over the roar of construction of a double-chocolate frappacin... frabucin...oh, to hell with it. There are, as near I can tell, no charging stations or other portals for laptops, though I am sure there is a drop or two somewhere around. I am pretty sure there is no Wifi...Wyfy... you know what I mean. You do not bring a laptop to Jake's, though you can read a newspaper, standing up.

Nor is he working hard to be quaint. There is not a single rocker here, unless he has one in the back for naps. But then I do not think the man even sleeps. There are just books, in a store where you are more likely to find Henry Louis Gates, Jr., than a pop-up book about some monkeys jumping on a bed (though, for the record, I have that one).

But what you do not see, at least at first glance, is the secret to its survival. "We've pretty much converted this joint to all signed copies," Jake told me, "and every year has been bigger than the last for twenty-two years. Our Signed First Editions Club is one of the largest, if not *the* largest in America, and we've been fortunate enough to have Philip Roth, John Updike, Richard Russo, Salman Rushdie, Geraldine Brooks, and so forth sign for our members…customers in all fifty states and fourteen foreign countries. We've hosted President Jimmy Carter, David Sedaris, Anne Rice, Christopher Hitchens, Ken Burns, Wendell Berry, and hundreds of others." He does not mean to sound like a salesman, like a man working it, he just can't really help it. When he made pants, he wanted to make good pants and sell them for as much as he could get and then sell some more. He sees no reason why the book business cannot be conducted in a similar fashion, without apology. I do not know where he finds the energy. When I am his age, I will look for a soft place to lie down.

He is so enthusiastic about his new business, he gets carried away. Introducing me, once, at a book event, he described in passionate detail how I bodily carried an elderly woman and her wheelchair into a crowded auditorium. I remembered it as a lovely young woman in one of those inflatable ankle casts. There was, however, carrying involved.

The people who make the money decisions in this craft recognize that enthusiasm and send people down here on more than just promises. They sell books at his store—lots of books. "When we request that big-time writers visit and New York publicists are a little reluctant about sending their superstars here, we remind them that Alabama not only produces the magnificent Mercedes and rockets that go to the moon, but author events that are out of this world, also. We usually partner with one of the city's nonprofits like Children's of Alabama, The Literacy Council, local NPR and public television…. We regularly produce sales that are tops on each author's tour."

I do not have the heart to tell Jake that we here in Alabama have not actually helped heave anyone to the moon in quite some time, but he is just so damn happy about it I hate to smudge up another good lie.

I think he is good for this craft, and his store is good for it. There are plenty of other places to sit in an old chair and sip some designer coffee and peruse the *Oxford American* or recharge your I-Whatever or check your email or pet a damn cat.

RICK BRAGG is the best-selling author of works of nonfiction, including *All Over But The Shoutin'* and *Ava's Man* and *Prince of Frogtown*, and winner of the Pulitzer Prize. He is a Harvard University Nieman Fellow, and Professor of Writing at the University of Alabama. He is also a winner of the James Beard Award and many other national writing awards.

Charles Brandt

Chapter One Bookstore, KETCHUM, IDAHO

Ernest Hemingway returned to live in Ketchum, Idaho, in 1959 with an unsettled heart. His beloved home in Cuba, his private paradise where he lived when he won the 1954 Nobel Prize, was soon to be confiscated by Castro.

So here he was, compelled to live in his second-favorite paradise on earth, compelled to live in a house on a hill on a bench above the Big Wood River in the high desert mountains, endless mountains with near-constant blue skies, invisible healing air, and world-class skiing in the adjacent celebrity magnet of the Sun Valley resort. It was in that resort's Lodge twenty years earlier in suite 206 that he had worked on *For Whom the Bell Tolls*, with his Silver Creek fishing buddy Gary Cooper in mind to play the hero. And it was in that house on the bench above the river where, in rapidly failing health, he felt compelled to live no longer and took his life with a shotgun in July 1961.

The Hemingway tradition flourishes in Ketchum with suite 206 still for rent in the Lodge, with the famous photo of Hemingway sitting in suite 206 at his typewriter blown up and hanging in the tourist office, with his marked grave alongside his wife Mary's at the Ketchum Cemetery, with a memorial bust in Trail Creek and an annual Hemingway conference, and with locals who knew him, like Rob the computer guy, who, at 4, was hoisted up by the great man for a hug.

Hemingway's granddaughter, the actress Mariel, isn't the only celebrity to make a home in Ketchum. If you know what you're looking for you can spot a celebrity pumping gas, shopping for groceries, or dining out. But the celebrities who live here value their privacy, and locals and tourists alike obey an off-limits energy field.

There is one special place, however, where you're likely to encounter a relaxed celebrity chatting amiably, with that off-limits energy field temporarily shut down. It is in Ketchum's oldest bookstore, Chapter One. As local architect Dale Bates puts it: "There is no community without a common resource."

I've hung out in lots of bookstores in my 70 years, including the unique Chartwell Booksellers off Madison Avenue in New York City, dedicated to Winston Churchill, jazz, and baseball; and the well-mourned Madison Avenue Bookshop, where one was apt to see Sam Shepherd getting advice from Gary the manager, and Barbara Walters on the cashier's line loaded with volumes of pleasure and enlightenment, asking if John Updike is really any good. But until I first set foot in Ketchum in 1985 I had never seen a bookstore so crucial to the well-being of a community as Chapter One. And our community itself knows that its "common resource," more than the store itself, is the store's owner and manager, Cheryl Thomas, a spiritual icon for decades in our valley.

> *...until I first set foot in Ketchum in 1985 I had never seen a bookstore so crucial to the well-being of a community as Chapter One.*

Cheryl and her right hand, Meg, who both read voraciously, can help you find the perfect book, including a first edition of *A Farewell to Arms*, even if all you want to do is hold it in your hands. At the same time, Cheryl can help you find the perfect dog from one of her sweet causes, the Animal Shelter. She not only fund-raises for the Hunger Coalition, but she tries to see to it that those in need have money for dog and cat food. She can help you locate a ticket to the usually sold-out Sun Valley Writers' Conference, where visiting writers like David McCullough will stop by the store for a chat. Cheryl works tirelessly on the Hemingway Elementary School Used Book Fair and at the annual Sun Valley Wellness Festival. Her collection of cutting-edge healing and energy books is unrivaled. Cheryl promotes and encourages local authors, whether self-published or well published. And yes, local authors are part of the celebrity world of Ketchum, a town of 2,700 residents.

One winter evening a few years past I came in the back door and headed to the front, where I could see in an aisle the back of a large man chatting amiably about Kosovo. I hung back and listened. He seemed to know what he was talking about. When his chat ended I could see it was ambassador and author Richard Holbrooke, who definitely knew a thing or two about the Balkans. On any Sunday a local such as singer-songwriter Carole King might be doing a signing of her memoir. The next Sunday it just might be a local ski legend.

Cheryl has got me delivering inscriptions like Domino's delivers pizza. If she has a customer who wants to buy one of my books, she'll call and ask me to stroll over and do a personal signing and chat a spell. Once, on call, I arrived to chat with a married couple. Kathleen Chamales had seen me speak at the Sun Valley Writers' Conference and wanted a book for their son. Her husband, Jerry, is an Entrepreneur of the Year recipient who had sold his business and was looking for something new to do. They owned the old Steve McQueen property. As we chatted I learned they were friends of Hollywood power lawyer Jake Bloom, who also has a home in our valley. We hit it off right there at Chapter One, and soon they bought an option on my book *I Heard You Paint Houses* (mafia-speak for murder), which is now in development at Paramount in a deal handled by Jake Bloom for a movie to be called *The Irishman*, to be directed by Martin Scorsese, starring Robert DeNiro, produced by their production companies and with a cast including Al Pacino and Joe Pesci. Oh, did I mention Cheryl is a matchmaker?

In his acceptance of the Nobel Prize, Hemingway famously observed that "Writing, at its best, is a lonely life." If Hemingway were alive, Cheryl would make sure that he came by the store, if only to chat a spell. It would be good for him.

CHARLES BRANDT is the author of the true crime bestseller, *I Heard You Paint Houses* and a novel based on major crimes he solved through interrogation, *The Right to Remain Silent*. He lives in Lewes, Delaware and Sun Valley, Idaho, with his wife, Nancy, and has three grown children.

Douglas Brinkley

BookPeople, AUSTIN, TEXAS

The summer sun pounded mercilessly down without a single layer of cloud to snuff out the UV radiation. In the scorching streets of Austin, it was dry and hot, with no gusts of wind to make the 104° Fahrenheit temperature any less suffocating. The heat was starting to make me irritable. Why wasn't I in some nirvana like the Hamptons or the Upper Peninsula of Michigan? That's when I directed my little Volvo to the only true oasis in this cowtown-cum-hipville: BookPeople.

Toward the back of BookPeople, near the bright-blue neon sign that advertises "Coffee Shop," is a gallery wall showcasing the wares of local artists. While the paintings rotate periodically, a blown-up, twelve-block comic strip by G.C. Johnson titled "An Illustrated History of BookPeople" is permanent. The installation—created in a style that could be called Early Keith Haring—documents the backstory of Texas's largest independent bookseller from its modest beginnings in 1970 as Grok Books, in a small house near the Original Oat Willie's, to the current 24,000-square-foot store conveniently located across the street from Whole Foods headquarters. Peace Corps veteran Philip Sansone bought Grok Books in 1978. Today, high-momentum bibliophile and aesthetician Steve Bercu, the CEO, continues to offer an avalanche of book titles, available both in the shop and online.

It seems to me the BookPeople is the hub of everything good and wise in progressive-minded Austin. It's the ideal escape zone in a city growing too fast. I've roamed far and wide visiting America's independent bookstores as both a consumer and an author on tour. I consider myself of expert caliber in judging bookstores, and so an eminently reliable character witness for BookPeople's excellence.

The store's name emanates from Ray Bradbury's dystopian novel *Fahrenheit 451*. At a crucial moment in Bradbury's story, the "Book People" take the banned books into the hills, determined to memorize them before the books are destroyed. I also like the store's name because it is egalitarian in spirit, like Howard Zinn's *A People's History of the United States* and Carl Sandburg's *The People, Yes*. What Bercu envisioned—and achieved—was a community meeting place where no matter what you were seeking, from politics to philosophy to poetry and beyond, that it would be stocked on the shelves. At any given time you'll find over 300,000 titles, instantly available. This isn't a strip-mall box store or Amazon warehouse, but the Town Hall of Weird Austin, bursting with personality, from *Moby-Dick* T-shirts to embroidered dish towels to offbeat candies at the cashier's desk.

The marvel is that nothing is ever rushed at BookPeople. Consumers purhasing products is not necessarily pramount to Bercu. Many visitors enter and fall into a browsing zone like none other in Texas. If Austin is the town that made the term *slacker* popular

> *This isn't a strip-mall box store or Amazon warehouse, but the Town Hall of Weird Austin, bursting with personality...*

(due to local filmmaker Richard Linklater's 1991 movie, *Dazed and Confused*), then let it be said that BookPeople is where browsing earned its golden spurs as an American pastime. I often loiter in the store for hours, flipping through merchandise, scribbling down notes from a book I don't want to buy. Never has one of the store's 125 employees reprimanded me. Loitering is part of the atmosphere. Clerks encourage me to graze both book-filled floors. Loitering is part of the flavor. Whenever I get blue, I take a drive to Lamar Boulevard, park my convertible, and seize the universe of knowledge on its shelves.

When I was a graduate student at Georgetown University, I used to visit Social Safeway. Like a scene from Allen Ginsberg's "A Supermarket in California," twenty-somethings would meet each other while pushing their shopping carts down the aisles, poking the pork chops and bananas while people-watching. Likewise, there are so many mating rituals taking place in BookPeople that it should be designated a National Wildlife Refuge.

Not that I'm part of such a dance anymore. My wife, Anne, and I regularly visit BookPeople to shop for our three children. And what an extravaganza of choices it is for little people. There is a huge tunnel house for the kids to play in as we shop. There is a children's reading area, complete with purple chairs. A blue stage is set up for performers. Storyteller events are a regular feature. Painted in huge yellow box letters on a backdrop next to a drawing of a friendly book-reading bat (a favorite mammal in Austin because the bats have a massive colony in town) is a sign that reads "What happens in Storytime... Stays in Storytime." Some happy employee actually set up displays of children's books in an imaginative fashion; for example, "things that go..." offers every flight of both fancy and reality imaginable on trains, boats, trucks, tractors, et al. If elementary school libraries were half this fun, America's literacy rate could be higher than those of Norway and Denmark.

We hear a lot of noise about independent bookstores dying in America. It's a sign of the hard times. But BookPeople—cosmic as a Willie Nelson concert at the Backyard followed by a breakfast burrito at Magnolia Café at midnight—remains the heart and soul of Austin. It's achieved institutional status.

DOUGLAS BRINKLEY is a professor of history at Rice University and a contributing editor at *Vanity Fair*. *The Chicago Tribune* has dubbed him "America's new past master." Six of his books have been selected as *New York Times* Notable Books of the Year. His book *The Great Deluge* won the Robert F. Kennedy Book Award. He lives in Texas with his wife and three children.

Liam Callanan

Boswell Book Company, MILWAUKEE, WISCONSIN

This is not a story about my friend, raised by a single mom, who got himself into an Ivy League School and then Teach for America after, only to discover that what he really wanted to do was medicine and only to realize there was no money for medical school. So he went to the overnight shift at UPS, which paid for him to go back and take all the undergraduate pre-med courses he needed, and then the Air Force, which paid for medical school. But no service, delivery or armed, was going to pay for his wedding, so he went back to his mom, and she figured it out, and no one who was there will forget the day: a beautiful ceremony, and an elaborate, raucous reception right downstairs in the church basement. "I always say," my friend proudly, if apocalyptically, explained that day, "that if the universe came to an end, and civilization needed restarting, my mom could do it, just her and a couple of friends, they could remake the entire world."

I feel the same way about Daniel Goldin, proprietor of my bookstore, Boswell Book Company in Milwaukee. And the apocalyptic reference seems entirely warranted: Not a day goes by that someone doesn't declare as nigh the end of publishing, much less bookstores. What this avenue of American industry needs, then, is not so much someone interested in selling a few books, but rather someone interested in selling a few books (and maybe a few gift items from a carefully curated stock) as a means of saving civilization.

Let the word go forth, then: The world has a future, and it starts in Milwaukee on an avenue named Downer.

I first met Daniel, and Boswell Book Company, when they were both something else. At that time, Boswell Books was part of a small, beloved local chain with a national reputation, Harry W. Schwartz Bookshops, and Daniel was its buyer. But not long after its legendary leader, David Schwartz, passed away, the store found itself facing its own demise. (Again: to write about bookstores is an inescapably eschatological activity.) Daniel stepped in, though the better verb is *stepped up*, pouring his own savings, and that of his extended family, into a little brickfront store on Downer Avenue a few blocks south of the teeming campus of the University of Wisconsin at Milwaukee, and a few blocks west of my house.

For the nonnative Milwaukeean, it's a sign of assimilation when you no longer find the name "Downer" ironic or funny or ominous, and a sign of true civic pride (not to mention literary engagement) when you start to refer to the bookstore no longer as "Boswell's" but "Daniel's."

As in: "Can we go into Daniel's, Dad?" As in: This is my daughter, just 3 at the time, whom I have brought to the Starbucks that neighbors Daniel's store just after dawn one Saturday morning. As anyone who frequents a weekend-dawn Starbucks knows, there are four categories of people there at that hour: doctors heading in to the hospital, hipsters who never went to bed the night before, people prepping for LSATs who wish they'd been out with the hipsters, and 3-year-olds and their fathers.

Oh, and there's one other category: bookstore owners.

Because just as soon as I start to explain to my toddler that there's a difference between coffee shops and independent bookstores—and it's not just that people will happily overpay for a cup of coffee that costs just pennies to make though prefer to pay pennies for a book that costs thousands to produce, but also that, generally speaking, people really need a cup of coffee at 7 a.m., whereas no one really needs a book until mid-morning, earliest, which is why Starbucks is open and Daniel's isn't—Daniel appears.

"Hi," he says, and addresses my daughter by name.

She responds in kind: "Daniel," she says, "I want a book."

My wife's college roommate was an author's daughter. The author was Calvin Trillin and among the many gifts he gave his children—and, by extension, my children—was this rule: If they ever found themselves together in a bookstore, he would buy them whatever they wanted. The rule, importantly, did not extend to toy stores or ice cream shops or pony stables. Just bookstores, just whatever they wanted. We've raised our children this way, and it is wonderful. It wears on the credit card, true, but children's books tend to be less expensive, and the benefit of having your kids think there's little difference between a bookstore and a public library—well, like our credit card company says: priceless.

"Of course," Daniel says, and takes my little girl by the hand, and they find the keys and unlock the store. He locks the door behind us: Indeed, he doesn't open for hours. That doesn't mean, of course, that he hasn't already been here in the back office toiling; the coffee-swilling surgeons, the test-preppers, the all-night hipsters: None of them put in anything like the hours Daniel does.

My daughter, blissfully unaware that any of this is extraordinary, takes her time weaving toward the back of the store, through the best sellers and bookseller picks, the calendars, philosophy, history, humor, the glass case of vintage bandage tins,* before careening left into the spacious, brightly windowed area that is the children's section. Thereupon she finds the largest, pinkest book about princesses that she can reach and promptly settles in to read it.

It's 7:35 a.m.

I apologize to Daniel for the intrusion, and he just laughs—he always laughs, which is one of the many things I've learned from him about books, bookselling, and surviving the looming end of anything: always laugh—and he says: Is there a better way to start a Saturday?

My daughter looks up, smiles, and then goes back to reading, and that's our answer: No, there is no better way.

I thank Daniel for going the extra mile, and then we both laugh, because he's gone about an ultra-marathon's worth of extra miles during his proprietorship—in some cases physically, as when he drove with me to a friends-of-the-library benefit reading I was doing an hour or so southwest of Milwaukee. The library had suggested I bring my novels to sell; I asked Daniel for some stock and he immediately offered to come along and handle the sales.

The reading went fine, though I went hoarse. It was an older crowd and they were not shy about asking me to speak louder. And louder. They were a bit shy, though, about purchasing books. This is not an uncommon phenomenon at library events. Unlike my daughters, library patrons—especially devoted friends—understand very well the difference between libraries and bookstores. At the library, the books are free. We sold two copies. I bought one for the librarian

---

*Of *course* there is a case of vintage bandage tins, as Daniel once explained on his blog: "It was the mid-1980s when I realized that the ubiquitous bandage tins I saw everywhere would soon disappear. There was a distinct trend away from metal in all things packaging. The bandage tin, however, is a beautifully designed container. Homage has been paid in the retro Accoutrements tins filled with bacon- and pickle-shaped bandages. And yes, I have a few of these. I love place and I love retail. When you think of cities, you might think of baseball teams or landmark buildings. I think of old retailers. I saw the regional food and drug chains consolidating at a rapid pace, and I panicked…and started collecting. The march against the bandage tin reminds me of what the soothsayers pronounce now for the book. And the examples I have remind me of the somewhat lost vibrancy of regional retailing. All of which explains a bit why I chose to open an independent bookstore in Milwaukee…."

who had invited me. And then I bought another for her mother, who had been looking on expectantly.

I dropped Daniel at his house fairly late that evening, not wanting to think how much this trip had cost him—if not him financially, at least his bank of free time—and how early he'd be appearing at the store the next day. I thanked him as profusely as I could; he just laughed and rolled his eyes and said, "Of course."

Of course Daniel opened the store for my daughter at dawn. Of course he'd driven hours into the night with me to sell two books. Of course he will be the one to save American bookselling, if not Downer Avenue. Because Daniel loves not only books, but bookselling. He loves retail. He can discuss the floor plan of almost any department store with all the excitement and attention to detail John Madden lavishes on a football field, or the floor plan of his own store: what goes best on a table or on a shelf, what his first shoplifted book was (Ian K. Smith's *The Four Day Diet*), and whether or not it's wise to stock robots.

On this last point—on just about every point—we agree; I once hosted a local reading by the poet Matthea Harvey. Just minutes before the event, I was tipped off that Matthea was a robot fan (what poet from Brooklyn isn't?), and so dashed over to Daniel's and double-parked on Downer. I ran inside and called out, "I need a robot!" Approximately sixty seconds later, I had a small, blue, marvelously movable wooden one in my hand. Matthea, needless to say, received the robot with great joy and installed him beside her at the podium.

In the end, the world doesn't ask much of booksellers—just to have a well-chosen selection of books and robots on the shelves, be open at all hours, be ready to travel all distances, be able to laugh at every obstacle that presents itself, whether they are dieting shoplifters, librarians' mothers, or literary doomsayers. Which is to say, we ask everything of them. Save this date for my reading. Save this pink princess book for me. Save us all.

My friend from college is a doctor now. The marriage has lasted. So, too, my memories of that happy evening in that church basement,

> *In the end, the world doesn't ask much of booksellers—just to have a well-chosen selection of books and robots on the shelves, be open at all hours, be ready to travel all distances, be able to laugh at every obstacle that presents itself...*

all whipped up out of nothing by his brave mother, who died, far too young, not too long ago.

I'm not asking Daniel to throw me a wedding reception anytime soon, but now that my friend's mom is gone, he should know that I'm looking to him to restart the world should it ever, however briefly, spin to a stop.

I sometimes wonder if our civilization did end a while back—it sure feels like it—and whenever I despair that it won't recover or that it's falling further, my daughter and I take a short walk to Daniel's honey-lit windows on Downer, gaze inside and realize, with relief: Here is the world.

LIAM CALLANAN is the author of the novels *The Cloud Atlas* and *All Saints* and has purchased something in every bookstore he's ever entered.

Ron Carlson

Changing Hands Bookstore, TEMPE, ARIZONA

You've got to know Tempe in the old days when it wasn't a tony theme park of franchise restaurants and shiny shops, but the main street was a funky collection of old storefronts which would come and go and that bright blue lake was not a lake but a dry ruined desert riverbed that flooded twice a year, three times if you were supposed to be somewhere in a hurry, and Arizona State was more like a big sprawling community college than the force-ten university it is today. If you climbed the butte there east of Main, you would have seen desert to the east, desert and farm fields to the south, Phoenix through the haze to the west, and the beginning scattered

> *People in a good bookstore use their feet differently; there is never a full step as we are reluctant to drift too fast past the anthologies of fiction, some familiar some new.*

cluster of Scottsdale on the north. It was a challenging and fully desolate place. Where was harbor? Where was oasis? Who would stop and make a mark in such a place? What I'm saying is that in those days, I was always—every single time—heartened and braced by walking into the sweet fixture of Changing Hands, new and used books, there on Main Street a block and a half from Monti's Mexican restaurant.

Stepping through the door changed the world; here was art, solace, a thousand hardback conversations on display on the homemade shelves and tables and some on the stairway that went up the weird mezzanine. Our pace changed. People in a good bookstore use their feet differently; there is never a full step as we are reluctant to drift too fast past the anthologies of fiction, some familiar some new. I was never in the store without running into someone I knew, literally, not just their books. Downstairs in the used books there was a spine on every shelf that we had at home. Invariably I would bump into Gayle Shanks or Bob Sommer who founded the place, and rather than trying to sell me this book or that, they always inquired about how my writing was going and if the book came out in January could we do a reading in the spring? Evenings we attended the readings there, great tiered circles of our friends and students and strangers, some sitting up on that second story. Pinna Joseph was always around with a good book in each hand and the same question: How's the writing going? It was a place absolutely full of books but which made me feel powerfully that there was a place for one of my own. When I read there in 1994 from a book of stories, I said impromptu what I meant: that this outpost was for me the heart of the village, and so—even having moved—it has remained in many ways the heart of Tempe.

Now the store has moved south in Tempe to the lovely new space, pressed to move by all the things Americans do to their hometowns; they put bricks in the sidewalks and six coffee shops and the price of beer goes up two dollars. Three. I'm in Changing Hands twice a year still, even though I live in California. Last time I nabbed the brilliant biography *Hemingway's Boat*, and I saw an old student, Cindy Dach, who I've heard is now even part owner. We talked in the stacks, trying to make eye contact despite the thousand books calling from behind. She asked me how my book was coming along. It is a special place, that store, and the spirit abides.

RON CARLSON lived in Arizona for 20 years and now directs the Programs in Writing at University of California at Irvine. His most recent novel is *The Signal*.

Kate Christensen

WORD, BROOKLYN, NEW YORK

A bookstore is a physical place, of course. But it can also be a state of mind.

I live in Portland, Maine, but my local bookstore is in Greenpoint, Brooklyn. It's the bookstore equivalent of a long-distance love affair. When I buy books, I order them from WORD. Whenever I'm back in my old neighborhood, I stop in to say hello to whoever's there—Christine, Stephanie, Jenn, or Jami—and I hang out and browse the shelves and sign copies of my books, and I feel at home again, as if I'd never left.

WORD is the only bookstore I've ever claimed as "mine." When it first opened, I lived right around the corner. The first time I went in, I saw they'd stocked all my books and asked if I could sign them. I ended up staying and hanging out for an hour and a half. Then I popped in as often as I could; I almost always walked out with a book or two or three. It was impossible to resist temptation: They always seemed to have in stock whatever books I was currently craving.

Since it opened, I've had all my book parties there, the way you have important, occasional parties in your family's house. After my marriage split up, when I still lived in Greenpoint and was feeling shell-shocked and exposed, I could always go into WORD and feel safe from any judgmental friends of my ex-husband's. If I

> *It was impossible to resist temptation: They always seemed to have in stock whatever books I was currently craving.*

ran into them there, it was my turf: They had to back off and leave me the hell alone, because Christine Onorati, the owner, has my back. (This is true: She told me if I ever committed a crime, she will hide me in her basement. I thanked her and promised to try never to put her in that position.)

When I was researching my most recent novel, *The Astral*, which is about a real building a block or two away from WORD, I asked around the bookstore one day for contact information for former and current tenants of the actual Astral Apartments. Three people in the store that day, it turned out, had lived there or knew someone who had. I whiled away a couple of hours asking questions and collecting stories. I never set foot in the real Astral. I got all my information at WORD.

I love WORD for other reasons, beyond the personal: It is a truly great bookstore. Everyone who works there is well read and passionate about books, young and energetic, influential in the world of books, and friendly. They're involved in the immediate community of Greenpoint as well as the wider community of writers: They have a basketball league and a dating board where you can meet people based on what kind of books you like. They throw readings that feel more like parties—festive, inclusive, and fun, often with wine and pizza or cookies, sometimes with music. I'm sad they're so far away. I keep hoping they'll open an outpost in Maine.

KATE CHRISTENSEN is the author of six novels, including, most recently, *The Astral*, as well as *The Epicure's Lament* and *The Great Man*, which won the 2008 PEN/Faulkner Award for Fiction. She frequently writes reviews and essays for many publications, including *The New York Times Book Review*, *Bookforum*, and *Elle*. She lives in Portland, Maine, where she is working on a new book, *Blue Plate Special: The Autobiography of an Eater*. Her food blog can be found at katechristensen.wordpress.com.

Carmela Ciuraru

The Community Bookstore, BROOKLYN, NEW YORK

F or starters, there's Tiny. It might seem odd to pay tribute to a bookstore by way of its formidable resident cat, but Tiny is no ordinary cat. He takes the notion of a charming curmudgeon to unprecedented levels, inspiring fear, awe, and affection in customers and employees alike. To disturb him for any reason is to do so at your own peril. Usually I stand at a respectful distance, resisting the impulse to address him as "Sir." Yet I can't imagine my favorite local bookshop without his inimitable presence.

The Community Bookstore has been a treasured resource in my Brooklyn neighborhood, Park Slope, since 1971. It's the borough's oldest independent bookstore and among the oldest in New York City. I love that the store sits between a toy shop and a liquor store. How great is that? It's also on the same busy block as a bank, a dry cleaner, a health food shop, and a grocery store, which means that I walk by all the time. I can rarely resist the urge to stop in, even when I have no money to spend and no time to browse. The selection of books is exquisite, and the people who work there are friendly and smart.

Like the best independent bookstores, the Community Bookstore does much more than sell a rather addictive—to bibliophiles, anyway—product. It's a kind of sanctuary. I can't count the number of times I've come in while having a stressful day, typically caused by frustration over my ability (or inability) to write. On such days, having abandoned a fruitless session at my desk, I'm welcomed like an old friend. When they ask how I'm doing, I can suddenly reply, "Great!" and the answer is honest.

After chatting about the books we've read recently, or what's going on at the bookstore, or the antics of my amazing dog, Freddy, I return home feeling encouraged, ready to get back to work. (Freddy often visits the store with me, and he is always rewarded there with treats, praise, and lavish attention.) The staff is probably unaware of their cheering effect; they treat everyone well. It doesn't matter whether you're coming in for the first time or the hundredth. You will feel as though your presence is valued. If you go to a chain bookstore, the experience is quite different and mildly depressing. Once, when I inquired at a giant chain store about the availability of *A Moveable Feast*, I was asked, "How are you spelling Hemingway?"

At the Community Bookstore, the employees are passionate and

> *Once, when I inquired at a giant chain store about the availability of* A Moveable Feast, *I was asked, "How are you spelling Hemingway?"*

knowledgeable readers. This is an algorithm-free space. Books are recommended by actual people who are eager to talk with you about the kinds of books you like and then offer suggestions. No one will judge you harshly for your literary preferences. You can further your literary education, as I have, by discovering "writers' writers" such as Mavis Gallant. But if you step up to the counter with more commercial fare, like *The Hunger Games*, you won't be met with a dismissive glare. At least one staffer has probably read whatever book(s) you have in your hand. Their tastes are eclectic. And I must add that one of the store's most impressive virtues is its relentless support of local authors. Lucky me: I am one of them.

Browsing there is a great pleasure, because you're likely to find another appealing book (or two, or three) while trying to track down the one you're hunting for. Of course, the best sellers and new-release titles are prominently displayed, but so too are graphic novels, oversized art books, literary journals, and beautiful blank notebooks, and there are shelves dedicated to smaller presses such as Europa Editions and Dalkey Archive.

The store takes its name seriously in its devotion to the community. There's a Frequent Buyers Club to reward loyal customers. The store donates generously to local schools. It will deliver books for free, anywhere around the neighborhood. And the staff will gift-wrap books, also free of charge. Whenever I wrap my own books, the results are dramatically different. In fact, the results are disturbing. My wrapping job always appears to have been attempted by a small child lacking fine motor skills; or a person fleeing the scene of an armed robbery; or a monkey; or just someone who uses too much tape and has never been taught how to cut in a straight line.

Stephanie Valdez and Ezra Goldstein, who bought the Community Bookstore in 2011, have done everything right. They are fiercely devoted to sustaining the neighborhood's literary culture. Not long before becoming an official co-owner, Stephanie told me about some of her hopes and plans for the store. It would change, but not too much. It would get cosmetic improvements, like new hardwood floors, but nothing fancy. She wanted the store to retain its wonderful character. I was excited by her ambitious vision for the store, but I was also struck by her kindness, intelligence, and warmth. I knew that under its new ownership, my beloved local bookstore would thrive rather than merely survive.

And it has. It's more vibrant than ever. There's an elegant new logo—hand-drawn by A.C. Harkness, an incredibly gifted artist who works at the store—and a new awning. There are newly designed bookmarks, tote bags, and T-shirts. There are more books in stock, more events, and even more customers. Wander around on any given day, and you'll find people browsing with deep concentration. Others are huddled in the back room, reading to their kids. (It's a space I love, filled entirely with children's books and leading to a lovely back-yard patio.) Tiny might be sleeping in a corner, offering a partial belly view. Some people will be chatting about the latest novel by a favorite author or sharing anecdotes from a recent family vacation. This is a place that inspires both readers and writers, but it's also just a favorite local hangout.

Whenever I'm asked about where I live, I mention the things I love: Prospect Park, the progressive spirit of the neighborhood, the historic architecture. And, I say proudly, "There's a great independent bookstore."

CARMELA CIURARU is the author of *Nom de Plume: A (Secret) History of Pseudonyms*, published by HarperCollins. She is a member of the National Book Critics Circle and PEN American Center, and was a 2011 New York Foundation for the Arts Fellow in Nonfiction.

Meg Waite Clayton

Books Inc., PALO ALTO, CALIFORNIA

When I confessed my favorite sin to the priest behind the screen each week as a girl, I stuck to the basics: I admitted to disobeying my parents, generally adding some random number of times to make it sound more real than I imagined it was. I was a good girl, with a good girl's propensity to go to church even on weekday mornings when I didn't have to. I contorted my early-grade-school shoulders in a failed attempt to gain the proper slant on my cursive without turning my paper upside down (which disconcerted the nuns), and brought home As in everything but penmanship, and yes, even played school with my friends on muggy summer afternoons.

If what I did under the covers in bed at night was a sin, I realized it only in that vaguest of ways expressed in those confessionals, and if caught in the act, I would have given up my brother Patrick; if he sequestered a flashlight and a book under the bedcovers, then surely it wasn't a sin for his little sister to do so. It's one of the guilty indulgences that has survived being a parent myself. Something about the illicitness of slipping a light back on after everyone is asleep makes reading all the more pleasurable. And it is similar after-hours bad behavior that shapes my affection for one of my favorite bookstores, Palo Alto's Books Inc.

My relationship with bookstores splits neatly into two periods, and at the pivot is Books Inc. A bookstore habit that began with childhood bike rides to the Book Bin in Northbrook, Illinois (run by book people who knew what a Judy Blume reader might like next), found its way to college years perusing the Ann Arbor Borders when it was a single jumble of a store, sans café. My early adulthood was spent in Dutton's Books (may it rest in peace), where booksellers introduced me, presciently, to the works of Irish-Catholic writer Alice McDermott, with whom I would later get to study. I began to hook my two sons on my bookstore habit at Nashville's Davis-Kidd, in whose fiction section I discovered not just the works of Ann Patchett, but the author herself.

By the time we came to Palo Alto, I was a story-and-essay-published writer, if not yet a book-published one, entering bookstores with the hope that I would find that next magical read, yes, but also that I would someday find a place myself on the shelves. The Palo Alto Books Inc. was in a mall across the street from Stanford University at the time. It was part of a small, locally owned bookstore chain that had just celebrated its sesquicentennial—150 years of selling books.

Books Inc. has the kind of history that is California: Man strikes it rich in gold rush and sets himself up selling books. Store thrives despite fires, relocations, changes in ownership, shifts in the market, and—because this is California, after all—shifts in the underlying land itself. Store grows into a chain of stores, which, after fifty post-war years under a single owner, is left to trusted employees...in a state of financial peril. (Did I mention this is California?) Two of the employees, Michael Tucker and Michael Grant, see the stores through a bankruptcy restructuring, emerging in 1997 with a four-location chain. Fifteen years later, twelve beautiful and well-run stores owned by Michael and Margie Scott Tucker—book people of the finest kind—employ some 200 other enthusiastic book people. The stores host over thirty reading groups a month, as well as dozens of literary events every week, authors connecting with readers in a more personal way than can ever be had online.

I first stumbled upon the Palo Alto store a few days after we moved to town, while shopping for new-home necessities. We hadn't even emptied our moving boxes, much less alphabetized the books on our new shelves, but I'd just received the amazing news that my agent had sold my first novel to a swanky New York publisher. I stood just outside the store, looking inside longingly, regretting the cup of coffee I'd bought before I'd realized there was a bookstore in the mall. The bookseller at the register invited me to have a look around, and when I suggested I would just find a bin to dump my coffee, he welcomed me to browse with coffee in hand. I left with a bag full of great reading that afternoon—and without my non-book shopping bag. I am forever setting bags or coffee cups or wallets down in bookstores without even realizing I'm doing so, and leaving them behind. No doubt it is subliminal. No doubt I'm looking for the easy excuse to come right back.

> *I am forever setting bags or coffee cups or wallets down in bookstores without even realizing I'm doing so, and leaving them behind. No doubt I'm looking for the easy excuse to come right back.*

Just over a year later, my husband called me from a payphone at the mall and told me there was something there he wanted me to see. And when he took me to the front table at Books Inc., I was flooded with the greedy anticipation that my novel might just be there.

I didn't see it at first. I was too excited to see my own novel right in front of me. When I did, finally, I started bawling. There was nothing I could do to stop the blubbering and the laughter over the fact of my book—my book!—actually being something a stranger might read.

Mac picked me up and twirled me around like he had when the priest at the front of the church pronounced us husband and wife.

"It's her first novel," he explained to the gawking shoppers. "It's the first time she's ever seen it. Not just in a store. Anywhere."

A young mom with a child in a stroller asked about the story, and bought a copy, and asked me to sign it, right there at the counter. She was from Pleasanton, across the bay, I remember. The bookseller handed me a pen, and I wrote the woman's name in my best back-slanting penmanship, along with a few words and my signature. The bookseller asked if I would mind signing the other copies they had too. Mind? It's the most enjoyable writing an author ever does, writing her name on the title page of her published book.

The hard part was keeping my tears from running the ink.

At home I returned to the penmanship practice I'd so unsuccessfully undertaken in the second grade. Write your name a hundred times. Surely you can make it look prettier than that! It's even harder when your forearm hangs over the edge of a book that will belong to someone else.

Ask any of the Books Inc. staff what they're reading and you'll learn a whole lot about books—perhaps even the ones you've written. I walked in one Sunday with a cup of Peet's to hear Jason at the register ask if I'd named Mrs. Peets, a minor character in *The Wednesday Sisters*, after the coffee shop two doors down, where I so often write. Clearly I had on some level, although not a conscious one. It's booksellers like these—booksellers who read broadly and thoughtfully and have opinions they love to share—who help new literary voices find an audience. Without their support—hand-selling my novels and keeping them front of store—I might well be back practicing law. If they dissappear, our choices as readers will narrow, and our lives as well.

The Palo Alto Books Inc. is now in a different location—a bright space less than a mile from my own bookshelves, which are so full of books I haven't yet managed to read that I ought not to be allowed to buy any more. I usually bike or walk to the store, out of choice rather than for lack of a driver's license now. The feeling is not unlike that of the kid I once was, biking to the Book Bin for the new Judy Blume. My dog, Frodo, will sit quietly tied to the bench outside for the time it takes me to buy a book I already know I want, but by the time I'm done chatting with the booksellers he has often chewed through yet another leash. It's been suggested I might bring him in with me, but it's one thing for a bookseller to keep a bag of coffee beans for the time it takes its owner to remember it, and quite another to keep a seventy-pound golden retriever who can't even read.

My favorite time in the store comes on the fourth Tuesday of each month, when we gather at seven with Margie to discuss that month's Fourth Tuesday Book Club read. Great company, great conversation, and great books. Or sometimes not such great books. Sometimes books some of us love and others of us don't. Sometimes books we all find disappointing. We have drinks. We have cookies or cupcakes or all those other things we aren't supposed to eat, much less in the clean, white space of a bookstore. The company and the conversation never fall short.

The sign on the door clearly states the store closes at eight, but we never leave by then. Some fourth Tuesdays, we're still there at nine, a full hour after the booksellers might have locked the doors and headed home to their own shelves of books. Shame on us.

"I stay after hours," I might confess in the dark safety of a confessional, except that the place I find solace now, and really always have, tends to hold more shelves than pews. In confessing one's transgression, too, one is supposed to commit to trying to do better, and I have no intention of trying to leave the store by closing time. If Margie stays after hours, then surely it's not a sin. And there is something particularly delicious about staying on in a bookstore well after the hour when the lights are meant to be turned off.

MEG WAITE CLAYTON is the nationally best-selling author of *The Four Ms. Bradwells*, *The Wednesday Sisters*, the Bellwether Prize finalist *The Language of Light*, and the forthcoming *The Wednesday Daughters*. Her novels have been translated into languages from German to Lithuanian to Chinese. Her essays and short stories have aired on public radio and appeared in commercial and literary publications such as *The Los Angeles Times*, *The San Jose Mercury News*, *Writer's Digest*, *Runner's World*, and *The Literary Review*. An Order of the Coif graduate of the University Michigan Law School, she now lives in Palo Alto, California. www.megwaiteclayton.com

Jon Clinch

Northshire Bookstore, MANCHESTER, VERMONT

The minute I heard the banjo music, I knew I'd arrived.

And by arrived, I mean *arrived*.

This must have been the hundredth time I'd walked into the Northshire Bookstore in Manchester, Vermont. I certainly can't remember the first. The first was probably ten years ago now, which would make it five years before the banjo music. My wife and I lived in Pennsylvania then, and we commuted to our place in Vermont as often as we could. Northshire was an important stop along the way—northbound, it was a signifier that we'd arrived in a better and far cooler place than the Philadelphia suburbs; southbound, it was a nearly irresistible reason to think about sticking around forever and ever.

Which we finally did. Statisticians may tell you that people cluster around jobs or transit or high-speed Internet, but some of us cluster around more important things. Like bookstores.

Anyhow, I'd never known a bookstore quite like Northshire. Make that *anything* like Northshire. Like so many suburban readers, I'd been a creature of the chains. Little B&Ns in shopping malls and sad downmarket outposts of Waldenbooks and end-of-the-trail remainder houses like Encore. In those days, a Borders was a big deal. Remember Borders? They had a better selection than anybody, grant them that. Kind of like Amazon, only without those flashing banners that tell you what other folks just like you have been buying lately, whether it's books or backpacks or barbecue grills.

Northshire was different. It was big, for sure. Big enough to get lost in. (What the heck kind of building did it occupy, anyhow? Was it a house? Was it two houses? A commercial block? Something else? I still can't quite get the hang of it, and I'm afraid there's a Borgesian quality to the whole business that I won't go into here.) But size and scope weren't the half of it. The main thing was that the instant you stepped inside the door *you knew that this was a place where books were honored*. There was a kind of respectful intelligence behind everything, and to make your way down the aisles was to engage in a conversation with whoever it was who'd arranged them.

This wasn't a chain store decorated with images of Twain and Faulkner and stocked with a sorry array of vampire books. This was a place where literature wasn't window dressing. Take it all around, Northshire was a revelation.

The place was always crowded with people, too. Locals and tourists and, above all, staff—real live booksellers worthy of that elevated title. And there was always plenty of conversation going on. Never mind the conventional hush

> ...*to make your way down the aisles was to engage in a conversation with whoever it was who'd arranged them.*

of the library or the cunning jacked-up motivational Muzak of the mall, folks here understood that books are things that you talk about. Things you need to talk about, because the more you talk about books, the more you understand the people you're talking about books with. It's as simple as that.

Speaking of which, I learned pretty quickly that a Northshire bookseller is likely to get excited about one of two things: a book he loves, or a book he's pretty sure you're going to love. Who wouldn't get excited about that? About approaching a friend with a little stack of books that you just *know* he's going to be crazy about? It's a gift, really. A gift to everybody. A gift that goes in both directions. And the only way it can happen is through conversation.

. . .

One conversation I never expected to have, back in those days at least, was the dreaded "I wrote a book" chat. But when *Finn* was coming, and word trickled down from my publisher that folks at Northshire thought pretty highly of it, there was no turning away. I had to make contacts on a new and entirely different level. But I didn't want to blow it. See, an author event at Northshire—a reading, a signing—was a prize to be sought after. All kinds of important authors stopped there on their way through New England, and I'd begun to hope that I might be able to do the same one day. So trust me when I suggest that a certain amount of trepidation went along with starting up the "I wrote a book" conversation. I girded my loins and had it anyway.

Do you know what changed as a result?

Not much. Which was good.

I got to know the names of some nice folks who'd helped me before. I got to meet some folks I hadn't met previously. And somehow or other, over time, I found myself talking music with Erik Barnum, Northshire's sales floor manager. It turned out that not only are both Erik and I frustrated folk musicians, but we also share a soft spot for the late and very great songwriter, fiddler, and Mississippi steamboat pilot, John Hartford.

Which brings me back to the banjo, and the night that I showed up for my first reading at Northshire.

It was the end of my tour for *Finn*, a book set on Mark Twain's Mississippi River. And no sooner did I sit down with a group of readers for a pre-event discussion than the music over the PA system shifted to Hartford's 1976 album, *Mark Twang*. To me there's no music more peculiarly American, no better sound track for the work I'd tried to accomplish in *Finn*. And there it was. In the air all around us. Because a very fine bookseller had been paying attention.

As I said, I had *arrived* at Northshire.

Again.

JON CLINCH is the author of *Finn, Kings of the Earth*, and the forthcoming *The Thief of Auschwitz*.

Mick Cochrane

Talking Leaves Books, BUFFALO, NEW YORK

All of us, not just writers, are susceptible to our surroundings. There are plenty of places that make me feel tense, lonely, and glum—hospital waiting rooms, most fast-food restaurants, all malls, especially the Mall of America. And there are a handful of places that make me feel safe and relaxed, unguarded—like myself, but maybe more interesting, more optimistic, more open to possibility.

The late A. Bartlett Giamatti, who, like me, was a student of literature, an academic, and a passionate baseball fan, eloquently described over the course of his writing career the special appeal and enduring lure of three very different, largely imaginative places, three versions of paradise: the garden found in Renaissance literary epics, the free and ordered space of the university, and the green world of the ballpark. While I have spent as much as time as anyone, I suppose, in classrooms and in the bleachers, there is for me still another place Giamatti never mentions, a place I seek out frequently for refreshment and renewal. It's not an academic building and not a ballpark; it's a bookstore, and not just any bookstore, it's *my* bookstore—Talking Leaves Books.

. . .

Jonathon Welch, the store's cofounder and owner, explains that the name derives from the way those unfamiliar with books characterized their unusual power: "Book pages were seen as 'leaves' that 'talked,' imparting wisdom and knowledge and spirit." The store's motto is "Independent and Idiosyncratic Since 1971."

The store is an expression of who Jonathon is, who we are, we his loyal customers, members, those who love and frequent the stores, Talking Leaves Nation. Today in the windows of the store there are posters and flyers announcing local concerts, readings, and other cultural and political events. In the spring of 1989, soon after the Ayatollah Khomeini issued his fatwa against Salman Rushdie, at the same time the chains were pulling his novel from their shelves, there were copies of *The Satanic Verses* in the windows of Talking Leaves. The meaning couldn't have been clearer: Independent and Idiosyncratic—and Fearless.

Just inside the front door for the past couple of years, there's been a life-sized Stephen Colbert cutout, a maniacally cheerful-looking cardboard greeter. He still startles me a little when I come in—he is just so, well, life-sized—and he makes me laugh. There's no corporate radio playing; most days, it's NPR or maybe some deep tracks from Fats Domino or Bob Marley, whatever Ken and the other clerks are feeling that day. There is sometimes an animal in the store, a cat curled on a chair in Philosophy.

Talking Leaves has great literary magazines, a cool collection of buttons, and postcards, but it's all about the books: 50,000 in the Main Street store, give or take. There's no danger of it turning into a technology or toy store, thank goodness. The store's mission has always been to stock books you won't find at the chains, books you won't find anywhere else. It's light on Nicholas Sparks and the various Chicken Soups for the Soul, heavy on literary fiction, alternative voices of all kinds, anything deeply original, challenging, quirky, and marginal. There's not a single copy of anything by Ann Coulter, but there are more volumes of poetry than I have seen anywhere else—Buffalo has always been a tremendous poetry town—a great wall of contemporary poets, Addonizio to Zagajewski. The self-stated goal of Talking Leaves is to make available life-changing books, books that "open us up to new worlds, or illuminate more clearly our own," books that "stretch and deepen our vision and our comprehension of the universe and its creatures, cultures and ways."

Talking Leaves—both the original Main Street store and its newer second location on Elmwood—is in the heart of our magnificent, scruffy, big-hearted, sometimes brilliant and sometimes blundering, too-often-misunderstood city. The 6,000 or so members come from every zip code in western New York: from the East Side and the West Side, from the waterfront condominiums and from university-district apartments, from every suburb, Cheektowaga to East Aurora. It is one thing we can agree on—we all love Talking Leaves. The mayor and the editor of The *Buffalo News* are members; so are my son's baseball coach and most of the writing students I teach at the college. The popularity of the current Sabres goaltender and the Bills quarterback ebbs and flows, but every time I have ever pronounced Jonathon Welch's name into a microphone at a literary event, it was greeted with enthusiastic applause.

Talking Leaves may be the only place on earth I'll ever be a regular, and I confess that I love it. Jon and his wife, Martha, and most of the people who answer

> *Talking Leaves may be the only place on earth I'll ever be a regular, and I confess that I love it.*

the phone in the store know my voice, and I know theirs. Jon knows which books I want to read before I do, and he sets them aside for me. Talking Leaves is there for me when I need it. Last November, when I came into the Main Street store right at closing time, in desperate need of a copy of *The Gambler*—a Dostoevsky emergency!—Jon walked me over to not one but two different editions and offered a brief, lucid overview of the different translations.

Jonathon Welch is one of those people I feel as if I've always known. I have no distinct memory of meeting him anymore than I can recall being introduced to my own brother. I am pretty sure that the first time I bought a book from him was soon after I moved to Buffalo from Minnesota in the 1980s: It was a copy of Gary Gildner's wonderful memoir *The Warsaw Sparks*, about the poet, on a Fulbright in Poland, coaching a baseball team. The reading was at the Polish Community Center, as I recall, on Paderewski Drive, and Jon was there, as he is at scores of readings and book signings each year throughout the city, with a carton of books and his credit-card machine. Wherever three or more are gathered in literature's name, it seems, Jon and Talking Leaves are there also.

Jon's office is as full of books as any professor's, crowded with enough paper to alarm, I suspect, a fire marshal. There are stacks of finished books and galleys and catalogs piled floor to ceiling. His phone rings constantly—customers, sales reps, writers interested in doing readings and signings. The back of his left hand is usually covered in blue-inked notes to himself, and there are Post-it notes everywhere.

But no matter what, Jon makes time for me. He welcomes me. He tells me about the new Stewart O'Nan novel I am going to want. He lets me know what his friend Morgan Entrekin at Grove Press is up to. He explains to me what World Book Night is all about. He asks who is visiting in my college's writers series so he can mark the dates. He is like the best professor you ever had: He never looks at his watch; he makes you feel smarter than you are; he embodies, he inhabits, a kind of passionate commitment you aspire to.

Jon and I, I like to imagine, have a lot in common. We're both Midwesterners, he from Wisconsin, me from Minnesota. We're both fathers, both politically 99 percenters, both a little skeptical about the way technology is changing the way we relate to one another. We both love writing and storytelling and books in ways so profound it would be impossible to put into words. Each in our own way, we're both educators, book evangelists. I am a novelist, and Jon is an artist, too, a great one. I believe that with all my heart. What John Gardner says about the true novelist's vocation applies equally to the true bookseller's: It "is not so much a profession as a yoga, or 'way' of being in the world, an alternative to ordinary life-in-the-world. Its benefits are quasi-religious—a changed quality of mind and heart, satisfactions no non-novelist can understand—and its rigors generally bring no profit except to the spirit. For those who are authentically called to the profession, spiritual profits are enough."

Talking Leaves, Jon's bookstore, *my* bookstore, our bookstore—Talking Leaves is his creative masterpiece, his own vast, teeming, inclusive, and open-ended epic poem, his *Leaves of Grass*, brave and untidy, fiercely independent and original, a clean, well-lighted place on Main Street, open six days a week. It is our very own retail Arden. It is a magic island, where we may both lose and find ourselves.

MICK COCHRANE is the author of two novels for adults, *Flesh Wounds* and *Sport*, and two novels for young readers, *The Girl Who Threw Butterflies* and *Fitz*. He is Lowery Writer-in-Residence at Canisius College in Buffalo, New York, where he teaches writing, directs the creative writing program, and coordinates the Contemporary Writers Series.

Ron Currie, Jr.

Longfellow Books, PORTLAND, MAINE

A confession: I am not a good literary citizen, in the sense that I've never cared much one way or the other about bookstores. For a long time I found myself looking around at the posture of communal support and gratitude displayed by other authors toward their favorite booksellers, and I wondered why I was so deficient, in this regard, by comparison. I didn't get all that excited by the notion of independent enterprise, didn't understand why it was such a big deal. More often than not I bought books through Amazon, and for the usual reasons: It was cheap and spared me the trouble of talking to people, and I could transition from book shopping to masturbation much easier than at a brick-and-mortar store.

As is standard practice these days, I blame my upbringing. Not my parents, but the community in which I was raised, which never really had an independent bookstore. During my childhood I got books primarily through the library, or else book fairs at school, the kind where the teacher would pass out those flimsy newsprint book catalogs and you chose the books you wanted (or could afford) and then waited in bittersweet anticipation, for six weeks, until they magically showed up one day and were distributed in class.

God, remember when we had to *wait* for things? What a sublime pleasure, now forever lost to us.

So anyway, then as a young man I transitioned, out of financial and geographical necessity, to buying only used books at a store here in town that opened, serendipitously, during my late teens. It was a somewhat dingy basement operation, and though I shopped there a lot and made some great finds, I never developed anything resembling appreciation—let alone loyalty—for the place. This was due in large part to the fact that I instinctively disliked the proprietor—he seemed stuffy, and a bit pretentious, and was mustachioed in a way I didn't care for, and always gave the impression that he suspected I was a shoplifter, even though I bought hundreds of books from him over the years. Once I tried to haggle with him over a signed first edition of *Going After Cacciato* that he was asking way too much for, and not only did he refuse to budge on the price, but did so with an air of dismissiveness that made me want to pull his fingernails out. This was the final straw for me—I haven't been in there since, though I do occasionally hear the clarion call of the hidden gems I know are sitting in all those stacks and stacks.

And so, you know, I moved on to my Amazon-and-masturbation routine, which seemed amenable enough and never put me in a position where I was one moment of lax-impulse-control away from assaulting somebody.

But then, shortly after my first book came out, I met a guy named Chris Bowe, the co-owner of Longfellow Books in Portland, Maine.

He's a shortish, intense dude, originally from one of the myriad hard-scrabble communities outside Boston, which as everybody knows are sort of breeding grounds for shortish, intense dudes. He loved my book, and he wanted to do whatever he could to make sure the world loved it too.

The thing about meeting Chris was, I'd never talked to anyone else about books in quite that way. Not agents, or editors, or even other authors. Chris transitioned from one writer to the next, one title to the next, at a breakneck pace, spouting cigarette smoke and equal passion for the writing he loved and the writing he loathed. Here, for the first time in my life, was a *bookseller*. And though Chris would prove to be an exceptionally dedicated and passionate example of that particular genus, what I learned from him was that booksellers in general, more than probably any other demographic, *live* for books, both aesthetically and practically speaking. And also that, when a good bookseller loves what you write, he will sell the living shit out of it. He will force it on every person who walks through the door, and push them toward the checkout counter before they have a chance to protest that they only read books about dogs and/or vampires. He will sell his own mother into white slavery in order to ensure cash flow to keep your book in stock. He will make you sign hundreds of copies, and he will move every last one of them. Moreover, he will do all this for the right reasons: because it builds community, and puts authors in direct contact with their audience, and makes everyone intensely happy—in short, because it's plain

> *...when a good bookseller loves what you write, he will sell the living shit out of it. He will force it on every person who walks through the door, and push them toward the checkout counter before they have a chance to protest...*

good business, in both financial and human terms.

So this was the first part of my education, regarding what book-sellers are, what they do, and why they're important. The second part came when I did my first reading at Longfellow. At that point in my career I'd had more than a handful of appearances at the chain stores, with mixed results. Sometimes the staff was prepared and attentive, and other times they made an announcement over the store PA five minutes before I read, then left me to police the crowd myself (one particularly bullshit moment came when I had to stop mid-reading, walk away from the lectern, and politely ask a woman yakking on her cell phone nearby to shut the hell up). Nothing like this at Longfel-low. First off, they'd managed to bring in a group of more than fifty people, and this on one of the first nice summer days we'd had after a very long, very cold, and very wet spring. As any author whose name is not Michael Chabon or Neil Gaiman can tell you, fifty people is a packed house. Moreover, these folks were not there on a lark, or because they happened to be in the store browsing at the time—they were already fans of mine, having been force-fed my books by Chris and company well before the date of the reading. On the first nice Friday evening we'd had all year, and with a large street festival with live music and beer gardens going on literally just outside the windows, these people had willingly, happily crowded into the store's small reading space to listen to me. And that, frankly, had very little to do with anything I'd written, and much more to do with the relentless efforts of Chris and the Longfellow staff to force them to pay atten-tion to my work.

At the appointed time, Chris took the floor and, with the same fierceness and conviction he'd displayed in our conversations, held forth about my books for those assembled. He said, as though it were a foregone and obvious conclusion, an inevitability requiring only time to be proven true, that they had the privilege of seeing a writer (namely, me) at the beginning of a long and important career. "This is like getting to see early Vonnegut," he told them. And then, when he was finished flattering me well beyond embarrassment, he yielded the lectern, but not before—and here's the coup de grâce—making certain there was a fresh, cold can of Pabst Blue Ribbon there for me to sip through the reading. And that was it. After this I would do, and have done, anything that Chris and Longfellow asked of me. I've signed more books than I can count, participated in benefits and holiday sales promotions and library events sponsored by Longfellow, talked with book clubs set up through Longfellow, and chatted at length with readers in the store when I'm browsing as a civilian and one of the staff brings someone over to say hello. I'd clean the toilets, probably, if they asked me to. Perhaps most important: I now buy almost all my books at Longfellow. Because now I get it. I get that booksellers are vastly more important than I am. I get that my contributions are meager compared to the daily trench work they put in. I write the stuff, sure, but they press its clothes and fix its hair and give it a swift pat on the butt and send it out into the world. Booksellers like Chris Bowe are the great beating heart of contemporary American literature, and without them, there's very little point to anything I do.

RON CURRIE JR. is the author of *God Is Dead* and *Everything Matters*. He's received the New York Public Library Young Lions Fiction Award, and the Addison M. Metcalf Award in Literature from the American Academy of Arts and Letters. A new book of his will be published in early 2013. He lives in Maine.

Angela Davis-Gardner

Quail Ridge Books & Music

RALEIGH, NORTH CAROLINA

Nancy Olson, the beloved owner of Quail Ridge Books & Music in Raleigh, North Carolina, reads, on average, four books a week. Four thousand people receive her recommendations in a regular email newsletter. Nancy's mission as a bookseller these twenty-eight years has been to transfer her passion for books to her customers. "I want to stuff the books down their throats," she laughs.

She's actually a gentle person, with a cap of white hair, blue eyes, dimples, a smile that animates her entire face, and an irrepressible sense of humor. Today she's wearing a rhinestone pin that spells out

READ in glittery letters.

We're sitting in a coffee shop talking, as usual, about books. She mentions a novel she's just finished. It could become an American classic, she says, if people just knew about it. She's indignant that *Publishers Weekly*—the almighty pre-publication arbiter of literary opinion—didn't review it. She's called them herself and asked if they'd consider doing a post-publication review. (She has cachet with *Publishers Weekly*: In 2001, they named her Bookseller of the Year.) *PW* has agreed to have a look at the novel; two copies are on the way.

"Oh, Angela, you've got to read this book," she says, leaning forward. "I'll lend you my copy. I want to know what you think."

The effect is hypnotic. As soon as we part ways, I drive to the store, where I've already been earlier that day, buy the book, go home, and dive in. She's right. I love the book.

Nancy has a genius for matching books and readers. People often ask her, "What should I read?" She knows her regular customers well enough that she can usually make an immediate suggestion. If she doesn't know the reader—or the reader's friend or aunt, for whom the book will be a gift—she asks about preferences, sometimes walking around the store, mulling it over with the customer until she has an answer.

A lifelong voracious reader, she has a substantial mental catalog to draw upon. She also knows her stock; all the books in the store were handpicked by Nancy and her staff and come from small as well as large publishers.

Nancy also has a rare capacity for attention. When she greets someone—in the store, or elsewhere—she comes to a physical and emotional pause. She takes you in. She wants to know how you are, and what you've been reading.

Only connect, Forster said.

Connection is the genius loci of this bookstore. Its motto, "Bringing Readers and Writers Together," is not an empty slogan.

Many people, myself included, think of the store as a second home. People who work there are like family. I go in so often that if

I miss a few days, a staff member might ask, with genuine concern, if I've been ill. People occasionally bring their lunch. One woman slept on the couch in the afternoons when she was recovering from chemotherapy. Some people come every night for the readings by authors, many of whom are famous; the store is a prime destination for writers on tour. (Their autographed photographs fill the walls of the cozy bathroom.)

There is no coffee bar. Before the last expansion, Nancy asked her customers if they wanted books or coffee. One hundred percent voted for more books.

Nancy's aim is to offer books not found everywhere, along with the expected titles. (Best sellers are on a shelf facing away from the door.) There's a section of international fiction, an impressive collection of books on writing and publishing, and an eclectic mix of paperbacks laid out on a table. (I recently discovered an Iranian novel there— *Women Without Men*, by Shahrnush Parsipur—and Eli Pariser's *The Filter Bubble: How the New Personalized Web Is Changing What We Read and How We Think.*) Classic fiction is shelved with the contemporary American and British work. Jane Austen occupies most of a shelf; Anthony Trollope stands beside Joanna; there are multiple editions of *War and Peace*. Occasionally I come across a tempting work of new experimental fiction tucked between books by established writers.

There's a large, separate area for children's books, overseen by children's-literature specialist Carol Moyer. The music section offers the only substantial collection of classical-music CDs in Raleigh, along with jazz and American traditional music.

The reading area, with its table and four armchairs, can be quickly transformed into a public space for readings and other gatherings.

The store hosts discussion groups (on topics as diverse as the Koran, health care, and Flannery O'Connor); writers' groups, including one for teenage writers; numerous children's programs; concerts; and quarterly town-hall meetings. In programs cosponsored by the local classical-music station, WCPE, the conductor and assistant conductors of the North Carolina Symphony give talks at the store about upcoming performances. Music director Grant Llewellyn prepared his audience for Mahler's Ninth with excerpts from the music; Shakespeare's influence on composers from Mendelssohn to Bernstein was the subject of another lecture.

An annual used-book sale raises money for Books for Kids, a nonprofit that Nancy founded for children whose families can't afford books. Since 1999, 50,000 children have received books through the program. (This effort is operated almost entirely by volunteers. Devoted volunteers also help in the day-to-day operation of the store, shelving and wrapping books.)

From the beginning, Nancy Olson has given strong support to North Carolina writers and Southern writers. The first author she invited to read at the store was Jill McCorkle, who had just published two novels with Algonquin Books.

Nancy scheduled the event on an afternoon that happened to coincide with a football game between North Carolina State and the University of North Carolina. No one showed up.

"I've learned a lot since then," Nancy says with a laugh. "But Jill was very gracious. We spent an hour or so going around the store, talking about books. We bonded for life."

She has also bonded for life with numerous writers whose books she has saved from oblivion, including mine.

. . .

A writer's career can rise and fall with stomach-dropping speed. My first two novels had done well, but my third, *Plum Wine*, made the rounds in New York for years without a sale. I finally placed it with a university press, which produced 1,000 copies of a beautifully designed volume, but the press didn't have money to promote it. *The New York Times*, *The Washington Post*, and the *Los Angeles Times*, which had given my earlier books excellent reviews, overlooked it.

Nancy Olson, who is quick to say that she is not necessarily drawn to each book by her many writer friends, happened to be passionate about this one. After a gala launch, the store gave the book what one staff member called "The Big Push." Customers could hardly get out of the store without hearing about *Plum Wine*. Nancy nominated it as a "Pick" for Book Sense, which is published by a national consortium of independent booksellers. The novel was chosen, featured in stores around the country, and began to sell. Nancy sent the book to an agent in New York who took on the book with enthusiasm. Suddenly I had a contract for four books: paperback editions of *Plum Wine* and my first two books, as well as a new novel. Nancy Olson saved my career.

She has also given boosts to dozens of other writers. She praised fledgling North Carolina fiction writer Ron Rash during an NPR radio interview; that day he received several calls from editors. (He has since won numerous awards for his fiction, and a movie based on one of his novels is in the works). Nancy saw promise for a wide readership in Jan Karon's first novel, *At Home in Mitford*, originally published by a small Christian press, and sent the book to an agent. Jan Karon now has a series of Mitford novels that have sold millions of copies.

In the decade before Charles Frazier published *Cold Mountain*, he often came into the store, and he and Nancy became well acquainted. She was a little anxious about what to expect of that first novel, she says, but when she read it, she was electrified. Quail Ridge launched the book with spectacular sales from the start, and Nancy was by Charles Frazier's side when he won the National Book Award for *Cold Mountain*.

Although Nancy Olson has become a major voice in the book world, she and her husband Jim started out in 1984 with a modest budget and no experience in bookselling, or in any form of retail.

Nancy had just retired from a government job in Washington, D.C., when she and Jim began to think seriously about opening a bookstore, Nancy's lifelong dream. Their research consisted of a national tour of twenty-four bookstores. "I saw what I liked and what I didn't," Nancy says. She decided that Raleigh, with its seven colleges, including one university, and at the time, no other independent bookstore, was fertile ground.

Since then, the store has grown from 1,200 to 10,000 square feet, with a stock of some 70,000 books. Customers drive to the store from other states and place orders from various foreign countries. (Just because a scientist or professor moves from this area to Sweden or Italy doesn't necessarily mean that he or she will leave her book home behind.)

Quail Ridge Books & Music, which *Newsweek* recently named one of the great bookstores in the country, has been phenomenally successful. Even in these hard economic times, the store is holding its own.

But as the years pass, and the culture shifts, the book business and bookstores have become increasingly fragile.

What if there was no Quail Ridge Books & Music?

An unthinkable question, but I've heard many people ask it. If we did not have this magnificent bookstore, I and countless others would lose a refuge, an intellectual home.

Since this particular store is so vital to our community, there's a good chance it will continue for decades, in one form or another.

But the possibility of an ending makes the existence of any living thing—and bookstores are live entities—more precious.

So read, Reader, read. And buy books, from stores.

> *What if there was no Quail Ridge Books & Music? It's an unthinkable question, but I've heard many people ask it. If we did not have this magnificent bookstore, I and countless others would lose a refuge, an intellectual home.*

ANGELA DAVIS-GARDNER has published four novels, most recently *Butterfly's Child*. Her novel *Plum Wine* was featured on NPR and was named a Notable Book by the Kiriyama Pacific Rim Prize committee for its contributions to East-West understanding. She lives in Raleigh, North Carolina.

Ivan Doig

University Book Store, SEATTLE, WASHINGTON

"Home. Home. I knew it entering." Richard Hugo's exalted greeting to a beguiling place of business that instantly and forever wins one's heart is hard to better, and though my late, great poet friend was saluting a Montana institution in "The Only Bar in Dixon" for *The New Yorker,* I can't resist hoisting that same 100-proof tribute to my home bookstore, Seattle's one and only University Book Store. Down through the years of readings and talks, I have hailed booksellers (and librarians) as the bartenders of information, and nowhere is the intoxication of reading more readily at hand than at the big store by the big U (of Washington).

The iconic UBS, which began in a cubbyhole next to the university president's office in 1900 and had grown to take up most of a city block by the time I arrived to the Seattle campus in the 1960s, was literally another world, bookwise, for me. In my college years at Northwestern, the available bookstores (two) drew notice only as to which would buy back used texts for fifty cents more. But the marketplace of tomes awaiting this slightly overage graduate student in the green and glorious Northwest, wowie. Here, an easy stroll from the grove (Douglas-fir size) of academe, my three years of giddy full-time reading began not on the UW campus where I was ostensibly enrolled, but at the shelves of just about the biggest and best-stocked emporium of authorial output to be found anywhere. I loaded up at the University Book Store, according to my handwritten list, all the way from Tacitus' *Annals* to Murray Morgan's contemporary saga of Grand Coulee, *The Dam*, with plenty of novels and poetry in between.

This new literary romance with the UBS got even better. My wife, Carol, and I, in mid-career as magazine editors, had abandoned all that and the Midwest and arrived to Puget Sound in a gunboat Buick intending to stay only as long as it took for me to snag a Ph.D. and become a journalism professor. The Ph.D. came on time, but we have never left; fourteen books authored by me seem to have gotten in the way. The very first of those, my Montana memoir *This House of Sky: Landscapes of a Western Mind*, was immediately championed by the Mr. Books of this end of the country, Lee Soper, and his fantastically intuitive buyer in the UBS trade department, Marilyn Martin (Dahl). What a ride that was for a first-time author, with

> *What a ride that was for a first-time author, with the University Book Store vigorously selling, oh, 15 percent or so of the national total as the book ascended all the way to the National Book Award finals*

the University Book Store vigorously selling, oh, 15 percent or so of the national total as the book ascended all the way to the National Book Award finals with Kazin, Boulding, and Matthiessen, to within a whisker of winning. Talk about a satisfied customer.

From there to, yes, my latest novel, *The Bartender's Tale*, my experience with the UBS has been both comfortable and stimulating. An instance of each:

—The back rooms of bookstores, where the staff and imagination run free, are one of the secret delights for an author on book tour. It is back there, before the readings and the Q&A sessions and the (hopefully) long lines of customers waiting for books to be inscribed, that the airport-raddled hoteled-out touring writer is treated to those necessary small comforts, someplace to sit and a restroom. Back there, too, are the stacks of advance galleys, the cartoons on the walls, the postings such as "A book is the only electrifying experience that won't kill you if you drop it in the bathtub." And, of course, the predilections of the word-mad tribe, booksellers. At their behest, backstage there, I have signed posters, walls, doors, tables, and more than once, booksellers. Yet the back room I most look forward to is one of those calmer ones, the offices of Lee and Marilyn's successors, Mark Mouser and events manager Stesha Brandon, where I know there will be a window looking out on the grandly wooded campus that began all this, with a foreground of high stacks of my books to be pre-signed. To this writer's eyes, it is old loved scenery, and I mean the forest of books as well as the trees.

—If memory serves, it was two or three books ago, in the UBS's fine loft area for readings, that a young woman in the signing line asked me what words of mine I would like to have tattooed on her ankle. She was not pulling my leg. She displayed a quite nice ankle with indeed a neat blue-inked circlet of sentence—quite nice in its own right—and explained that she would like to match it with a sentence from one of my books. Which particular set of words took some fast thinking, but we came up with it, she and I. And so it is a lovely thought to me that somewhere among us, even today, walks a magical woman with Norman Maclean's unforgettable ultimate line from *A River Runs Through It*, "I am haunted by waters," on that first ankle, and on her other, my lyric one from the title song of *Dancing at the Rascal Fair*, "Feel love's music everywhere."

And so it goes on, blessedly, in my bookstore where I am author, shopper, customer, and grateful browser, now and then, along that certain shelf on the second floor of the University Book Store where fiction is housed and the inhabitants happen to be Dickens, Doctorow, Doig, Dostoevsky...

IVAN DOIG is the author of three nonfiction books and 11 novels, including *The Bartender's Tale* (2012). A recipient of the lifetime Distinguished Achievement Award from the Western Literature Association, a record six Pacific Northwest Booksellers Awards, the Wallace Stegner Award, and many other honors—including an Audie for his audio reading of *A River Runs Through It*—he lives and writes in Seattle, Washington.

Laurent Dubois

The Regulator Bookshop, DURHAM, NORTH CAROLINA

"Can we go to the Regulator?" Among the many different questions I get from my 9-year-old son, Anton, when I pick him up from school, this is by far my favorite. He well knows by now that—in contrast to many of the other requests for exciting outings he might make at 5 p.m. on a Tuesday afternoon—the answer will always be an easy and emphatic "Yes!" An outing to the Regulator has its attendant attractions, to be sure: a dinner at Dain's, our favorite 9th Street pub, concluded either with their only dessert item (Oreos and a glass of milk) or a milkshake at Ox &

Rabbit, an old soda shop converted into hipster heaven. We'll likely run into some friends as we wander up the sidewalk. But this is just preparation for the main course: sauntering into the Regulator, where Anton runs back to the kids' section of the bookstore while I stop to talk about the latest soccer news with Wander (whose life history includes a stint in a Dutch youth soccer academy) or Tom, the store's benevolent sovereign.

More often than not, there's a hefty stack of books waiting for me, the ones I've ordered online from the store. When I pick them up I get the pleasure of some sincere questions about precisely why I might be reading a self-reflexive ethnography of West Africa, a recent book on soccer in Mexico, the latest collection of critical essays on NGOs in Haiti, and a classic work by Amitav Ghosh. But unless I'm in a rush I know better than to pay for these ordered books when I arrive. It will be tough for me to get past the tables inside the door, decked out with recent titles of perpetual diversity, many signed by authors who have recently made the necessary stop to a store that has, over the years, helped to define the intellectual culture of our funky, changing, contented post-industrial city.

The Regulator opened its doors in 1976. It was, as one of the store's founders and its current owner Tom Campbell wrote in 2006, "a small and perhaps improbable bookstore."[1] At the time, Durham's 9th Street, which is just two blocks from Duke University, was largely defined by a closer neighbor: a large textile mill that sat basically across the street. Back then it was packed with workers who went to 9th Street for meals and errands. All the stores that were there in 1976—including McDonald's Drug Store, a hardware store, and a series of grills that served breakfast and lunch—are gone now. The Regulator is the oldest business on a street that now caters to Duke students and Durham residents looking for coffee, toys, hip T-shirts, records, yoga classes, and, of course, books.

[1]Tom Campbell, "The Story Begins Like This," http://www.regulatorbookshop.com/localbestsellers/286278.

The building that houses the Regulator was, at the time, home to a small local printing press—the Regulator Press. The name, probably gleaned from a history class taken by some of the Duke graduates who worked there, honored a locally famous bunch of precocious North Carolina rebels who, years before the American Revolution, carried out an uprising against the British. It was, as Tom Campbell recently summarized to me, both "local and rebellious," which at the time captured the spirit of the store. It still does.

While the name preserves a bit of local history, the store also commits itself to offering customers a wide selection of books about North Carolina. Since I moved to Durham five years ago, the Regulator has been where I've learned about the sedimented stories that define my adopted home. The town's history is defined, even dominated, by tobacco. Though the city no longer smells like Brightleaf being dried and cured, the red brick factories loom everywhere—though most are now converted into apartments, studios, offices, shops, or restaurants. Because it really didn't exist until after the Civil War, Durham was defined less by the plantation than by the factory. It became home to a prominent and successful African-American middle class, famously boasting a "Black Wall Street" and touted as a model by Booker T. Washington. North Carolina Mutual, long one of the largest African-American business in the country, was founded here by an ex-slave. One of the country's oldest historically black universities, North Carolina Central University, makes its home here. It abuts a neighborhood known as Hayti, so named as the city was built because—like the country in the Caribbean—it was a place where people of African descent could rule themselves and build their own institutions. As it happens, I'm a historian of Haiti, so the fact that I can find myself in Haiti while in Durham—and can take my various Haitian visitors home, in a way, when they are here—is something that gives me particular pleasure. Durham has long greeted seekers like myself—immigrants with various convoluted stories who have found in North Carolina something nearing the home they'd long imagined.

Like any rapidly changing community, Durham has gotten

increasingly self-conscious lately—there are T-shirts and bumper stickers that announce, with slight aggression born of supercilious comments made by friends in New York, "Durham: It's Not for Everyone." Others demand, with the fear of recent arrivals who are worried that the next arrivals will destroy what they came to enjoy, "Keep Durham Dirty." Sometimes it does feel as if Durham is a rapidly gentrifying neighborhood in Brooklyn. Still, there's something true and good about the desire to keep things local. And it is a striking fact that within downtown Durham itself you'll find almost no chain stores (beyond the inevitable McDonald's). The city has gotten rather famous for its ever-proliferating food culture; every week, it seems, a new food truck appears, and within a few months it becomes a store, and then another follows, until it's become quite difficult to decide precisely where to get a cupcake or *pain au chocolat*, not to mention a delectable meal of all locally produced food, on any given day.

Artwork by the author's son, depicting his favorite characters reading from their own books in The Regulator. From left to right: Greg from *Diary of a Wimpy Kid*, Vordack from *Vordack the Incomprehensible*, and Nate from *Big Nate*.

But among all these local businesses the Regulator holds a particularly central place. Part of what Durham is, in so many ways, is the intersection between Duke University and the broader community, and the bookstore is pivotal in that relationship. It is a hub around which much life in Durham circles, bringing together readers and talkers in a swirling, open way.

My son's reading life circles around the Regulator too. The day a particular book is released—the latest installment of *Big Nate* was the last one in question—we speed from school to the shop. He dashes out of the car as soon as we park along 9th Street, and by the time I manage to catch up with him at the counter he's already holding the book, handed to him with a "Here you are, Anton!" Then it's the dash back to begin reading, then and there. If there's no book waiting, he skips past the counter with a quick "Hi!" and I'll find him, minutes later, sitting down amongst the bookshelves, engrossed. We used to read together; now I'm basically superfluous (except for my wallet, of course), but I do get to look at particularly hilarious or notable pages in the books he's reading. Sometimes he'll make a pitch that his school desperately needs a particular book in its library. Each year his school holds a two-day event at the store where kids read favorite books, as well as some of their own writings, and parents can buy books requested by the teachers. I love that he's learned that we each play a role in the big warm web of books: choosing, giving, reading, writing. With two writers as parents, he's already kind of surrounded by the idea of reading and writing books, but the Regulator is what makes that experience truly one of community in the largest sense.

There's a spot in the back of the Regulator, at the crossroads between the children and young-adult books and the "Society" section of recent nonfiction, that always has the feel of a twenty-first-century salon. There's a small area with a comfortable couch, a chair, and a long pillowed bench, where you'll usually find a group of people sitting and reading together. They might chat occasionally about what they're reading. Anton and I can spend hours there, slouched and paging through different books, chatting with others doing the same.

Sometimes a writer happens by, and we buy a book and have him or her sign it. Sometimes there's a reading downstairs, and it might include a short concert of blues music, a heated political argument, or cascades of delirious laughter. There are political meetings, book-group meetings, and the more informal meetings that make up the texture of daily life in a place worth living in. The work of the bookstore is, ultimately, to create that kind of space. At the Regulator, they do it through their books, of course, through the events that, week after week, bring a remarkable group of writers and thinkers to the store. But they do it as much through the cultivation of a space that says to anyone and everyone: Come on in, take your time, stay for two minutes or two hours. And because of the time spent inside, you'll walk out into a world that's a little bit different from when you came in.

LAURENT DUBOIS was born in Belgium and grew up in Bethesda, Maryland. He graduated from Princeton in 1992 and received a doctorate in anthropology and history from the University of Michigan in 1998. Since then, he has taught at Harvard University and Michigan State University and is now Marcello Lotti Professor of Romance Studies and History at Duke University. He is the author of *Haiti: The Aftershocks of History* (Metropolitan, 2012), *Soccer Empire: The World Cup and the Future of France* (University of California Press, 2010), and *Avengers of the New World: The Story of the Haitian Revolution* (Harvard University Press, 2004) and is currently writing a history of the banjo.

Timothy Egan

The Elliott Bay Book Company, SEATTLE, WASHINGTON

The floors have to creak, of course. There should be a bit of a chill inside—not dank, or damp, but enough to bring on thoughts of curling up somewhere with one of the bound companions. If the table displays, favorite picks, and the like have a quirky randomness to them, in defiance of the latest imperatives from publishers, all the better. And placing the erotica section not far from religious tomes shows social engineering skills rare among bibliophiles.

All of this you take for granted at The Elliott Bay Book Company in Seattle. Or did, in the years when the store was hard by Puget Sound. After they decided to move up the hill to a new home, for survival, there was much concern about loss of the ambient charm. The personality, I'm happy to report, is intact.

But with the move you realized that Elliott Bay, as with all great bookstores, is only partially about physical space. You remember all the nights when you forgot where you were. There is Terry Tempest Williams paying raspy reverence to the slickrock canyons of the Southwest. Here is Sherman Alexie making you laugh so hard you gasp for breath. And here, there, and everywhere are the many obscure poets who arrive on Tuesday nights in January only to find that they are not obscure, not at Elliott Bay, an author's affirmation shrine.

Joe Lelyveld, a fine writer who also served as executive editor of *The New York Times* (full disclosure: Joe is my former boss, a likable one at that, and a friend), told an Elliott Bay audience not long ago how lucky they were. How so? You can walk nearly the length of Manhattan, he said, and not find a bookstore with such devoted readers as Elliott Bay's.

He did not have to convince me. For a time, I traveled almost 50,000 miles a year throughout the American West, looking for stories. A Carnegie Library, planted, say, on a patch of prairie somewhere more than a century ago, stood in many a town that had lost everything else. Rare was the well-tended, well-stocked independent bookstore—not just a haven, not just a refuge, but damn near a miracle. To return home and see a store like Elliott Bay housing all those stories and, nightly, all those storytellers, made me a fierce partisan of the indies.

We consider ourselves in Seattle—often with a bit of smugness— to be the most literate, best-read city in the nation. If you look at number of books sold per capita, the percentage of people with advanced educational degrees, and support for visiting authors, Seattle ranks near the top in all categories.

Is this Elliott Bay's doing? No, of course not. But you can't have one without the other. An informed, enlightened, well-read community needs an anchor. In Seattle, the only big city in the nation that people move to in order to get closer to nature, as the British expat Jonathan Raban said, our lives are defined by the natural world close at hand. But equally important are the interior spaces where we gather in order to tell each other stories. The climate, no doubt, encourages the latter—especially during the rainy season.

And while that "institution" (a word I use with caution in regard to Elliott Bay) must change with the times, as formats and "content platforms" sprout from tech labs in the digital revolution, certain things should remain constant. In Elliott Bay's universe, the written word is second to nothing. As it should be. As it will be.

> *…as the British expat Jonathan Raban said, our lives are defined by the natural world close at hand. But equally important are the interior spaces where we gather in order to tell each other stories.*

TIMOTHY EGAN is a Pulitzer Prize-winning reporter and the author of six books, most recently *The Big Burn: Teddy Roosevelt and the Fire That Saved America*, a *New York Times* best-seller and winner of the Pacific Northwest Booksellers Award and the Washington State Book Award. His previous books include *The Worst Hard Time*, which won a National Book Award and was named a *New York Times* Editors' Choice. He is an online op-ed columnist for the *New York Times*, writing his "Opinionator" feature once a week. He is a third-generation Westerner and lives in Seattle.

Dave Eggers

Green Apple Books, SAN FRANCISCO, CALIFORNIA

I feel weird choosing just one Bay Area bookstore, because at different times in my twenty years living out here, I've frequented Black Oak and Pegasus Books and Cody's and Moe's in Berkeley, Book Passage and the Depot in Marin County, Books Inc. and Modern Times and Dog Eared and City Lights in San Francisco, and many others in between. The Bay Area has the most independent bookstores in the country—maybe the world—but for the purposes of this collection I'd like to mention the first store I had a relationship with in San Francisco, Green Apple Books. They're also the ones who mentioned this book about indies, the one in which you're reading this essay, so they get dibs.

> *The first many times I passed by, driving or walking on the other side of the street, I thought, huh, another fruit market, and moved on. But it's a bookstore, and it's a world-class bookstore, and people love it deeply, and I love it deeply.*

My brother Toph and I lived in the Laurel Village/Richmond area for a few years, and when we did, the bookstore we went to was Green Apple. Like a lot of great bookstores, on the outside, Green Apple is deceptively simple, humble, even misleading. At first glance, you'd think it was actually a fruit market. There's the store's name, of course. Then there's the green awning, the global symbol for produce. There are even a few bins outside, where fruit would normally go. The first many times I passed by, driving or walking on the other side of the street, I thought, huh, another fruit market, and moved on. But it's a bookstore, and it's a world-class bookstore, and people love it deeply, and I love it deeply.

It was started by a former soldier named Richard Savoy, who in 1967 borrowed a few hundred dollars from a credit union to rent a storefront on Clement Street in San Francisco's Richmond District — a wonderfully diverse, predominantly Chinese and Russian neighborhood also known as The Avenues. The store originally carried used paperbacks and comics and magazines, but it was successful from the start and grew steadily over the years, into new books, and collectors' books, and every genre available, while always expanding physically, too. Into the second floor, and over into some of the neighboring storefronts; it's gone from 700 square feet to 8,500. Not bad for an independently owned store opened by a guy with no experience in the business.

Mr. Savoy ran the store for forty-two years, until 2009, when he handed the reins over to three longtime staff members—Kevin

Hunsanger, Kevin Ryan, and Pete Mulvihill—who own the store and run it together. I've known these guys for about fifteen years now, and I have to say there are no purer book people in the world. They know their store, they know their customers, and of course they know books. They know everything Green Apple carries, which is more or less everything—new books, used books, antiquarian rarities, humor oddities, coffee table masterpieces, paperback thrillers. The crazy thing about Green Apple is that everything, even a cat calendar, seems far more interesting and wantable in their hands.

This is the beauty of atmosphere and careful, inspired curation. First, a few words about atmosphere. Green Apple's floors, most of which are over a hundred years old, creak wherever you go, and when you walk upstairs, there will be small clouds of dust. The place is old, and smells old, in the best sense; it smells like paperbacks and sun and paperbacks faded in the sun. It smells of 1904, when the building was erected, and it smells of every decade and era in between. It smells of ink and leather shoes. The shelves occasionally bend in the middle. The hallways are narrow and the upstairs rooms are often small. It is a warren. It is a labyrinth. It has the feeling of the Winchester Mystery House, a building that seems to go on forever and into impossible directions and illogical spaces. But it never feels cramped. Instead, there is the feeling you get when walking into a house of worship with fifty-foot ceilings and stories told in stained glass, a feeling of grandeur and possibility.

There have been marriage proposals proffered in the store. Former employees have married each other. People, or at least one person, has died in the store (he had a heart attack, and, for the first time anyone could remember, just afterward, a bird flew in, alighted briefly, and left through the window). The store is frequented by children, by tourists, by older women seeking Patricia Highsmith, by students, by sellers of used books (the store has six full-time buyers), by passionate young readers, by last-minute holiday shoppers, and by Robin Williams.

I may need to check the data on this one, but my informal research says that no one has ever left the store empty-handed. I have personally never left the store without buying something.

There is a lesson here. I think stores should be well organized and have self-contained sections where you can find your philosophy books, your nonfiction, your books about fast cars, on and on. But there is equal, and possibly greater, benefit, in having these sections closely intermingling, or even overlapping. When you walk into Green Apple, the new and best-selling books are right there, in your face, but just to the left are the oversized art books, and there's always something that jumps out at you there, or just a few inches from those, where they keep fifty or so different new paperbacks, carefully curated, reminding you of all the books you missed in hardcover but would be a fool to miss now. Within a few feet are the humor books, the topical ones about zombies and shark-fighting. And again, in Green Apple, everything seems essential. Even without their thousands of handwritten notes of recommendation—which of course are heartfelt and urge-creating—even without these, something in the building casts a light of wonder and inevitability on everything they carry. Maybe it's the history of the building, which predates and survived the earthquakes of 1906 and 1989 and has the psychic wounds to show for it. Maybe it's the history of the business, which is after all the history of small family businesses in America. Maybe it's just the feeling that if a bookshop is as unorthodox and strange as books are, as writers are, as language is, it will all seem right and good and you will buy things there. And if you do, it will persist, and small publishers will persist, and actual books will persist. Anyone who wants anything less is a fool.

DAVE EGGERS is the best-selling author of *Zeitoun*, winner of the American Book Award and Dayton Literary Peace Prize and *Hologram for the King*. His novel *What Is the What* was a finalist for the National Book Critics Circle Award and won France's Prix Medici.

Louise Erdrich
Magers & Quinn Booksellers

MINNEAPOLIS, MINNESOTA

November 2004. George Bush just reelected. Dejection and apocalyptic dismay. But on the bright side, I am on my own, working on a book I love, happy in a complicated, messy house with my singular daughters. The great elms around my house have survived a drought. I've started running again. Then a man asks me out for coffee. I haven't been asked out by a man I wasn't already friends with, ever. I ask my date-guru friend, S., what to do? At our age, she says, having coffee with an interested man is like first base.

She advises me to scout out the coffee shop a few minutes early and choose the table with the softest lighting. She tells me that after he falls in love with me, he won't care what I look like. I don't want him to fall in love with me, but still, I choose a table lighted to my advantage and am waiting at Dunn Brothers with my chai latte when he arrives. He's tall and very attractive in a youthful, silver-fox sort of way; he has a dimple on one side of his South Dakota grin. But he's not my type, a businessman, a tile importer in building supply. Sure, I like tiles, but they have no irony. I'm ready to go home. Then he says, what next? Want to go to Magers & Quinn?

I remember catching glimpses of him as we walk the aisles of books, absorbed, then checking in with each other, then getting lost in the books again. He is wearing a black corduroy jacket, pressed jeans. Oh my god, *pressed* jeans? Actually, it occurs to me, I love the smell of ironing. I haven't ironed in years. We keep browsing. People love independent bookstores for the same reasons they love other people—looks, personality, interesting mind, smell. Magers & Quinn has been a boyfriend of mine ever since I moved to Minneapolis. I wonder if this man intuits that he is making himself part of a landscape I love?

When I first started visiting Magers & Quinn, signing my books even though it broke my heart that they were remaindered, I worried that the Borders across Hennepin Avenue would put Denny Magers out of business. Orr Books was across the street too, tiny but lovingly curated and with a passionate following. When I started my own bookstore, I asked Denny for advice. He didn't send me to a twelve-step program to try and stop me. Instead, he offered to let me go through the pallets of books in his basement and choose the new books, which he would sell to me for practically nothing. I found out that's how real book people are—delighted in the existence of other small bookstores, supportive of anyone crazy enough to start one. He would have done the same thing if I'd opened up next door to him, probably. As I hand-chose the first books I would put on my shelves, I had a feeling that our stores would both, somehow, survive.

My first date bought his books, I bought mine, and as we walked back to our cars he handed me a book he'd chosen as a gift. It was on Druids. I was slightly freaked, but he looked at me intently and asked if I also had a thing for trees. I told him about my elms. He saw that my car was a decisive date killer, a Ford Windstar minivan, and he looked troubled. Then he manned up and gave me the other book he'd chosen for me—the collected poems of Theodore Roethke. As we stood in the parking lot he began to recite, *I knew a woman, lovely in her bones...*. I looked into his eyes to detect some irony—there was none. But I'd already had lots of irony—maybe I had gotten it wrong. Maybe I needed not an ironic man but a man who ironed. Four years later, I did the only thing I could do.

Bookstore Lovers, I married him.

He still presses his jeans.

And Magers & Quinn is now old enough to vote for Obama. Happy 18!

> *My first date bought his books, I bought mine, and as we walked back to our cars he handed me a book he'd chosen as a gift. It was on Druids.*

LOUISE ERDRICH's books *The Round House*, *The Antelope Wife* (new and revised) and for children, *Chickadee*, will be published late summer and fall of 2012. She is the owner of Birchbark Books, in Minneapolis.

Jonathan Evison
Eagle Harbor Book Co.
BAINBRIDGE ISLAND, WASHINGTON

The little island on which I've lived most of my life has changed considerably over the decades. The bowling alley where we loitered as teens is long gone, along with the Jiffy Mart and the Island Bazaar. The Kell-in burger joint owned by our overweight gym teacher was paved over for a shopping center. American Marine Bank, where my mom worked for twenty-nine years, is gone. The Country Mouse, Yeakels Shoes, Torvanger's Gas Station—gone, gone, gone. The names, the faces, the personalities long associated with these local institutions are goners, along with their Fourth of July floats, their

Little League sponsorships, and their ads in the *Review*.

We've got a Safeway on the island now. A Rite-Aid, a McDonald's. They've got a Walmart just over the bridge in Poulsbo. A Barnes & Noble in Silverdale—even a Costco. Heck, these days, a guy can procure just about anything from 30 weight oil to Chicken McNuggets 24/7/365 around here. And once Amazon starts selling fast food at impossible prices, a fella won't even need to leave his house to get a fake beef cheeseburger! Oh, joy! Just think: We can all get fatter and lazier and more vaguely dissatisfied, and we won't have to deal with other human beings! Plus, since we will no longer have to slog all over town supporting local shops and paying an extra buck or two, and talking to actual people, we'll have twenty extra minutes a day to watch TV advertisements, and we'll have a few extra bucks we can spend on lotto tickets and phone apps!

> *Thanks, Eagle Harbor Book Company, for being made out of bricks and mortar, so I can soak up your atmosphere, haunt your shelves, and turn my own books face out when nobody's looking.*

All of this is just a long way of saying: Thank heaven for Eagle Harbor Book Company! For the names, the faces, and the personalities that make EHBC so quintessentially local—so Bainbridge Island. Victoria and Janis and Morley, and Andrew, and Jane and Allison—along with Jan, and Mary, and Paul, who preceded you with the same spirit and energy. Thanks, Eagle Harbor Book Company, for being made out of bricks and mortar, so I can soak up your atmosphere, haunt your shelves, and turn my own books face out when nobody's looking.

Thanks, Eagle Harbor Book Company, for letting me drive ten minutes out of my way to get to you, and thanks for letting me spend a few extra bucks to buy what I could purchase cheaper sitting on my ass at home without having to make any effort at all. Thanks, because effort matters. Effort is key to the survival of anything healthy or meaningful. Double thanks, Eagle Harbor Book Company, for putting that few extra bucks I spend by not shopping online or at a box store right back into the community, for bringing your resources into our classrooms, for sponsoring local events, for championing local authors, for encouraging book clubs, for providing your community with a venue for discourse and discussion. Thanks for ordering obscure titles for me. For answering questions, for making suggestions, for letting my kid trash your children's section three times a week, and for blowing his mind with your recommendations.

Above all, thank you, Eagle Harbor Book Company, for representing—for being exactly what you are: totally unique and personable in an increasingly uniform and impersonal world.

JONATHAN EVISON is the *New York Times* best-selling author of *All About Lulu*, *West of Here*, and *The Revised Fundamentals of Caregiving*. He lives on Bainbridge Island, Washington, with his wife and son.

Kathleen Finneran

Left Bank Books, ST. LOUIS, MISSOURI

As with many things in my life, I did not discover it until I was in my twenties and moved from the suburbs of St. Louis, where I grew up, to a small apartment in the city, where I grew up again. I knew little about literature, even less about the world. When you know little, it is easy to assume you know a lot. In knowing little, I assumed it was named for the Left Bank in Paris (it is) and that it was a tribute to Hemingway and Fitzgerald and Stein and the other expatriate writers who lived and wrote there (it isn't).

I worked nights as a proofreader and aspired to be a writer (knowing little, assuming much). I knew so little about what it meant to

101

be a writer that I thought the way to begin was to buy a hefty volume called *Writer's Market* (The Most Trusted Guide to Getting Published! Completely Revised and Updated! 3,000 Listings to Help You Sell What You Write!). I hadn't written anything, but I was eager to sell it.

The woman working the cash register asked if I was a writer. I hope I wasn't arrogant (or naive) enough to say that I was, but whatever my response, it led her to recommend another purchase: *Poets & Writers Magazine*. She went and got a copy off the shelf and showed me the classifieds section in the back with its Call for Manuscripts, Contests, Conferences, Residencies, and Retreats. I remember feeling respected, taken seriously, understood. Yes, I did feel all those things in the slight time span of that transaction. And I was naive enough (and, yes, also arrogant enough) to think that she was personally responding to me and my self-purported future and not just skillfully increasing her sales.

In fact, she was doing both. Doing both, I suspect, is one of the reasons Left Bank Books has survived for over forty years. The cashier that day was Kris Kleindienst, an aspiring writer herself, who co-owned the bookstore with Barry Leibman, an artist. Both had been employees of the original shop, a source for underground newspapers and leftist literature started by a collective of student activists from Washington University who named the store, then located nearer to campus, in recognition of the protests that took place in Paris in the spring of 1968, the year before Left Bank Books began.

I did not know, that day, who the woman was that waited on me, but she influenced me greatly from that first day forward. I became a regular customer, and as such, I was the benefactor of her taste and intellect and values. The decisions she made about what books to stock in her store became the discoveries I would make when browsing with that kind of idle intention that good bookstores inspire. Indirectly, and without my conscious consideration of it, she was as much a mentor to me as any of the writers I went on to study with later.

At Left Bank, my browsing always began outside the store. I found

> *Indirectly, and without my conscious consideration of it, she was as much a mentor to me as any of the writers I went on to study with later.*

it impossible to enter without surveying the flyers, postcards, handbills, and rental notices—Register to Vote Inside! Keep Art Happening! Pelvic Workshop for Women!—that filled the community bulletin boards framing the store's corner entry. That entryway! Without it, would I have learned of some of the more obscure readings, concerts, plays, and exhibits I attended in my twenties? Would I have plotted my imagined moves to apartments that promised more character than mine, more love, more life? Would I have become a true citizen of St. Louis? Would I have encountered my pelvis? Perhaps. Perhaps not.

Once through the door with its long, oval window, I tended always to descend the stairs that led to the store's lower level—offices and an art gallery on one side, used books on the other. Essays were my weakness. And autobiography too (it would be another ten years until memoir came into its own). In time, I gained enough sense to realize that writing was not about publishing but about reading and seeing and thinking and listening and developing a sense of one's self. And, yes, about putting words on paper. I acquired sacks and sacks of used books from Left Bank's basement and occasionally splurged on new books from the store's main floor, where I favored the set of shelves labeled "Belles Lettres."

For years, "Belles Lettres" was located opposite the cash register. It has since been moved further back. Because I spent a lot of time in "Belles Lettres," I often stood in the shadow of the sales desk. It is situated, roughly, in the center of the store, and elevated slightly. The salesclerks sit higher still whenever they are perched on their tall wooden stools, busying themselves with paperwork and special orders and whatever other tasks fill their time between transactions. Something about this spatial arrangement satisfied me, especially when I stood in "Belles Lettres," the casual chatter and banter of bookstore business—book recommendations, on-the-spot reviews—occurring just over my shoulder.

Shortly after my first visit to Left Bank, I became a subscriber to the magazine Kris had recommended, and several years later I sent off a manuscript in response to an advertisement in its pages for a scholarship to attend a summer writing workshop in Vermont. The next year, through connections made at the workshop, I got a clerical job in New York City and moved away from the Midwest to make a life in Manhattan, land of many bookstores.

Curiously, I never became a regular at any of them. I lived a life nearly barren of books except for one: the one I was writing. A few weeks after I moved to New York, on the basis of an essay I wrote at the summer writing workshop in Vermont, I was offered a book contract to write a memoir. Even now, so many years later, it's difficult for me to admit how little I read during the decade I spent writing that book. The deprivation was born of fear, I suppose, fear that I would never write something equal to anything I read, fear that I would borrow someone else's voice before I found my own, fear that the limited hours I had to write at night and on the weekends could get easily lost to reading. During that time I mainly went to bookstores to hear other writers read from their work, or, more honestly, to see other writers read from their work, but I had left my habit of browsing back in St. Louis, along with all the books I had bought at Left Bank, stored now in boxes in my parents' basement.

When my book finally came out, it had what is known in the industry as a "quiet" publication. But before it settled into its obscurity, it enjoyed one night of immeasurable attention. I was scheduled to read at Left Bank. I flew home to St. Louis the day before the reading, and the next morning I realized that I had left my only copy of the book—an advance reading copy—in New York. I hadn't yet received my box of hardcover copies from the publisher. I panicked. I had planned to spend the morning selecting what to read from the book, timing it and rehearsing it. Although I had no real experience giving readings, I knew that I was no natural at it and that showing up that night and reading cold would make for a less than impressive debut. I was staying at my parents' house in the suburbs. I drove to the new big-box bookstore up the road to buy a copy, but they didn't have my book in stock. (A week or so later, they did begin to carry it, but since the book was about my younger brother's suicide, they shelved it in a section of the store called "Family Psychology" far away from the shelves of literature and memoir, and few people found it.) I drove a little farther down the road to the mall, to the small chain bookstore I frequented when I was a teenager, with its single catchall shelf marked "Literature," but, again, no luck. So I drove across town to Left Bank. Since I was reading there that night, they would have to have copies.

I didn't browse the bulletin boards that morning before going in that oval-windowed doorway that I loved. I know this for a fact because I was stopped short by a single flyer announcing my reading there that night. It was the first publicity I had seen for my book, and the sudden surprise of it made me start to cry. Not wanting to enter the store crying, I walked around the bookstore's Central West End neighborhood a bit. Like the bookstore, it was a neighborhood that fought hard to sustain itself, one that had been revitalized by urban pioneer retailers and restaurateurs, Left Bank an early anchor.

I made my way back to the bookstore and went in. I hadn't been inside in over a decade, but it was still as I remembered, light-filled, calm, simple, and straightforward, a contrast to its ornamental early-twentieth-century terra-cotta exterior. New nonfiction was displayed and shelved on the left. New novels on the right and beyond that the children's corner, always looking somewhat suitably disheveled, signifying a place where curiosity is encouraged. Straight ahead, the stairs to the lower level, where now a sign—More Books Below—hangs overhead, featuring the painted cutout silhouette of a black cat, with the store's actual black cat, Spike, slumbering or slinking somewhere below it.

I walked over to "Belles Lettres." I knew my book wouldn't be in that section—it wasn't a book of essays of the sort that filled those shelves—but I suddenly felt self-conscious about going directly to wherever it might be. For all the time I had spent writing my book, I had never really thought about what it would be like for it to exist in the world, or for me to exist in the world with it. It was my first time being in a bookstore in which some other part of me was there as well, some shadow self, some better, truer part perhaps. I browsed a bit in "Belles Lettres," and when I felt more settled into this new circumstance—me here in person, me here in print—I proceeded to look for a copy of my book to buy.

I didn't have to look far. In fact, I simply looked up and there on the sales desk were several stacks of my book, with a sign above them saying I would be reading at the store that night. I took one from the stack and handed it to the salesclerk. She said something that created an awkward moment. I don't remember her words exactly. She either told me about the reading or asked me if I planned to come. I stood there—the me here in person, the me here in print—feeling somewhat embarrassed. Should I admit that I was buying my own book?

(Several years later, my book out of print, I got into the routine of checking online book sites for used copies that were marked in "like new" condition and selling for under five dollars. Every couple of months I would buy a few to replenish my own supply. Once, after buying a copy online, I received an email almost immediately from the seller saying she couldn't help but notice that my name was the same as the name of the person who wrote the book. Did I know the author, she asked. I am the author, I replied. Within minutes, she sent another email explaining that my book had been required reading for a class she took. Now that the class was over, she said, she had no reason to keep it. "I'm happy to sell it to you," she wrote. "It's not a book I'd ever want to read again.")

On the day of my reading at Left Bank, faced with the salesclerk's question or comment, I decided I should say who I was. After all, I would be returning a few hours later. If she was still working at the time of the reading, wouldn't it be even more awkward to have her recognize me and wonder why I hadn't introduced myself earlier? I told her the book was mine and explained why I was buying it. I'm relieved to say she got excited (more than the woman years later who unmasked me online). She put the book down and walked around to my side of the counter, telling me that I had to meet Kris, one of the owners, who loved the book and would be introducing me that night. She took me to the back of the store where Kris was meeting with a book rep from Random House.

It may seem unimportant that the book rep was from Random House, and maybe it is. But she was the first (and only) representative of Random House that I have ever met, and I felt a little starstruck in her presence. When I was a child and spent much of my time alone wondering about random things, one of the random things I wondered about was Random House. As a child, I had few books. One, a favorite, was *Bennett Cerf's Book of Laughs*. Just thinking about the yellow cover of that book with its multicolored, multi-patterned drawing of a giraffe still makes me smile, and often even laugh. It's one of the few reliable responses I have to anything in the world. As a child, I spent a lot of time with that book, reading it mostly with my older brother, who fancied himself as funny as Bennett Cerf, but wasn't.

We had a few other books too: *Bennett Cerf's Book of Riddles*, *Bennett Cerf's Riddles and More Riddles*, *Bennett Cerf's Book of Animal Riddles*, and when we were older, *Bennett Cerf's Treasury of Atrocious Puns*. With the exception of *Bennett Cerf's Treasury of Atrocious Puns* (a book of more-sophisticated wordplay written really for adults, which we mostly didn't understand but laughed at anyway), all were published by Random House Books for Young Readers. I was drawn to those words "Random House" and wondered about them maybe more than I should admit. I'm sure I even often said them out loud—Random House, Random House—in the privacy of the room I shared with my sister. Rhythmically, they were, to me, words worth repeating.

When I was in fifth grade and assigned to write a report on my favorite author, naturally I chose Bennett Cerf, and in my research solved for my young self the mystery of those alluring words, Random

House, suggested by Cerf as the name for an enterprise undertaken by he and his friends "to publish a few books on the side at random." (Note: As a benefactor of all the laughter he provided in my childhood, I willingly overlook Cerf's role in founding the infamous Famous Writers School and admit that if I had been of age to enroll in that seemingly specious correspondence school, vanity and Bennett Cerf fandom would likely have led me to do so.) And so for me, among its many significances, Left Bank will always be the place where I met one of Bennett Cerf's descendants. And recognizing my name (recognizing my name!), the rep from Random House congratulated me on a review of my book she had read in her hotel room that morning in *USA Today*. I had had no idea that my book had been reviewed in *USA Today* that morning—it was my first review—and without her mentioning it, I doubt I would have heard about it, much less had a chance to buy a copy before one day's edition became the next's. Thank you, thank you, rep from Random House. Thank you, thank you, Sam I Am. (Yes, of course, I also had *Green Eggs and Ham*, a book that my fifth grade research revealed was written by Dr. Seuss when Bennett Cerf bet him that a good book could not be written using only fifty words.)

Kris did not remember me from my earlier era of browsing at Left Bank, and there was little reason why she should. After that initial purchase to launch my publishing career with *Writer's Market*, there were few times that she actually waited on me, although I noticed her working whenever I came to the store. In truth, I was both in awe of her and intimidated by her back then. We were roughly the same age, and while I had accomplished little in life at that point, she had accomplished much, not only sharing in the ownership of a bookstore but contributing significantly to the vitality of our town.

On the day of my reading, when I officially met her, she refused to sell me a copy of my book, insisting that I take it with the store's compliments, and she asked me how many people I thought they might expect that night. I counted up the members of my extended family and the few friends I had kept up with since I left St. Louis and delivered a high-end estimate of forty to fifty. She showed me the space where I would be reading, where later they would roll several sets of bookshelves to the back of the store and set up chairs in the area between children's books and my beloved "Belles Lettres." She showed me the podium they used (of the pulpit sort) and asked me if I'd like to stand behind it with my book opened to see how it felt. I sensed that she could tell I'd not had much experience reading before an audience and that she was introducing me to any details she thought might make me feel at ease. When she finished familiarizing me with the setup, she offered to call some newsstands to see who still had copies of USA Today. It was late in the afternoon by then, and she was worried I might not find one. All the while, I had been keeping her from finishing her work with the rep from Random House, but she made me feel as if I was the most important matter of the day.

When I returned for the reading a few hours later, there were over 150 people filling the store. More shelves had been rolled aside, more chairs set up, and still people stood on the sides and in the aisles. People from my childhood, people from my siblings' childhoods, people even from my parents' childhoods. There were people from my parents' neighborhood and people from their parish. Teachers from my grade school, high school, college. People I didn't know who were there with people I did. Connections and reconnections were made that night that still astound me. The best man at my parents' wedding came with his wife. He and my parents had lost touch over the fifty years since they'd been married. The man came especially to tell my father that they, too, had lost a son to suicide. And most moving to me, friends of my younger brother came, young men and women now in their thirties whom I had not seen since his funeral when they were 15.

There will never be another night like that. I imagine it will always remain the biggest night of my life. And it was the beginning, too, of a closer, more personal relationship for me with Left Bank, and with Kris, and with her partner Jarek Steele, who is the newest of the store's co-owners. I have learned a few things about bookselling from them. I have learned, for instance, that if a book is published "quietly," as mine was, with not much publicity and only a handful of reviews, it can still find its way in the world, thanks to the kind of "hand-selling" that is the strength and specialty of good booksellers. My book would have had a much shorter life were it not for Kris's promotion of it. It became a BookSense 76 pick and gained the notice of other independent booksellers, whose collective attention resulted, three years later, in a paperback version, something the publisher had not previously planned on bringing out.

I have since moved back to St. Louis and have become a regular again at Left Bank Books. They now have a second location downtown, but by habit (and proximity to my house), I still tend to frequent the original store in the Central West End. I admit I no longer dawdle in the doorway reading notices and announcements. I'm in my fifties now, and for better or worse, the need to fill my days and nights with things other than those with which I'm already familiar feels less urgent.

Unlike in my twenties, I tend to buy more new books now than used. Still, I find myself drawn to the "Rare Books and Collectibles" section in the rear of the store, with its two glass-fronted antique bookcases and the wooden bench that sits between them. There is not much turnover in the inventory on those shelves; selfishly, this pleases me. I like to look at (but can't afford) the first-edition or near-first-edition copies of *Twenty Years at Hull-House* by Jane Addams, *Tambourines to Glory* by Langston Hughes, *Mastering the Art of French Cooking* by Julia Child, all seven volumes of *The Diary of Anaïs Nin*, a children's book called *Betty, Bobby, and Bubbles*, George Orwell's *1984*, J.D. Salinger's *Franny and Zooey*, and my favorite, Virginia Woolf's *The Waves*, with an inscription that reads: "J, if this book is good, I'm glad; we will discover an unknown (to us) author together. – R."

I feel happy for J and R whenever I read that. Certainly they found Woolf's novel good, and were glad, and went on to discover many other unknown authors together. I feel happy, too, when I pull from the bottom shelf of "Rare Books and Collectibles" the copy of St. Louis author Constance Urdang's book of poems *The Picnic in the Cemetery*, signed by the writer and inscribed to Erika, presumably a resident of either the East Coast or the West: "For Erika, From MidAmerica," Urdang wrote. Her wit makes me smile. As did the words and wit of her husband, the poet Donald Finkel, and the poets Mona Van Duyn and Howard Nemerov and John Morris, and the writers Stanley Elkin and William Gass, and others who gave St. Louis a lot of its literary shine when I was in my twenties, and still do. "For Erika, From MidAmerica."

As for me, happily once more in MidAmerica, I am pleased to say that when I sit on the bench in "Rare Books," either browsing or reading or eavesdropping or watching people pass by the bookstore window, I am completely comfortable in the knowledge that around the corner, in "Biography and Memoir," my second self is also present—the me in person, the me in print. I am confident too that Left Bank is the only bookstore where I could ever claim that double existence. My book is a few years beyond its paperback issue and would be considered well past its shelf life in any other store.

KATHLEEN FINNERAN is the author of the memoir *The Tender Land: A Family Love Story*. She teaches writing at Washington University in St. Louis.

Fannie Flagg

Page & Palette, FAIRHOPE, ALABAMA

Dear Reader,

As a longtime author and a lifetime lover of books, I have had the opportunity both personally and professionally to visit hundreds of bookstores over the years—large and small, independent and chain-owned. Knowing this, you might guess that being asked to pick out just one bookstore to write about would be hard, but (unlike writing books) for me this is an easy task.

I can say without any hesitation that my very favorite bookstore in the entire world, hands down, is Page & Palette, a longtime family-owned independent bookstore located in Fairhope, Alabama. And luckily for me, it just happens to be about two minutes from where I live.

But first, before I tell you about the store, let me tell you a little something about Fairhope. It is an absolutely charming town located in South Alabama that sits high on a bluff overlooking the beautiful Mobile Bay, and fortunately, unlike a lot of other small towns across America whose local stores have fallen victim to the large shopping malls and closed, Fairhope still has a bustling and thriving downtown area, and if you should happen to visit and walk around Section Street, you would soon learn that the hub of most of that downtown activity is the Page & Palette bookstore. And if you were to go inside, the other thing you might quickly observe is that Fairhope people, visitors and locals alike, just love to read. Why?

Well, other than the fact that they are a highly intelligent and curious bunch, I think it all began in 1968 with one woman, Betty Joe Wolff, and with her love of books.

In fact, Betty Joe just may be the reason we still have so many readers and book buyers today. For as long as I can remember, customers have come in the door and called out, "Hey, Betty Joe, I need a good book—what do you recommend?" And Betty Joe, a delightful brunette with bright green eyes and a smile for everyone, always seems to have time to find just the right book for you, whether you are 6 or 70.

> *For a small store in a small town, Page & Palette has the biggest heart of any bookstore I know.*

For a small store in a small town, Page & Palette has the biggest heart of any bookstore I know. And Betty Joe's customers appreciate it and are fiercely loyal. Even today, old-guard Fairhopeians wouldn't dare be caught dead with a Kindle or, God forbid, a book ordered from Amazon.com. I once heard the mayor's wife say, "Why, I wouldn't even consider reading a book unless Page & Palette recommended it!"

I personally came to know Betty Joe just by being one of her many customers, and then, in 1981, when my first novel was published, Betty Joe hosted my very first book signing, and I will never forget it. As I mentioned, it is a family-owned store, and at the time, Betty Joe's two little skinny 10-year-old twin granddaughters, Karin and Kelley, were on hand to help open books and hand out cookies. And now, seven books and some thirty years later, it is still my favorite place to go for book signings.

From an author's point of view, book signings can be long and tiring, but Page & Palette signings are always special and a wonderful and fun event. You never know what will happen; for instance, when my novel *Can't Wait to Get to Heaven* came out, as a complete surprise to me, the store had everyone in town come to the signing dressed as angels, complete with halos, white robes, and wings!

Of course, times have changed. A wonderful café and coffee bar was added to the store, and now some events draw as many as 800 or 900 people, but the feeling is still the same. Betty Joe claims she has retired, but she still comes in every day to visit. Best of all, those two little twin granddaughters have grown into lovely young women with families of their own. Karin and her husband now run the bookstore, and Kelley and her husband own the art store next door. And both continue to carry on Betty Joe's legacy. So, if you do visit Fairhope and you love books, just go into Page & Palette and browse around the wonderful Southern Writers Section or sit down and have a cup of coffee and a sandwich in the café. I can guarantee you, at some time or another, you will be sure to spot hometown authors like myself, Winston Groom, Mark Childress, Carolyn Haines, W.E.B. Griffin, Jimmy Buffett, or Rick Bragg wandering in and out. And you might be surprised to see, in this day and age, when expediency and convenience seem to rule, that people in Fairhope are still shopping in person for books in an honest-to-God real store, with real people behind the counter to talk to.

Why have the customers and authors remained so loyal all these years? I think it's because Page & Palette has always been, from the very beginning, from the owners right down to the staff, an effort of love. They care about their customers and their authors, and in a time when more and more bookstores all over the country are closing down every day, Page & Palette's continued success says a lot. We know they love us and we love them back. It's that simple.

Sincerely,
Fannie Flagg

P.S. Like I said, you never know what to expect at a Page & Palette book signing. Just minutes before my last signing, poor Karin locked me in the broom closet by mistake and had to call a locksmith to get me out. But the good news is that I did get out and had another wonderful event. I can hardly wait for the next one (neither can my publisher), but then that's another story.

FANNIE FLAGG is the author of *Fried Green Tomatoes at the Whistle Stop Café* and several other novels including her latest titled *Welcome to the World, Baby Girl!* She lives in California and Alabama.

Ian Frazier

Watchung Booksellers, MONTCLAIR, NEW JERSEY

Montclair is a long and narrow suburb of New York City. It is a hills-and-valleys sort of place, with the town mostly in the valleys and the bigger houses on the hills. The commuter train runs through a valley as it has done since 1854—this is a very old suburb, one of the first—and the train's whistle, often accompanied (at my house) by the rattle of ice cubes in a cocktail glass, marks the end to the suburban day. The hills are what remain of ancient mountains called the Watchung Range. Watchung is pronounced WATCH-ung, a fun word to say, like "Watch it!" but with an "ung." It's the kind of Jersey word you can imagine the Sopranos saying, but I don't think any of them ever did, though parts of that show were filmed here.

I am a writer who usually works at home, but when I do go into the city Watchung Plaza is where I get the bus or the train. The plaza is a modest one, with a flagpole in memory of the town's World War I servicemen and a few benches and a bus shelter and some hedges and a lawn. Along one side of the plaza stands a row of businesses, including a Chinese restaurant called Wah-Chung. Once I asked the people in the restaurant if, by coincidence, "Wah-Chung" meant something in Chinese, but they said it didn't. Watchung Booksellers occupies a corner of the plaza; the store has been there or in a location nearby for sixteen years, three years longer than we've lived in Montclair.

It's only a small exaggeration to say that we moved here because of the independent bookstores. Montclair used to have five of them, and now it has two—a regrettable decline, but two independents is still not bad for a town of 34,000. Watchung Booksellers quickly became my favorite. If I return from the city at night when all the stores on the square are closed, I notice the lights in the windows of the bookstore as I come down the train station steps, and I walk by to see what books are on display. The pleasure of leaving noisy New York and disembarking in this peaceful place settles in as I take a moment while the cars that have come to pick people up from the train drive off. I appreciate this good bookstore somehow even more at this late hour, when it is closed and empty of staff and customers and it sits there quietly diffusing its warm, intelligent light.

As someone who makes a living by writing, I feel a kinship with Margot Sage-EL, the store's owner. Writing books, and trying to sell them, seem equally ill-advised ways to spend one's time. Of course you do it for love. Robert Frost once wrote, "Only when love and need are one/And the work is play, for mortal stakes/Is the deed ever really done/For heaven and the future's sakes." Like a poet writing to make the rent, an independent bookstore exists at that heart-quickening juncture of love and need. I always take encouragement from the lights in Margot's bookstore because they tell me that, at least so far, our mutual and sometimes dicey enterprise is succeeding.

I go to the bookstore to buy—will writers be the last remaining purchasers of books? I don't think so, to judge from the crowds I often find at Margot's—and to examine the author photos and the paper stock and judge the all-round quality of production. You must actually touch a book to discover that. When I publish a book of my own I do readings there, as does my wife when her books come out, as do others of our writer friends in Montclair. The readings are held in a part of the store not much larger than a one-car garage. If the audience exceeds about a dozen and a half, some must sit in an overflow area among bookshelves where they can't see the author or vice versa. To me that is the best kind of crowd, and when I go to readings there I don't mind being in the zero-visibility section myself. That's part of the reason I became a reader, and a writer, in the first place—to be off in a corner and yet part of the grand adventure of literature.

In the bookstore I am in this bricks-and-mortar shared place on Watchung Plaza in the town of Montclair, not adrift in some cyber Nowhere. A very wise writer I know said recently, during one of those inescapable modern discussions about books and their future, "A book is public." I can't exactly explain why I think that is a brilliant observation, but I know "A book is public" is true just the way I know when a joke is funny. A book is public because it takes what is inside a writer and brings it out for readers so they can make it part of what is inside themselves. No writing exists until that transfer occurs. Writing exists not in the writer only and not in the reader only, but in a shimmering plane midway between the two; and the region where the encounter occurs is the book. A book is a physical thing and physical occasion like a person met by chance on the street. You can summon a book out of cyberspace and read it on your e-reader, but that experience is too private for the exchange to really count. To read a book is to possess

> *A book is a physical thing and physical occasion like a person met by chance on the street.*

it physically and hang out with it. At some point you should be seen with it in public as if it were a friend you're proud to have or a scar you're not too modest to show.

At Watchung Booksellers there's a daily rhythm to the life of books. Kids are running around—a bookstore like this is where kids are first brought into the wider world of reading—and there are the sounds of conversations about books, and the humming quiet of the browsers, and the crisp tearing and folding of gift-wrap paper at the counter, and it smells like books, with that fresh, subtly seductive smell. Independent bookstores such as Margot's collaborate with writing in an intimate way that makes cyber bookselling seem merely retail. They are where the public aspect of the book, its real publication, plays out. I often travel the country to promote my books, and sometimes when I'm doing a reading a person in the audience will ask me what I think will happen to books and bookstores in the future. My answer usually is, "Well, we're all here right now, aren't we?" Books imply the future, but we write them, and we read them, and they begin their public existence, not in some unknown future but right now. Watchung Booksellers is, valiantly, a place where all of us who love books can be right now.

IAN FRAZIER is the author of 10 books, including the nonfiction *Great Plains, On the Rez,* and *Travels in Siberia,* and the comic novel *The Cursing Mommy's Book of Days.* His work often appears in *The New Yorker* and other magazines.

Mindy Friddle

Fiction Addiction, GREENVILLE, SOUTH CAROLINA

Book touring can be lonely for authors. You're on the road after being sequestered at your writing desk. For months you've been perfectly content to hold imaginary conversations with characters, only to be thrust now into the world of commerce, blinking like some soft, startled creature from under a rotting log. You grip your signing pen and smile. Your extroversion muscles have grown slack with disuse, but you're expected to chat with real humans and display some charm, not to mention field questions with wit. (Most authors will tell you the number one question they're asked at their book signings is, "Could you tell me where the restroom is?")

So when I discovered an event on my book tour that worked— ravenous readers, attentive listeners who *buy your book!*—it was cause for celebration. The event is an author series called Book Your Lunch, and it's the brainchild of bookseller Jill Hendrix, owner of Fiction Addiction, an independent bricks-and-mortar bookstore in my hometown of Greenville, South Carolina. Book Your Lunch is a fantastic way to bring readers and a wide range of authors together— from mystery writers, to award-winning novelists, to nonfiction and cookbook authors. Fiction Addiction sells tickets in advance, and the featured author reads from her work, or gives a short talk, followed by a Q&A session, a delicious lunch, and then an on-site book signing.

I was lucky to be included in the birth of Book Your Lunch, to be in the delivery room, as it were, as this exquisite event was brought forth into the world. It all started nearly three years ago when I sat down with Jill to brainstorm. I'm a writer. I love brainstorming. Jill wanted my thoughts on how Fiction Addiction could create success- ful author events. She was then prepared to fashion my ideas into an actual plan with spreadsheets and a win-win business model. We talked about the Moveable Feast, Litchfield Books' wonderful literary luncheon series held Fridays at a variety of restaurants in Pawley's Island, South Carolina (another bright spot on my book tour). Might Fiction Addiction tweak and tailor such a luncheon series to an author event in our own community? We listed potential names—puns are my specialty—and came up with Book Your Lunch. Once Jill made sure the domain name was available for a website, Fiction Addiction's inaugural luncheon series was born.

In 2010, when Picador published my second novel, *Secret Keepers*, in paperback, I had the honor of being a featured author for Book Your Lunch. I looked out onto a roomful of people—and I wasn't even related to most of them. I had to use a microphone, a sure sign of a successful reading, as far as I'm concerned. Fiction Addiction sold a pile of my books afterward, and as soon as I inhaled my free lunch, I had one of my most enjoyable book signings ever.

Now, two and a half years after it began, more than fifty Book

Your Lunch events have been held, an average of two luncheons per month. Fiction Addiction has increased sales of books thanks to Book Your Lunch—and weathered the economic downturn just fine, thank you. A number of authors have stopped in Greenville, South Carolina, for the first time and cultivated new readers. (Author Dorothea Benton Frank gets the prize for the most books sold at one luncheon—250 audience members, and 300 books sold!) Word has spread. Publicists and authors now regularly contact Fiction Addiction about appearing at Book Your Lunch. Imagine that: readers, publicists, authors, an independent bookstore—all happy! I call that a win-win-win-win.

> *I had the honor of being a featured author for Book Your Lunch. I looked out onto a roomful of people—and I wasn't even related to most of them.*

MINDY FRIDDLE's novel *The Garden Angel* was a National Public Radio Independent Booksellers' pick. Her most recent novel, *Secret Keepers*, won the 2010 Willie Morris Award for Southern Fiction.

David Fulmer

Eagle Eye Book Shop, DECATUR, GEORGIA

I've spent time in independent bookstores on three continents—
or is it four? A few have been famed: City Lights, Gotham Book
Mart, Shakespeare & Co. Others I've visited are less legendary, but no
less an experience, like Partners & Crime and the Mysterious Bookshop in New York City and Faulkner House Books in New Orleans.
I almost got into a fistfight in one and was cornered by a predatory
female fan in another. Don't get me wrong; we're talking decades
here. It's not like every bookstore experience is a walk on the wild side.

I've had my longest and happiest history with Eagle Eye Book
Shop in Decatur, Georgia, which is a contiguous part of the city of

123

Atlanta, where I live. It's been a narrative in and of its own, with my role shifting from customer to published author to writing instructor. And I was a dad all along.

This began one morning as I was walking from ChocoLatté, one of my coffee joints, to visit Sukru, the computer doctor who has saved my book files a half-dozen times. I passed Eagle Eye and stopped. The facade spanned two normal storefronts. Had this place been here before? How did I miss it?

When I got to the computer shop, I found the patient still on the table with its electrical guts on display. Sukru was muttering in Turkish and I figured he'd be happier with me out of there, so I wandered back to the store.

I found neither another hole-in-the-wall nor an antiseptic waiting room. The first thing I noticed was how roomy, light, and airy a space it was. I trolled long aisles and found books for every brain, thousands of them, new and used and in-between. A children's section in the corner offered sounds like the gabbling of baby ducks. Then I wandered into a back room that was lined on three sides, floor-to-ceiling, with oddball collectibles. Such as a set of H. Irving Hancock's Dick and Company series (no, really) from 1911. A heavy tome on shipbuilding in Russian. An atlas the size of a café table, with maps so richly colored they appeared edible. The point is, even among indie stores, this was what you call one of your more eclectic establishments.

I became a regular. At the beginning, because I *needed* books for my shelves and for my daughter Italia's room. I was simply a customer until my career as a fiction author got off the ground. I did book launches there, and that brought out my friends and theirs.

In other words, I became a truant part of the family. The staff was a mix too. Young and not-so, girls and boys, and a dog now and then. I mean a canine. It was like a cast from a series. I wish I could say more, but these are real people, not cutouts. Every one of them had something interesting going outside the store. You can use your imagination.

> *Even among indie stores, this was what you call one of your more eclectic establishments.*

It was at Eagle Eye that I had my closest brush with the notorious rare-book thief who had been making the rounds of the Atlanta stores. As a mystery writer, I was intrigued by this guy's M.O. Every bookseller in the city knew him on sight, but he still made his scores. One afternoon, he and I were in Eagle Eye at the same time and I didn't know until after he had evaporated. He was one character and there were others. Independent bookstores invite independent individuals of every stripe.

I had been teaching a writing program I called Fiction Shop for a couple of years and kept on losing my home through no fault of my own. I made a deal with Eagle Eye to use the Reading Room in back. Like a salon kind of deal. It worked. Interesting people from all over the map showed up. The staff welcomed them, even when it got weird. They still drifted out before, after, and during breaks and spent money. The vibes back and forth were pleasant.

Well, mostly. One incident jumps out. I had a—how do I say this—*challenging* student in one of my eight-week classes. She was a little out of control. A chemical imbalance, to put it in recent parlance. Some nights she was a perfect lady. Other times, she was out there, chattering to herself and to others. When it came time to read the exercise I had assigned, she would either freeze or begin rewriting on the spot. She was unaware of the disruption she was causing and was oblivious when I left her babbling and moved on to the next student. During the break, she would disappear, sometimes for a half hour. I had no idea where she had gone.

The class and I had put up with her for six weeks. On the seventh, she arrived in a manic state. This night, she spoke out of turn one too many times. I barked like a dog on a chain. "Andrea!" Not her real name. "Enough!" (This from someone who chastises students for their use of exclamation points.) Everyone in the room froze, and I heard dead silence from the store. Now I was feeling like a monster for picking on this poor woman. On the other hand, she was carrying those meds for a reason.

The good news was she didn't totally freak out and the class ended without another incident. After we wrapped up, I went to the front desk and apologized to the clerk and whatever customers had been on hand for yelling like that with customers in the store.

Instead, I received a small round of applause. The clerk said, "I can't believe it took you this long." Try that at your big-box store.

The one other piece of the story has to do with the modern family. My daughter has been around Eagle Eye for half of her life. We've bought books for her room and books for school. The store happens to be located halfway between her mom's house and ours and became the weekly pass-off point. Italia loves the place and says she'd like to work there one day. And maybe she will. That would please her dad, too. It's that kind of place.

All the above could have transpired only in an independent store. They are by definition unique, bless their souls, with their own rare personalities. Let's hope this doesn't go away.

Because they will be the salvation of books on paper.

As the author of seven critically acclaimed historical mysteries, **DAVID FULMER** has been nominated for the Shamus Award for Best Novel, the *Los Angeles Times* Book Prize, the Barry Award, and the Falcon Award; has won the Shamus Award for Best First Novel and the Benjamin Franklin Award; and has been nominated to numerous "Best of" lists, including *New York Magazine*'s "Best Novels You've Never Read." He lives in Atlanta.

Henry Louis Gates, Jr.

Harvard Book Store, CAMBRIDGE, MASSACHUSETTS

One of the changes alumni visiting Harvard generally lament is the loss of many mom-and-pop businesses, and especially of so many independent bookstores. Harvard Square has, famously, long been a mecca for bookworms and bibliophiles (readers and collectors alike), and returning former students in search of memories and mnemonic devices want to know where those storied bookstores from their young adulthood have gone. It's a fair question. After all, if this capital of learning and erudition won't support independent booksellers, then who can? Who, indeed?

I thank the good Lord every day that Harvard Book Store not only remains, but thrives. I have worked in Cambridge for twenty-one years now, and the last decade or so I have lived just a few blocks away from the store. I can walk there in under five minutes, which is very useful when I am doing one of its fabled early-evening lectures and book signings. I have lost count of the number of titles I have purchased within those marvelous book-and-mortar walls over the past twenty-one years, and in fact long before, since I first visited it when taking pre-med classes in the summer of 1970. (Yale thought summer school devalued the brand, until they realized how very profitable it could be!) However, I value Harvard Book Store not only for the books I have purchased there, but for the untold thousands I have thumbed through, considered, shelved...and reconsidered.

I've often wondered how a store that seems to have been made for browsing can make a profit. Seated quite solidly at the corner of Massachusetts Avenue and Plympton Street, the bookstore's wall of windows make it possible, from almost any of its aisles, to lift your eyes from the book you are devouring and see the widest variety of residents and tourists silently slipping by on the streets outside. Or, book in hand, you can easily ignore these passing throngs and just by lowering your eyes be transported to any one of the thousands upon thousands of places or periods for which these books serve as portals, or be transformed into as many different people or things you could never otherwise be. This store induces a sense of place—I should say "places," if I could find the right grammatical construction—that no online shopping experience can even attempt to approximate. And Harvard Book Store, with its generously schooled and learned staff, induces its own sense of place like no other bookstore I have visited—and you might say that, since my undergraduate days at Yale, I have been "collecting" bookstores, on almost every continent and in many, many countries.

On its corner across from the gates of Harvard Yard, Harvard Book Store creates a sense of community as well. It is a study in multiplicity and mixing, a place where Harvard students, faculty, and staff commingle with Cambridge residents and tourists from seemingly every part of the world. Harvard Book Store is situated on Massachusetts Avenue immediately next to another Harvard Square institution, Mr. Bartley's Gourmet Burgers (which has given me the great and privileged honor of having a burger named after me), and two storefronts down from the legendary Hong Kong Restaurant, where many a greasy midnight meal has been enjoyed by more than five decades of inebriated undergraduates. Its Plympton Street neighbor, the Grolier Poetry Book Shop, is perhaps the block's most "civilized" resident, Harvard Book Store's genteel aristocratic cousin. In the midst of these other ventures, Harvard Book Store is central to the fabled identity of Harvard Square as a place not just for writers and scholars, but for anyone who loves to learn, for thinkers of all stripes. Sometimes I wonder which I enjoy more: sitting at the counter at Bartley's and hearing the Book Store's activity through their shared wall, or smelling the tempting aromas of Bartley's indefatigable grill as I browse the bookshelves on the other side!

Wandering the aisles of the store upstairs, or perusing the phenomenal used-book collection in its basement, gives one the most profoundly comforting feeling that we are, in the end, readers, and that each of us fortunate enough to wander up and down these aisles is a participant in the vibrant world of ideas housed by this magical and magnificent place.

> *...each of us fortunate enough to wander up and down these aisles is a participant in the vibrant world of ideas housed by this magical and magnificent place.*

And the history of Harvard Square itself is palpable there, inscribed. On a brick wall across Massachusetts Avenue that winds its way around Harvard Yard are plaques, literally framed by ivy, for Robert Bacon (Harvard class of 1880 and the 39th secretary of state) and Theodore Roosevelt (also of the class of 1880 and the 25th president of the United States). Just down Mass Ave, at the intersection with Quincy Street and Harvard Street, is a park dedicated to Josiah Quincy, the fifteenth president of Harvard University. And immediately across the street from the store is a tiny park dedicated to Sen Lee, founder of that very Hong Kong Restaurant. An immigrant to the United States, Sen Lee came from China in 1929, at the age of 13. Here he attended public schools, fought in World War II, started a laundry, and opened up the restaurant in 1954. This one corner is a microcosm of the histories of Harvard, the City of Cambridge, the Colony and then the Commonwealth of Massachusetts, the United States, and our marvelously various world, but also the life of the mind itself. And there could be no better companion to this history than Harvard Book Store, situated squarely at the center of the Square.

Harvard Book Store has been especially kind and generous to me as an author these past two decades, and I hope its extraordinary staff knows that it delights me beyond words (if such a place exists) every time I am invited to read on the store's cozy left side, or whenever I see one of my books as one of their staff picks, or if a title of mine is lucky enough to make their "Select Seventy." If all politics is local, as Tip O'Neill so masterfully observed, so, I suppose, are all honors. And nothing is more gratifying to me as a writer than the warm embrace of readers and booksellers at this store that I haunt in order to imagine.

HENRY LOUIS GATES, JR. is the Alphonse Fletcher University Professor and director of the W. E. B. Du Bois Institute for African and American Research at Harvard University. He is the author of 16 books and has made 12 documentaries, including the PBS series, *Finding Your Roots with Henry Louis Gates, Jr.*, which examines the histories and family genealogies of a number of well-known personalities. He is the recipient of 51 honorary degrees and numerous awards, including the MacArthur "genius grant." He was named to *Time*'s "25 Most Influential Americans" list in 1997 and to *Ebony*'s "Power 150" list in 2009 and its "Power 100" list in 2010. *The Henry Louis Gates, Jr. Reader*, a collection of Professor Gates's essays, was published in 2012.

Peter Geye

Micawber's, ST. PAUL, MINNESOTA

When I was a kid, my grandma used to take me shopping on my birthday. We'd catch a bus and head downtown, where I'd spend my allotted ten dollars on some bric-a-brac from the dime store's toy aisle. Oftentimes, after I'd made my selection, she'd spirit me to the top of the IDS Tower for a hot chocolate and cookie or take me to the restaurant inside Dayton's department store for lunch. Those were wonderful times. Some of the happiest in my memory.

The thing is, for all the years and all the gifts (I'm sure we went every year from the time I was 6 or 7 until I was a couple of years out of high school), I can only remember one present. This would have been the year after I graduated from high school, when I was working hard at becoming the Serious Literary Fellow I was then intent on becoming. We went to Baxter's Books, and for the same ten dollars I'd so often blown on forgettable toys, I bought Thoreau's *Walden* and Dante's *Inferno*. They were Signet Classics, as the spines on them advertised. I brought them home, read them piecemeal over that summer, and for the first time in my young life felt like I was becoming who I wanted to be. They were the first books in my personal library, or the first books I'd selected myself, with earnest intent. I still have them on my shelf.

In the years between then and now, I've become a proper bibliophile. When last my wife and I moved five years ago, I had fifty boxes of books. There are many reasons I love books: for the worlds they show me, for the things they teach me, for the way they feel in my hands or in my satchel, for the way they look decorating my house, for the questions they arouse from my children, for their mystery, for their cold or warm truths, for their lies, for their promise. But mostly I just love being transported to some place outside of my everyday life.

As a book nut, it stands to reason that I enjoy shopping for books, and this is true. Just ask my wife, who still (after fifteen years together) can't understand how date night inevitably ends with us browsing bookstores.

Over the years, as my taste in literature has evolved, so has my taste in bookstores. When I was in college at the University of Minnesota, I used to haunt the Book House in Dinkytown or Biermaier's just up Southeast 4th Street. It was in those shops that I discovered the likes of Camus and Dostoevsky. Biermaier's is gone now, but I still creep into the Book House every time I pass through Dinkytown.

After college I lived and worked in downtown Minneapolis, and on my walks home up the Mall, I'd stop at James & Mary Laurie Booksellers almost every day. The rare-book room in the back of the store was like paradise, and there were Fridays when the better part of my paycheck went toward first editions I'd been coveting on those rare-book shelves for months.

My wife and I lived in the Uptown neighborhood of Minneapolis when we were first married. At least two or three times a week we'd walk from our rented house up to Hennepin and Lake and have dinner. After dinner, inevitably, we'd stop at Magers & Quinn or Orr Books. Twice that first year of our marriage I had to invest in new bookcases in order to accommodate what I was bringing home from those dates. And though Orr Books has gone the way of Biermaier's, I still consider Magers & Quinn to be a wonderful store.

But there's another shop in the Twin Cities that I find myself gravitating toward these days. Tucked away in one of the quaintest neighborhoods in St. Paul, halfway between downtown Minneapolis and downtown St. Paul, Micawber's Books is like the answer to the question that all the bookstores in my past have posed. We're exactly copacetic, Micawber's and I. Like my favorite pair of broken-in shoes.

Setting aside its charm and warmth and the benefit of its being in such a great location, Micawber's is a straight-up kick-ass store. This is in no small part thanks to the ownership tandem of Tom Bieleberg and Hans Weyandt. I've never been in the store when one or the other (if not both) wasn't present. And not present in a back room sort of way, but standing at the cash register or talking to customers in the children's section. I admit, just having the boss around isn't sufficient to guarantee great service or a great experience, but in the case of the boys who own Micawber's, their presence means better service than I've ever had in a bookstore. In any store, for that matter.

The last time I visited, Hans saw me milling around a table of new books. He came over, said hey, we talked about baseball and business, our kids, my new book. The usual. But then he put on his bookseller's cap. He stepped around the table and took a book from a small stack.

"Have you seen this?" he said. "M. Allen Cunningham has a new book out." He handed me the book.

I looked at the cover. "I haven't seen this. What's the story?"

"He started his own press. This is a limited-edition collection of stories. It's gorgeous, where both the writing and the book itself are concerned. You're a fan of his, aren't you?"

"I am," I said. "Thanks."

This might seem unremarkable, but consider a couple of the variables that went into this conversation. One, Hans had to remember a conversation we'd had years ago in order to recall that I was a fan of Cunningham. I didn't remember this conversation myself until he recommended *Date of Disappearance*. This alone is impressive. Hans must have twenty conversations each day about which books people like to read. But more impressive still is the fact that *Date of Disappearance* was on the table in the first place. Here's a book that was printed as a limited edition—only 300 numbered copies—by a small press that I can guarantee not a hundred other booksellers in the country even know about. That it was in Micawber's speaks not only to the depth of knowledge the boys at Micawber's have, but to their unwavering commitment to small presses and lesser-known authors.

As I stood there looking the book over, I began to feel as though Hans had ordered it to have in stock just so he'd be able to recommend it to me personally. I know this isn't true, but it's a hell of a feeling to have. In fact, as a customer, it's about as good a feeling as I can imagine. But it's not even the best indication of what great advocates the boys at Micawber's truly are.

When Hans finished a galley of my most recent novel, he didn't send me an email to say how much he enjoyed it. He didn't talk about it on a panel at a trade show. He didn't wait for the next time I visited his store to impart his kind words.

> *As I stood there looking the book over, I began to feel as though Hans had ordered it to have in stock just so he'd be able to recommend it to me personally. I know this isn't true, but it's a hell of a feeling to have.*

What he did was look me up in the phone book. He dialed the number to my house. And he told me over the phone that he was excited about the book. He said he was looking forward to hand-selling it when it was released. This all sounds self-congratulatory, I realize, but by mentioning it I only mean to describe the sort of grassroots work the boys at Micawber's are doing. Of course it means a lot to me that he liked the book, and that he's going to be hand-selling it when it releases. I'd be a bald-faced liar if I said otherwise. But the greater truth is that it's just another indication of how committed they are to providing a unique book-shopping experience. And it's because Hans has undoubtedly made countless other such calls that I love his store so much.

Over the course of the past couple of years, as my career as an author has gotten under way, I've had the great fortune to meet many of this country's best booksellers. I'm amazed on a regular basis by the general good feeling, by the enthusiasm, by the commitment, by the generosity. I have no doubt that there are other bookstores and book-sellers out there with as much to offer as Micawber's. I'm sure other booksellers reach out to local authors and encourage their careers. I have no doubt book buyers think of individual customers when they stock a title. I'm sure they keep inventory on their shelves for years simply because they love a book or writer and know that one day, the perfect customer will come in and find it. I'm just lucky that Micawber's is a fifteen-minute drive across town. Most of the most recent books that have made their way onto my own personal shelves have come back across the river with me from Micawber's. Then they sit on my shelf right alongside those Signet Classics from twenty-odd years ago.

And if my wife is sometimes dismayed by the quantity of those books, which she is, I tell her it could be worse. Rather than collect-ing books and spending the bulk of my free time reading them, I say, I could be buying motorcycles or exotic pets. This is usually justifi-cation enough, but it's nice to add that those same books have been helping to make me the man that I am. Often as not, she's pleased with who that is. I thank Thoreau and Dante and the hundreds of others between them and M. Allen Cunningham for that.

And I thank the boys at Micawber's.

PETER GEYE is the award-winning author of *Safe from the Sea* and *The Lighthouse Road*. He was born and raised in Minneapolis and continues to live there with his wife and three kids.

Albert Goldbarth

Watermark Books and Café, WICHITA, KANSAS

I *tried* to talk Skyler out of our getting married. "It's so wonderful right now. Why rock the boat?" But evidently that language was Martian; and evidently she was from Venus.

The no-brainer, uncontested part was the venue: Watermark Books, Wichita's premier (well, *only*) full-service independent literary bookstore. When I arrived in town in 1987 the business was already a decade old. It has been the undercurrent of my Wichita life for as long as I've had a Wichita life, and day by day it's been enriching a community that ranges from the overspill crowd for Republican senator Bob Dole to the overspill crowd for hottie rocker Pat Benatar—a community that, but for this bookcentric haven, would have by now spent thirty-five years grazing on a much thinner, less sustaining Kansas pasture of social and intellectual possibilities.

Sometimes a contrasting background allows for greater appreciation of what is otherwise taken for granted. Of late, my benighted governor's misguided decision to defund the state arts council (among other, similar strikes against free expression) serves to especially highlight the necessary role of Watermark Books in maintaining the privileges and pleasures of unconstrained reading. But even without that fabular context in which the Forces of Biblio-Goodness combat the Drooling Armies of Repressive Limitation, who could not automatically smile on entering through these doors, browsing the staff recs, checking out the soup of the day?

One afternoon, an ebullient, matronly gathering Q&A'ing its way through the signing for a cookbook's release; another afternoon, bright beelines of bikers riding in from a three-state area for a vintage electric-guitar show. Here, a 5-year-old zoom-zooming an Olivia doll above a jerry-built skyline of Olivia books; over there, a 25-year-old woman intent on *Siddhartha*. Somebody solo; someone here for a book club. *New York Times* best sellers hobnobbing companionably with local poet Jeanine Hathaway's new ribbon-bound chapbook. Art on the walls. Java in the urns. There's Carol Konek! There's Dan Rouser! Hey, there's Tim! Howzzit goin'? Drawn here by the book-surround comfort. A neighborhood of—you'll know what I mean—unalike like-mindedness.

> *Drawn here by the book-surround comfort.*
> *A neighborhood of—you'll know what I mean—*
> *unalike like-mindedness.*

Sarah Bagby, once-upon-a-time guitarist ("a sweet little Gibson SG") for Wichita all-chick rock group The Inevitable, wouldn't have had any notion that, a number of transformations down the time line, she'd be—as the owner of Watermark Books—an ABA board member. But America is made for such stories. Here she is, with President Obama, both of them smiling over an open book, in a recent White House photo op.

And there we were, at Watermark Books, on November 27, 1989, a small group bent on big doings. Sarah was there. And her husband, Eric (back then, he managed Maple Grove Cemetery, which unknowingly loaned a few of its foldout chairs to the cause). Shirley and Robert King, on the bride's side. John Crisp, up from San Antonio, Texas, on mine. We screened that 1930s cartoon in which Mickey croons "Minnie's Yoo Hoo" by way of courting the femme mouse of his dreams. We played Bonnie Raitt singing "Baby Mine." Skyler Lovelace said "I do" and Albert Goldbarth said "I do" and the thousands of witnessing books seemed to nod in affirmation.

Time goes by. Time can't be talked out of that. And I haven't always been Mr. Perfect Husband, believe it or not, but on rare occasions I do Get It Right. When my latest book was published in January 2012, of course I kicked off my modest tour with a Watermark reading. Well attended, by Wichita standards: 150 people or so. What Skyler didn't know was that an hour into what would be a two-hour event, John Crisp, on cue and fresh up from Texas, would briskly walk up to the podium, seemingly out of nowhere, interrupting my inter-poem gab. That was my cue for my essential line: "Skyler Lovelace, come on dooooown!" Shirley King was whisked up to the podium too, and Skyler's friend Cindy, and rare-book dealer Kris Strom. Sarah officiated. Snazzy headgear was donned. Beth Golay saw that the wine appeared. And twenty-two years after our Watermark wedding, Skyler said "I do" and Albert said "I do," renewing our vows to Van Morrison's "Crazy Love" before the second half of the reading commenced.

Things change, I know. One of John's hips is plastic now. The Watermark Books of 2012 is three locations removed from the Watermark Books of 1989. But here we are, still; and here's the store, still, having outlasted both of Wichita's Borders stores and one Barnes

& Noble. Do we take the books on Watermark's shelves, again and forever, to be our companions, our life enhancers, our manifold loves and exasperations and hopes and assuagers and lights in the dimness, both in lean times and rich times?

We do.

ALBERT GOLDBARTH has been publishing notable books of poetry for 40 years, two of which have received the National Book Critics Circle Award; the latest is *Everyday People* (Graywolf Press). He is also the author of five collections of essays and a novel. A staunch computer refusenik, his fingertips have never touched a computer keyboard.

John Grisham

That Bookstore in Blytheville, BLYTHEVILLE, ARKANSAS

When my first novel was published in 1989, I hit the road with a trunk full of books in a valiant but misguided effort to create some buzz and launch a new career. After a month or so of miserable sales, I had learned the painful lesson that selling books is far more difficult than writing them. While libraries, coffee shops, and grocery stores were generally more welcoming, most bookstores could not be bothered with an unknown author's first novel published by a tiny company too poor to even produce a catalog. The first printing of 5,000 went unsold, for the most part, and there was no talk of a second printing, no dreams of paperbacks or foreign editions.

The fledgling career was on the rocks.

However, a handful of wise booksellers saw something the others did not, and enthusiastically pushed *A Time to Kill*. There were five of them; one was Mary Gay Shipley, of That Bookstore in Blytheville, Arkansas. I've always suspected Mary Gay had a soft spot because I was born in Jonesboro, Arkansas, not too far away. When I was a kid I visited my grandfather's music store on Main Street in Blytheville, so Mary Gay and I had some common ground, shaky as it was.

> *...a handful of wise booksellers saw something the others did not, and enthusiastically pushed* A Time to Kill.

I soon abandoned all dreams of seeing my first novel on the best-seller lists. I got tired of hawking copies of it from the trunk of my car. Instead, I concentrated on finishing my second novel, *The Firm*. Mary Gay read an advance copy of it and said things were about to change. I agreed to do a signing in her store and arrived there on Sunday, March 17, 1991, St. Patrick's Day. Her husband, Paul, had found some green beer to go with the green popcorn and the like.

It was a raw, windy March day, not that pleasant, but Mary Gay had called in the chips and there was a nice crowd. I signed books, posed for photos, chatted with each customer, and, in general, had a grand time. The book was selling, and I was on top of the world. The day was significant for another reason: *The Firm* debuted that Sunday on the *New York Times* best-seller list at number 12. I suspected life was about to change, though it was impossible to know how much.

In the rear of her store there is an old potbellied stove surrounded by children's books and rocking chairs. Late in the day, we gathered around the stove and I read from my novel. I talked about the writing of it. I answered questions with little regard for time, and the crowd showed little interest in leaving.

As soon as *The Firm* "hit the list," I was inundated with requests from bookstores to do signings, but I declined, and not out of some sense of revenge. I'd rather spend my time writing, and besides, book tours are not that enjoyable. However, it's always been easy to remain loyal to those first five stores, especially That Bookstore in Blytheville.

I returned the following year with *The Pelican Brief*, then *The Client*. By the time *The Chamber* was published in 1994, the signings were going on for ten or more hours and everyone was working far too hard. We changed the rules and shrunk the crowds, but the signings still felt like marathons. Eventually, we stopped them altogether, and for the past several years I have sneaked into Mary Gay's back door and signed 2,000 copies of each new book. This takes a few hours and we enjoy the quieter times. There's a lot of local gossip, and I've picked up more than one idea for characters. Old friends stop by, and on several occasions, I've had lunch with my mother and her three sisters.

Blytheville is an old, declining cotton town, and many of its Main Street stores are empty. Mary Gay has kept hers open through hard work and the sheer will of her personality. With independent bookstores vanishing at an alarming rate, I wonder how long she will hang on, or if someone will take her place. She and others like her had a huge role in the early success of my career and the careers of many rookie authors. Without their encouragement and support, it will be even more difficult for first novels to have a chance.

Over twenty years have passed since that cold Sunday in March when we sipped green beer by the stove, celebrated all things Irish, and toasted the country's newest best-selling author, but it remains one of my fondest memories as a writer.

JOHN GRISHAM is the author of 24 novels, one work of nonfiction, a collection of stories, and three novels for young readers. He lives in Virginia and Mississippi.

Pete Hamill

Strand Book Store, NEW YORK, NEW YORK

In the summer of 1957, home from a year in Mexico on the GI Bill, I found temporary lodging in paradise. That is, in an apartment on Fourth Avenue and 11th Street in New York City, right there in Book Row. I shared the rent with a friend of a friend, a student who attended school a few blocks south at Cooper Union, and though we talked through many beery evenings about art, I was already on the way to becoming a writer. My university was Book Row. My personal classroom was called the Strand.

The bookstore was almost directly across the avenue, at 81 Fourth Avenue, flanked by the other bookstores, all of them visible from the front windows of the apartment where I was living. On days of rain or snow, I could vanish into its shelves and tables, examining the endless literary treasures. There I bought my first volume of poetry by William Butler Yeats, my first copy of Balzac's *Lost Illusions*, and I found my way into Winesburg, Ohio, with Sherwood Anderson as my guide. I also found a copy of Hemingway's parody of Anderson, *The Torrents of Spring*. All at prices I could afford on my job as an assistant in the art department of an advertising agency.

> *On days of rain or snow, I could vanish into its shelves and tables, examining the endless literary treasures. There I bought my first volume of poetry by William Butler Yeats, my first copy of Balzac's* Lost Illusions, *and I found my way into Winesburg, Ohio, with Sherwood Anderson as my guide.*

Then, in the late fall, I retreated to Brooklyn, to be closer to Pratt Institute where I was trying to sharpen my skills as a designer (and learned many other things). My journeys to Book Row and the Strand were restricted to Saturdays.

And then one Saturday in 1958, the Strand was gone. Someone had bought the properties on that east side of Fourth Avenue. The Strand's $110-a-month lease was canceled, along with the leases of its immediate neighbors: the Arcadia, the Friendly, Louis Schueman, Wex's. What the hell do we need with all these cheap books? The true god of New York, which is real estate, had prevailed.

For a while, I was forlorn. One thing that had vanished with the Strand and its neighbors was serendipity—that extraordinary sense of surprise and delight when you enter a bookstore in search of one book and discover another. You are looking for a copy of Irving Shulman's

The Amboy Dukes and you leave with Emily Dickinson. Or both. You are desperate to find Malcolm Cowley's *Exile's Return*, to replace one you lost in the subway, and find a hardcover copy of Faulkner's *As I Lay Dying*. Every time I enter a bookshop, I still feel the same way, filled with a sense of possibility. It's like going to a dance when you're 21.

But then came news that the Strand was not dead. It was moving to Broadway and 12th Street. In those days, when every New York block felt like a different hamlet (or shtetl), this felt oddly ominous. Many of us had already lived through the traumatic move in 1957 of the Brooklyn Dodgers and New York Giants to neighborhoods on the far side of the continent. Our unease was soon relieved: The Strand quickly flourished, rising four floors above street level, becoming a kind of vertical Book Row.

In June of 1960 I was given a tryout as a reporter at the *New York Post*. And the Strand again was there when I began to focus on all the great journalists who had preceded me. I was working nights at the *Post*, which gave me time to get to the Strand (particularly on payday) and move into a darker area of the store, to the left, where I could find A.J. Liebling and Joseph Mitchell, Heywood Broun and Westbrook Pegler, Martha Gellhorn and Damon Runyon, H.L. Mencken, Jimmy Cannon, I.F. Stone, W.C. Heinz, John Lardner, Paul Gallico, Rebecca West...the list seemed without end, and I learned from all of them.

At the *Post* I met Murray Kempton, whose column I loved. And in the Strand I found his marvelous 1955 book, *Part of Our Time*, and had him sign it for me. Then I started seeing him again, wandering the side aisles of the Strand. Lost in the possibilities that were boarding on the shelves. Another one of my unpaid teachers was Joe Wershba, also at the *Post*, later to become one of the founding producers of *60 Minutes*. Joe was like me: He never entered a bookstore he didn't like, but he liked the Strand most of all. When he suggested I read a book, old or new, I always did. I've lived long enough now to see my own books on those hallowed shelves. But when I left the Strand in those early days, I joined many others, not all of them writers, who rode home on the shoulders of giants.

PETE HAMILL is a veteran newspaperman, columnist, editor, and novelist. He has published 22 books, 11 of them novels, including best-sellers *Snow in August*, *Forever*, *Tabloid City*, and the memoir *A Drinking Life*. He lives in Tribeca with his wife, Fukiko.

Daniel Handler and Lisa Brown

The Booksmith, SAN FRANCISCO, CALIFORNIA

DANIEL HANDLER is the author of the novels *The Basic Eight*, *Watch Your Mouth*, *Adverbs*, and *Why We Broke Up*, recently awarded a Michael L. Printz Honor. As Lemony Snicket, he is the author of far too many books for children.

LISA BROWN is the best-selling author and/or illustrator of a growing number of books, including *Vampire Boy's Good Night*, *The Latke Who Couldn't Stop Screaming*, *Baby, Mix Me a Drink,* and *Picture the Dead*, an illustrated Civil War ghost story for teens. She sporadically draws the *Three Panel Book Review* cartoon for the *San Francisco Chronicle*. Lisa lives in San Francisco.

Elin Hilderbrand

Nantucket Bookworks, NANTUCKET, MASSACHUSETTS

For the past nineteen years, I have been blessed in the most specific and wonderful way: I have lived on an island that has not one but two independently owned bookstores. No Amazon for me, no Barnes & Noble, no Hudson News, no Books-a-Trillion, no Chinaberry catalog. I used to go to Shakespeare & Co. when I was in New York City and Waterstone's when I was in Boston, and I will always live in awe of Prairie Lights in Iowa City and the Tattered Cover in Denver…but really, none of those stores have been mine the way the Nantucket stores are mine.

For our purposes today, I am going to talk about Nantucket

Bookworks, although Mitchell's Book Corner is also a unique and amazing place. You will trust me on that.

Nantucket Bookworks is a free-standing one-story building with the look of a cottage about it; probably it has a provenance other than a bookstore. Decades ago it might have been an ice cream shop or a private home for someone like Angela Lansbury. It is on quaint, leafy Broad Street, sandwiched between a famous hotel, the Jared Coffin House, and a famous restaurant, the Brotherhood of Thieves. In fact, let's say the first time I discovered Bookworks, I was standing in the very, very long line outside of the Brotherhood, waiting for a table. Bookworks was conducive to browsing, and I was a budding writer; a good browse was my favorite form of free entertainment. Bookworks is cozy and not unlike a rabbit warren—shelves and shelves of books, nooks and crannies, places to sit, folk art and gifts and greeting cards and cool jewelry and funky handbags…but mostly books.

My second summer on Nantucket, let's call it the summer of 1994, when I was on the island not to visit, but to live, I would ride my ten-speed (that's a bike) to Bookworks several times a week. I had no job other than to write, and writing was hard and often discouraging, and since anything was preferable to actually writing, I did a lot of reading and a lot of biking and a lot of browsing. That summer, I read Lorrie Moore's short stories and then proceeded to become maudlin and discouraged, because there was certainly no way I could ever write anything that good. I would stand in the literature section at the H's and try to visualize a slender volume with my last name on the spine—Hilderbrand—between Hemingway and Hillerman. Standing and visualizing was preferable to actually writing the volume that might someday be placed there.

Years passed; things changed. I attended the University of Iowa Writers' Workshop (where I frequented Prairie Lights, but only once a week at the most; I had serious writing to do). Shortly after I returned to Nantucket and shortly after I, yes—hear me roar—had my first novel, *The Beach Club*, accepted and published, Nantucket Bookworks was purchased by a young woman (my age) with small children, a woman named Wendy Hudson. In one of life's awesome synchronicities, Wendy's growth as an independent-bookstore owner mirrored my own growth as a novelist. We became friends, then good friends, and now she has a treasured seat in my inner circle of confidantes. It is impossible to say if we are better matched personally or professionally.

We all know that a bookstore is just bricks and mortar—even Barnes & Noble has managed to accomplish that. A good bookstore is a welcoming space with staff picks and the occasional reading and signing. But I would argue that a truly great bookstore depends on the people who work there. When Wendy took over Nantucket Bookworks, she magnetized a staff that is unparalleled in their friendliness and knowledge. It would be impossible to pick a favorite, and yet a favorite I do have.

Dick Burns looks like the mad professor in *Back to the Future*. He has a sonorous voice that is probably best suited to reading T.S. Eliot aloud. He knows a lot about books, but so do most bookstore employees worth their salt. Dick is singular because his sensibility is my own. His opinion has become valued and treasured. A few years ago, he recommended John O'Hara's old and all-but-forgotten novel *Appointment in Samarra*, a book that instantly became one of my top three favorite novels of all time. Dick and I talk about Alice Munro and Marilynne Robinson like they're our neighbors—sometimes we're reverent, sometimes we're catty. On one rarified occasion, I was able to do Dick a favor. We were both reading Tom Rachman's novel *The Imperfectionists*. This was a book we had both been anticipating greatly after the front-page article in the *New York Times Book Review*. I bought it first and read it first. Dick was reading it also, and he was dismayed to find that the copy he had bought was not a first edition. I offered to switch books with him—he could have my copy, a first edition, and I would take his. Never have I seen someone so delighted! And certainly never have I seen someone so delighted by a first edition. But that's the thing: To Dick, books matter. They are not to be downloaded and deleted. Books are loved and treasured. It

> *But that's the thing:*
> *To Dick, books matter.*
> *They are not to be*
> *downloaded and deleted.*
> *Books are loved and*
> *treasured. It is this*
> *love, this appreciation*
> *of the written word,*
> *that suffuses the air at*
> *Nantucket Bookworks.*

is this love, this appreciation of the written word, that suffuses the air at Nantucket Bookworks.

In closing, I will say this: I am not a political person. I have never campaigned for anyone; I have never marched on Washington. I don't care if you return your cart to the front of the supermarket or leave it to block the parking spot for the next person. I don't care if you buy a tomato out of season or dismiss organic milk as too expensive. But I would implore you to buy your books from independently owned bookstores. Places like Nantucket Bookworks, and people like Dick Burns, have a quality that is hard to find in the world today. They are authentic.

They make the world safe for budding writers on ten-speed bikes with big dreams.

ELIN HILDERBRAND is the author of 11 novels, including *Summerland*, published in June 2012. She has lived on Nantucket Island year-round for 19 years and is the mother of three children. Elin is passionate about running, NFL football, cooking, travel, and good Champagne. Her favorite novelists are Jane Smiley, Richard Russo, and Tim Winton.

Ann Hood

Island Books, MIDDLETOWN, RHODE ISLAND

The first bookstore I ever walked into was a Waldenbooks at the Warwick Mall in Rhode Island. And I, a bookstore virgin, fell immediately in love. This was somewhere around 1971 or '72, long before books could be bought online. Until that moment, the only books I'd read came from libraries or the backs of my classrooms, so I did not know the difference between chain bookstores and independent ones. I only knew that past the greeting cards and magazines and the cute, green-eyed boy at the cash register, hundreds of books waited for me. For just a few dollars, I could own a paperback copy of *The Outsiders*, take it home, underline my favorite parts, turn down the corner of the pages I wanted to go back and reread. No one was waiting for me to return it. No one cared what I did with it. The book was mine.

My taste in books back then was confused, eclectic. I could not differentiate between highbrow and lowbrow, so I bought with abandon. *Anna Karenina* one week; *Hawaii* by James Michener the next. For my cousin Gloria-Jean's birthday, I bought my first hardcover book: *Love Story*, and read it half open so as not to break the spine before wrapping it and handing it over. The sounds of the mall faded as I stood before all of those books, touching their spines, staring at authors' photos, reading first lines and jacket copies. Years later I would understand that this was how love felt: Everything faded in the face of it.

Eventually, I grew up and moved to Boston, where on weekends I would walk up Washington Street to an enormous Barnes & Noble and spend hours roaming its aisles. My reading taste had not really improved much, though I discovered Stephen King and John Irving there. I worked as a flight attendant for TWA then and I liked fat books, books that would get me through my constant jet lag, flight delays, and bouts of loneliness. So I bought *Les Misérables* and *Doctor Zhivago* along with more James Michener and Harold Robbins. One rainy afternoon, as I was leaving the store, I spied a hardcover copy of E.E. Cummings's *Collected Poems* on sale and added that to my stash. For a few years, that was one of about a dozen books that lined my bookshelf, along with a few saved from college and other collections—Edgar Allan Poe, Ogden Nash—bought on sale at that B&N.

Eventually I moved to New York City, and wandering the streets of my Greenwich Village neighborhood I happened upon a tiny bookstore called Three Lives. I almost didn't go inside. How many books could it possibly have? But the windows boasted signed copies and a promise of a reading by Deborah Eisenberg and Laurie Colwin the next night. Until that moment, I had no idea that either of these marvelous things occurred, that authors signed their books and went to read from them at tiny bookstores.

Inside was just as curious. Tables piled with books I'd never heard of, written by writers I'd never heard of. Travel books and cookbooks and poetry all had their own little nooks. The best sellers that Barnes & Noble kept in racks up front seemed hardly to be in evidence here at all. As a lifelong reader, a lover of books, I had no idea how to choose one in such a bookstore. In fact, I fled.

However, I did return the next night, undeterred by a cold driving rain. Late, I entered the crowded store with its smells of books and steam heat and wet wool and was pointed to a spot on the floor where I should sit—right at the feet of the two writers. As each of them read from their short-story collections, I stared up at them, mesmerized. It was easy to follow the others there and buy those two books. But too shy to have them signed, I quickly left, tucking the bag under my coat to keep the books dry.

How could I have known on that long-ago night that someday I would be one of those writers that stands at the front of a crowded bookstore and reads from her just-published book? How could I have known then that across the country—the world!—small independent bookstores like that one helped readers choose what to read next, brought communities together, gave writers the opportunity to visit and sign their books? That night I knew only that despite all the hours I'd spent in them, my Waldenbooks back home and the cavernous Barnes & Noble in Boston had not given me the thrill that this one short hour had.

Since then, I gave up my TWA wings and began to publish books. In those twenty-five years, I've visited more bookstores than I can count, and every time I walk into one of them, I get that rush of first love again. Yet Island Books, technically in Middletown, Rhode Island, but close enough to Newport for Newporters to take credit for, rises above all of

> *I've visited more bookstores than I can count, and every time I walk into one of them, I get that rush of first love again.*

them. There are prettier stores. Fancier ones. Bigger ones and more intimate ones. Its aisles are a bit crooked. It's tucked into a tiny slip of a strip mall. And it is perfect. For me, Island Books has everything a bookstore should have. The owner, Judy Crosby, knows books and loves books. In fact, whenever I read there, she presses her most recent favorite into my hand, telling me I need to read it. She sends me books for my 7-year-old daughter, Annabelle, if she reads one that might suit her. And if Judy isn't there, or even if she is, Pat will be behind the counter, quietly running everything. What other bookstore staff, when you go to read there, has just read a short story you wrote or your op-ed in *The New York Times*? And cut it out and made copies for everyone? What other bookstore knows you prefer chardonnay over pinot grigio and always has some waiting for you?

Fans of Island Books are loyal and possessive. Once, when I mentioned I had just been there, a woman frowned and told me, "But that's my bookstore." Give a reading there and it will be standing room only. Even if they've never heard of you, they will come because Judy invited you and they trust her. She and Pat move the shelves around and bring in seats. They bake cookies and serve cheese and crackers and wine. In warm weather, they set up the snacks outside under little lights, and everyone lingers. Because Island Books makes you want to linger there.

Here is a good example of how wonderful Island Books is. One afternoon I got an email from the coordinator of an event I was doing the next evening. *Bring along some books to sell*, the email told me. But writers do not have books to sell; the twenty complimentary copies we receive go to our parents and friends and disappear pretty quickly. How was I going to get a few cases of books in twenty-four hours? I sent my own desperate email to Judy. The idea seemed preposterous: Could I "borrow" as many of my own books as she could spare? I held my breath. For as amazing as Judy and her bookstore are, would she really let me take a few cases of books without buying them, trust me to collect the right amount of money, and then bring them back to

Middletown, which is about forty minutes from my house?
By now, you already know the answer. Of course she did. I sold those books and we sat together doing the accounting. I signed whatever others she had in the store. And then, instead of going right back home, I lingered. Because that's what you do there.

ANN HOOD is the author of 13 books, most recently the best-selling novels *The Knitting Circle* and *The Red Thread*.

Pico Iyer

Chaucer's Books, SANTA BARBARA, CALIFORNIA

There are books in piles all along the narrow aisles, and other books in towers on the top of every shelf. There are books laid out on tables and set out in the window, and books in special cases in the middle of the store, offered as "Staff Favorites." There are books from many years ago, long out of print, and books that more corporate shops would long since have sent back to be pulped or remaindered. There are seven editions of *Moby-Dick,* all at embarrassingly low prices.

Around the books are greeting cards. Above the cards, stunning and unexpected, are nine framed photographs—a bangled woman in a golden sari, an old man's eyes under a turban, a woman brushing the empty steps above the ghats in Varanasi—taken by the shop's owner, Mahri Kerley, on a recent trip to India. There are books you won't find in the public library, and a whole room, as large as a regular bookstore, for children's books—and toys and games—where a kindly woman will guide you toward just the perfect work for the 13-year-old brother of a goddaughter in faraway London.

A longtime friend from Asia gift-wraps even the smallest paperback so that it looks as if it just came from a temple in Kyoto. Another vibrant pal who sets up Graham Greene mini-displays on the main table tells me about what she learned at Kenneth Rexroth's knee (when writing of an old love, write only of what you loved in her). Another, when I buy a Nicholson Baker volume, tells me he'd love to know what I think of it, because his father was a conscientious objector during World War II.

One of the youngest workers, a small, elegant man barely out of college (he had earlier told me about a very obscure book on Werner Herzog), now presses into my hands a copy of Thomas Bernhard's *Wittgenstein's Nephew*. "You should try this," he says. Many, many of my more literary writer friends have tried to sell me on Bernhard, and none has succeeded. But when someone from Chaucer's suggests it, how can I turn away?

I buy two of the Austrian novelist's books and promise to come back to tell the other man at the cash register, who reads everything, how they compare with W.G. Sebald.

. . .

A bookstore is, at its heart, like any of the novels you may choose to buy in it. The shop itself is just the title page—you can find any work you want, after all, in many other places—and its holdings are the table of contents, the portal to the real experience. What ultimately makes the place sing, and live in you forever, is something else, much deeper: the characters you meet in it, the emotions that arise in you there, the sense of patterning—and being without pattern—that turns the story of a bookstore into the story of a life. What I recall, when I step out of an expedition to a bookshop, is not so much the works I've just acquired as those two chiming enthusiasts behind the front desk who pressed on me Geraldine Brooks's *March*, because they recalled I'd loved *Ahab's Wife*, or the former graduate student in literature who led me to the Food section to find *Eat, Pray, Love* and so let me fall into the pages of M.F.K. Fisher.

Is it any wonder, then, that Chaucer's, "my bookstore" in Santa Barbara, has been my sanctuary, my talisman, my spiritual and social and literary home and inspiration for thirty-seven years now, ever since I was gobbling down Ursula K. Le Guin's Earthsea books in my teens? (Now I return to Chaucer's to acquire them for my goddaughter's brother.) It is my de facto office, my classroom, my place of worship, my site for dates, and (not unrelatedly) my ideal location for getting lost. All of this is a way of saying that it's not a shop so much as an old friend's home, a place where thousands of us feel welcomed, woven into a circle, and surrounded by like-minded souls. Over the years, I've met the son of the wonderful owner, Mahri, visiting from Vancouver; run into her husband (now deceased) near the signing table; and been to dinner at her house, to find a treasury of books that could almost rival the one she shares with the world in her shop. Sometimes, she even leaves advance galleys of books she thinks I'll like at the front desk for me to take back home to enjoy.

> *It's not a shop so much as an old friend's home, a place where thousands of us feel welcomed, woven into a circle, and surrounded by like-minded souls.*

. . .

Chapter 1 of the story that is Chaucer's might simply describe the place itself and how it looks to the innocent newcomer. She will walk through its doors to find stacks of free newspapers and magazines that focus on matters literary and local, as well as a copy of this week's *New York Times Book Review*, offered gratis, if she wants to read about what's just come out. She will see little notices here and there recording the latest winners of the National Book Critics Circle Award or the Man Booker International Prize; she will encounter calendars from around the world, and audiobooks along one wall, and books in Spanish as well.

Very quickly, too—since the beginning of a book has to offer more than mere facts—she will see that a bookstore is not just a place for books; it's a place where you store something richer, in the way of memories and companions and collections of photographs too expensive to purchase, encyclopedias too hefty to carry home. It's a place where I've bought haiku cubes at the cash register, and books on Maine Coon cats after I've left the store (and seen them in the window as I was exiting).

It's a place that is really—like Sir John Soane's house in London— the concrete external geography of a mind. In every last corner you'll find some forgotten passion, a whimsical interest, a byway to some larger stream of associations. And it's only by following a train of thought that you arrive at another, which you'd never expected to come upon. Many books in Chaucer's are shelved in more than one place, so I go looking for Abraham Heschel and run into *The Light Inside the Dark* by the Tasmanian Zen poet and wise man John Tarrant. I let someone lead me to a biography of Arthur Miller, and, right next to it, is a gripping account of the Cuban missile crisis. Chaucer's never remainders books or offers discounts—though it does hold book fairs to raise money for schools and offers standing discounts of 20 percent for teachers—which is a way of saying that it sees the value of books and never treats them as mere goods.

Santa Barbara is rich in elegant little paseos and chic, custom-made shopping streets; Chaucer's—like those fabled seven-star sushi restaurants in Los Angeles that don't even have a name and are known only to Jack Nicholson and Warren Beatty—sits inside a somewhat featureless shopping mall in one of the city's less glitzy areas. On one side of it is Glenda's Party Cove, selling balloons and piñatas, and on the other is a small, locally owned drugstore that still hasn't been driven out by CVS. It would be hard to find a more perfect location for a place that draws from the festive spirit of one neighbor while offering the medicines for the soul that the other doesn't always have room to stock.

Few first-time visitors to Santa Barbara are likely to stumble upon it, therefore, yet for more than a third of a century now, people have been driving from every corner of Santa Barbara County to do their shopping (to see their friends, to pick up their copies of the *Los Angeles Times*, to hear Salman Rushdie and Buzz Aldrin read, or to get their books signed by sometime Santa Barbaran Sue Grafton) there. The county as a whole is singularly well supplied for books: the Book Den, across from our library and museum of art downtown, is the oldest used-books store in California, and in quiet and privileged Montecito, to the south, a beautifully bespoke and compact bookstore, Tecolote, almost as old, has been hand-selling elegant new books for eighty-six years (and was saved five years ago by local residents, who banded together to buy it when its former owner decided to retire). But Chaucer's is something unique—town hall and free library and source of local pride—and I usually allow hours for every visit there, because I'm almost certain to run into long-lost classmates, to find a book (by Terry Castle or Sigrid Nunez or Ivana Lowell) that I have to read then and there, in the aisles, or to realize that this is the perfect place, better than any website, to check on the principal parts of the irregular ancient Greek verb *baino*.

One employee drives 100 miles each way, arriving before dawn each day, to disappear into the back of the store and help buy the books that will save our lives.

Chaucer's is the first place I go when I return to Santa Barbara from traveling abroad, and—a little embarrassingly—it's the last one I visit before I leave (to fill my suitcase with books to take to Ethiopia or Easter Island). My friends who work there often see more of me than does my own mother, whose residence in Santa Barbara is meant to be the reason I'm revisiting. I've done readings at Chaucer's, next to its cash registers, and I held my first-ever signing there, almost a quarter of a century ago. I've had public discussions, on the nature of travel, at its front table, and I've gotten to see T.C. Boyle there, in the audience of a reading by Jane Smiley.

I've learned about the seasonal patterns of monarch butterflies from one of its longtime workers, and another has told me about her life growing up in Peru. Often I've startled my friends at the front desk by buying copies of my own books there, as last-minute gifts for a dentist or a mother's gynecologist; sometimes I've arranged for strangers to leave books at the cash register if they want me to sign them.

Chaucer's is where I've gone to make phone calls, or to pass an hour or two between doctors' appointments; it's where I raced through the life story of Van Morrison and where I order my magazines when I'm out of town. When I'm very far away—in my sometime flat in Japan—I stay up in the quiet autumn evenings, making long lists of all the books I have to collect the next time I'm at Chaucer's.

I was lucky enough to be born and to grow up in Oxford, England, where every last corner of Broad Street seemed filled with secondhand-book sellers, shops dealing in art books, places offering only kids' books, and outposts of one of the world's largest bookstores, Blackwell's; I later lived in Boston and New York, home to some of the world's great independent bookshops. As a writer who's been touring with new books for more than two decades, I've come to know some of North America's most sumptuous independent bookstores, from Seattle to Toronto, from Corte Madera to Iowa City, from Pasadena to Miami.

What I've found—and the same is true of books, of course—is that each of them has its own particular color and spirit, yet all are involved in the same enterprise, almost as partners, or players in the same orchestra. A novel, as a schoolteacher in Julian Barnes's *The Sense of an Ending*, reflects, "is about character developed over time." So, too, is a bookstore.

. . .

A book lives, to some extent, off its tension, and in the story that is a bookstore there has been no shortage of conflict in recent times.

Every day brings new reasons not to go to a bricks-and-mortar shop, as friends tell you about e-readers and online discounts, while publishers sometimes seem to be racing about in panic like passengers on the *Titanic*. My literary home in Kyoto, Maruzen bookstore, where I've spent much of the past twenty-five years, suddenly, and without fanfare, closed down; the extraordinary Village Voice in Paris, as discerning and tasteful a collection of English-language books as could be found on the planet, recently met the same fate. Every time I return to Cambridge, Massachusetts, or to Berkeley—communities more or less consecrated to the word—I find old friends and classic volumes among bookstores vanished.

A book will arrive on your e-reader at a click, friends tell me, for less than half the price I'm paying. A computer will give you recommendations on what to buy next. There are things it won't do for you, however, and would think of as heresy. Once, when I was in the Village Voice, I asked the man at the front desk, Michael, for a copy of George Painter's biography of Proust; it was out of print, he told me, so he'd bring me a copy of his own, for me to keep, free of charge, if I came back the following day ("Paperback or hardcover?" he asked, and the next day was as good as his word).

A bookshop isn't just about business, in short; it's about shared passion. It's a conversation, a spirited exchange, the kind of thing you'd enjoy with that other Pynchonian who has just tracked down another reference to Vinland in old Norse literature. It's not what passes between hands at the cash register that matters so much as what passes between minds, as that person who sees you buy a copy of Siddhartha Mukherjee's *The Emperor of All Maladies* tells you how she was once diagnosed with cancer, but that not all such dire developments prove fatal.

So just when you expect to turn a page and find Chapter 11 in the history of a brave little independent bookstore that's swimming against the tide of digital sales and big-box convenience, you find something that defies expectation on the bottom line as well as all the sentences that lead up to it. The penultimate chapter in my story of my bookstore would begin eight years ago, when another small shop selling books on travel—as well as travel equipment—opened its doors downtown. As soon as I went in to explore this new place of wonders, its manager corralled me. He wanted to put this place on the map, he said, to encourage a community of readers, to remind the public of the private delight of books. He was going to organize huge readings, advertise them everywhere, and rent a room in the public library down the street to make them real events.

Would I be a part of this?

How could I not support the books that have supported so many of us, as writers, readers, and just lovers of our city? Without them, I'd be without a livelihood, as well as a reason for living.

I instantly said yes, therefore, and we agreed on a date four months later, when I'd have a new book out. The night arrived, and I came to the fresh, upstart store to find that no advertisements had been organized, no extra room had been reserved, and, in sad fact, the manager had neglected even to get any copies of my new book to sell.

I looked at the customers who'd given up their warm spring evening to be here—they filled several rows of grey folded chairs—and called my inner 911.

"Of course," said my old friend David, at Chaucer's, the second he picked up the phone. He would collect every copy of my books he could find in his store, drive them all down here in the next twenty minutes, and, in effect, help a new rival sell the books it had been too lazy even to stock.

The point was not which bookstore claimed the profits, he might have been saying; it was that people should have access to the books they need.

. . .

At the end of many a great novel there's often a coda that puts everything you've just read and learned into perspective. So let these be my final words on Chaucer's, for now.

Several years ago, Borders came to the very heart of downtown Santa Barbara and erected a vast and alluring three-story citadel at the central intersection on our main shopping street, next to a large public parking lot and one of our five-screen cinemas. There were always kids hanging around outside—it stayed open till very late—and there were often musicians striking up impromptu concerts, to draw people toward its entrance. There were free restrooms inside, there was a hip counter selling coffee and cakes, there was a top floor full of CDs, which even my book-hating friends began to haunt.

There were aisles upon aisles of magazines, and free computers to guide you to what you were looking for; there were readings and comfy chairs and all the props of an indie store that a crafty major retailer knows how to turn to advantage.

Right across the street from Borders, as part of our most stylish new shopping mall, was a sprawling Barnes & Noble.

The writing was on the wall for little Chaucer's, we all sensed, off on the wrong side of town, hidden away in a mall, with only Mahri, and no multinational, to support it, a typical casualty of the hard and the corporate times.

In January 2011 Borders closed its doors, forever. Almost the same day, Barnes & Noble across the street also stopped doing business, driven away, perhaps, by Santa Barbara's terrifying rents and dozens of tourist shops. The Borders near our large public university closed. Chaucer's, meanwhile, only grows bigger and bigger, to the point where many of us suspect it would devour much of the mall around it if only its neighbors would say yes.

It might almost be a parable, or a Tom Hanks movie, that Mahri and her twenty-six employees are enacting. The little shop stocks more books—150,000 and counting—in its happily crowded space than the downtown Borders did in a space five times as big. Twenty-four of its employees are full-time workers (by marked contrast with the business model in the chain stores), and many have been working at Chaucer's for more than ten years, thanks in part, no doubt, to the 100 percent health coverage offered and Christmas bonuses. And when the two behemoths closed down, Mahri expressed her regret, because more books are preferable to fewer. After she first opened

Chaucer's, with a modest bequest, as a small paperback shop, in 1974, she and her husband had to dip into their life-insurance funds to keep it going.

The last time I visited Chaucer's, one of its newest employees—24 years old, from back East, who'd just moved to Santa Barbara to try to become a writer—lit up when I bought a book on Iran. "Oh, you're the guy who's into long sentences," he said, and then we were off on an escalating passion of rhythm and flow and how no staccato works could catch the effects of a Melville or Pamuk or Sir Thomas Browne. My bookstore is the place where I find myself, as well as my home, my passion—and my reason for trying to do what I do.

PICO IYER is the author of two novels and eight works of nonfiction, including *Video Night in Kathmandu, The Lady and the Monk, The Global Soul,* and, most recently, *The Man Within My Head,* an exploration of the way writers can live inside us. Though based since 1992 in rural Japan, he spends much of his time haunting bookshops from Rio to Bhutan.

Ward Just

Bunch of Grapes Bookstore

VINEYARD HAVEN, MASSACHUSETTS

S omeone at dinner was going on and on about Zola, his provoca-
tions, his headlong narratives, his fierce and spacious conscience,
his embrace of controversy. The novel being discussed was *Thérèse
Raquin*, scandalous when published (in 1867), scarcely less so today.
Wonderful descriptions of the erotic life, the more erotic for being
clandestine, and the murder that results. The denunciations from
church figures and others was so fierce that Zola was obligated to
write a preface to the second edition defending himself, which he
did with tremendous relish. "The critics have given this book a hostile

and indignant reception. Certain righteous individuals, writing in no less righteous newspapers, have picked it up between thumb and fore-finger, screwed up their faces in disgust, and thrown it on the fire. ..." Well! Who can resist that? So I took myself downtown to the Bunch of Grapes Bookstore, where *Thérèse Raquin* was nestled against another Zola novel called *The Kill*, and that was not all. Next to Zola was the Israeli novelist A.B. Yehoshua, and a little further up the line all the literary wolves, with their various spellings, Virginia, Thomas, and Geoffrey. I walked out of the store with half a dozen novels, and therein lies the definition of a full-service bookstore of the sort called "independent."

This sort of thing happens all the time, and if Bunch of Grapes doesn't have the book they'll order it. And often on the flimsiest description. My memory is not what it used to be, and what it used to be was not exactly investment-grade so the clerks are obligated to make huge leaps of the imagination and with the same alacrity and good cheer as Zola's roughing up an archbishop.

I heard about a novel last night. I forget the title.

Who's the author?

I can't remember that either, except he was a professor of English somewhere in the Midwest.

Maybe Kansas.

Recent book?

No. Published years ago.

Ummm.

It's in paperback. I think it's a New York Review of Books book.

Ah! That would be *Stoner* by John Williams. Beautiful novel.

That's the one!

I'll have it for you by Friday.

Walk into these bookstores, either on a mission (*Thérèse Raquin*,

Stoner) or simply to graze, and your reading life passes before you—the first time you read *The Old Man and the Sea* in *Life* magazine, sitting in a chair by the big window in your parents' house in the suburb north of Chicago, the light failing and you so caught up in the sea and the old man that you could not stop long enough to switch on the reading light—and here, more than sixty years later, through God knows how many printings, the old man lives once more. Scan the shelves and recall the books you put aside after an hour or two, knowing the failing was not the author's but your own and promising to pick it up later, when you are older and have more patience or perhaps understand the world a little bit better. *The Man Without Qualities*, Robert Musil's novel, the lovely two-volume edition published by Knopf, rests in my library to this day, a rebuke; one of many. Comforting also to see the books of friends, Kib Bramhall's meditation on the art of fishing, Jon Randal's search for Osama bin Laden. Remain in the stacks long enough and your whole damned life passes before you.

> *Walk into these bookstores, either on a mission or simply to graze, and your reading life passes before you...*

WARD JUST's 16 previous novels include *Exiles in the Garden*, *Forgetfulness*, the National Book Award finalist *Echo House*, *A Dangerous Friend*, winner of the Cooper Prize for fiction from the Society of American Historians, and *An Unfinished Season*, winner of the Chicago Tribune Heartland Award and a finalist for the 2005 Pulitzer Prize.

Lesley Kagen
Next Chapter Bookshop

MEQUON, WISCONSIN

Like a kid with her first report card, I skipped over to Next Chapter Bookshop with the galley of *Whistling in the Dark* clutched in my sweaty little hand.

After pats on the back and much oohing and ahhing, the book-sellers went back to work doing what they do so well, and I sneakily moseyed over to their best-seller stacks. Glancing over my shoulder to make sure no one was watching, I set the book down next to the big guns, just to see how it'd look. Never for a second entertaining the thought that someday it might earn that spot. Me...becoming an award-winning or *New York Times* best-selling author? Please. I loved and believed in my book, but knew it took more than a solid story to exist in the rarefied air of those top shelves. Connections matter. Publisher support too. It's also quite helpful if you're a gorgeous twenty-something blonde from LA or NYC with a nice chest and an MFA, and not a 57-year-old mousey brunette living in Mequon, Wisconsin, who anticipated the need for a bosoms belt in her near future. Before I'd completed the novel, the last thing I'd written of any consequence was a book report on Helen Keller.

A few weeks later during a lunch chitchat, my editor, who happened to be paying a serendipitous visit to nearby Madison, buttered her roll and said, "I'm curious. If you could make one wish for your book, what would it be?"

I'd given that some thought. As a lover and supporter of independent bookstores, I'd already asked my fairy godmother for a waving of her wand. "More than anything," I answered, "I'd love the book to be selected for the Book Sense list. Do you think that could... ah... happen?"

From across the table, violent croissant choking erupted, which I took as my editor's somewhat dramatic but enormously effective way of saying *fat* chance.

But tables can turn, and a month later, she left this stunned message on my answering message: "I can't believe...your book...it made the May Book Sense list! How? I mean...wow!"

Lanora Haradon, that's how. The owner of Next Chapter Bookshop had been holding my hand on a road to publication that had been fraught with potholes. My manuscript had been rejected for representation by well over a hundred literary agents, and only one publisher had made an offer. Despite the detours, Lanora believed in me and the novel and it wasn't just lip service. Well, actually, it was. Behind my back, the little rascal had been talking up the book with other independent booksellers, had written a recommendation for the Booksense list, and had encouraged others to do so as well.

When the real books arrived at the shop months later, Lanora rang me up and suggested I get my bum over there. She led a weak-kneed me to a table, thrust a Sharpie into my hand, and returned a few minutes later with two cartons of *Whistling in the Dark*. There I was... signing my books in *my* bookstore. Cool customer that I am, I burst into tears. Of course, the launch party for the novel was held at my home away from home. Considering that the story is set in 1959, Lanora thought it'd be fun to serve pigs-in-a-blanket and button candy and, of course, cheapish wine, which works to liven up any era. When she took the podium to deliver a heartfelt speech about the novel, I had to plug my ears. It was too much happy to take in.

> *There I was... signing* my *books in* my *bookstore. Cool customer that I am, I burst into tears.*

Surrounded as I was by friends, family, and other book lovers, the shindig was a celebration of a destination reached. Who could ask for more? Not me. No way. There is nothing more humbling for an author than standing in the middle of a bookstore. Gazing upon shelf after shelf lined with thousands of other writers' hopes. Even with the much-wished-for Book Sense recommendation, I knew it'd be a walking-on-water miracle if my book sold more than a modest amount. But within a week, the Next Chapter staff had hand-sold fifty copies; by the next, another forty; and on and on it went and still does in their store, across the country, and around the world. *Whistling in the Dark* eventually made the *New York Times* list and won the Midwest Independent Booksellers Association award that sits next to my bed alongside the other unexpected gifts. (Imagining readers paging through my books while sitting on the Great Wall of China and below windmills in the Netherlands and whatever-the-heck landmark Turkey has to offer can keep me occupied for hours.)

Five years and four novels later, it still takes everything I've got not to burst into a chorus of "You Light Up My Life" and drop to my knees in gratitude when I step through the doors of the store to sign my works, attend author events, or shoot the book breeze with the team that makes it all possible. (So far, I've managed to keep it to joyful humming and a simple genuflection, but I'm not making any promises.)

Bless you, Lanora.

Bless you, Next Chapter Bookshop.

LESLEY KAGEN is a mother of two, an actress, a former restaurateur, accomplished equestrienne, and award-winning *New York Times* best-selling author of *Whistling in the Dark, Land of a Hundred Wonders, Tomorrow River,* and *Good Graces*. Visit her at lesleykagen.com.

Stephanie Kallos

Third Place Books, LAKE FOREST PARK, WASHINGTON

Defining Third Place
third place \ 'thərd 'plās \

1: a term coined by urban sociologist Ray Oldenburg; used in the concept of community building to refer to social surroundings separate from the two usual social environments of home (first place) and work (second place). ⸢What suburbia cries for are the means for people to gather easily, inexpensively, regularly, and pleasurably—a place on the corner, real-life alternatives to television, easy escapes from the cabin fever of marriage and family life that do not necessitate getting into an automobile ~ Ray Oldenburg⸥ 2: an open, light-filled public space offering a variety of food and drink, furnished with large sturdy tables that have been sliced from the massive trunks of salvaged Douglas firs, and employing a waitstaff that is completely unconcerned with rapid customer turnover 3: deluxe amenities of some third-place locales include bookstores, bowling lanes, live music and/or juke boxes, upright pianos, beanbag and/or barber chairs, community kiosks, photo booths, beer and wine licenses, wood-burning stoves, and giant chess sets 4: the monthly meeting venue for The Commoners, a five-person writing group to which you belonged for ten years, through marriages and divorces, house sales and purchases, the deaths of parents and dear friends, the births of children and grandchildren, job firings, unemployment, and job retrainings 5: the place where your writers' group spends seven of those years critiquing every chapter of your first novel, Part One of your second novel, and half a dozen short stories—all this beginning in 1996, long before you even dared to dream that anything you wrote would actually be published 6: where, season after season, your writers' group offers smart, insightful, and kindly voiced variations on one of two things that all writers need to hear in order to become better: (1) Keep going. Don't give up. It's wonderful. (2) Keep going. Don't give up. It's not good enough. 7: comments involving variations on <it's not good enough> sting less because they are offered over lattes, herbal tea, and calorically generous pastries provided by Honey Bear Bakery 8: it is where you nurse your second baby on the first Saturday of the month from November 1997 through April 1998 while drinking decaf and nibbling disks of fruit panettone sprinkled with generous amounts of organic sugar and fennel <an aid to lactation> and listening to your writers' group continue to critique your first novel—the one you began writing before this baby was even *conceived*, the one you won't finish and finally publish until he is 7 years old and his older brother is 10 9: where your sons play with the giant chess set as soon as they are slightly taller than the rooks 10: in the fall of 2003, where you spend many hours over the course of several weeks sitting at one of those expansive wooden tables editing your first novel after it is accepted for publication, your notes executed in a ragged, barely legible scrawl because ⁀having recently discovered that the cooling effects of an ice-skating rink provide fabulous relief for menopausal hot flashes⁀ you signed up for a private ice-skating tutorial, fell ten minutes into the lesson, and fractured your right radius. It is your first broken bone ever. The novel you are editing is called *Broken for You*. **11**: where you go to meet your writers group as usual on the morning of January 7, 2006: the first Saturday of the New Year, the morning after you held vigil and watched your mother die almost a year to the day after your dad; you go because one of your earliest memories is of your mother's hands demonstrating the right way to open a book; because it is from your mother that you inherited a sanctified love of reading; because she wept when she read the first draft of your first novel; because she would have wanted you to go; because there is no place in the world you can imagine being—not even the first place of home—that will comfort you today like this place and these people **12**: you will for-ever bear a grudge against a famous American movie star/daughter of movie stars who shall remain nameless because at a huge third-place event promoting her latest children's book she was cruel to your bookselling buddies **13**: you will forever adore Alan Alda even more than you already did because at a similar event promoting his autobi-ography he was kind to them **14**: since you have a habit of inscribing all book purchases with the date and place of purchase, you know it is where you acquired the following volumes: *Edwin Mullhouse and A Girl Named Zippy*; *Four Letter Word: Invented Correspondence from the Edge of Modern Romance*; *Strange as This Weather Has Been and Defining the Wind*; *The View from the Seventh Layer*; *How Green Was My Valley*; *Poemcrazy*; *Stuffed*; *Saul Bellow: Letters*; *The Brief History of the Dead*; *The Face on Your Plate*; *The Face of a Naked Lady*; *Woe Is I*; *Words Fail Me*; *Writers on Writing, Volume II*; *A Writer's Time*; *Reading Like a Writer*; *Pitching My Tent*; *Border Songs*; *The Great Good Place* ⁀there are many more books bearing third-place inscriptions in your house; these are only the ones culled from your office shelves⁀ **15**: it is where you step onstage in December of 2008 to launch your second novel—the one you wrote in the wake of grief, the one dedicated to your deceased parents and a writer friend who committed suicide 16: it is where you teach the audience the Nebraska fight song, flanked by Third Place bookseller/friend Cheryl McKeon and PGW rep/friend Cindy Heideman who hold up large poster boards bearing the lyrics: "Oh, there is no place like Nebraska; dear old Nebraska U; where the girls are the fairest, the boys are the squarest, of any old place that I knew…" 17: it is where the Q&A is initiated when beloved author/buddy Jim Lynch stands up and asks: "How do you write with such authority about the dead?" ⟨It occurs to you as you're writing this essay that this is the kind of question only a third place would inspire⟩ 18: it is where booksellers know you, greet you by name, ask how the next one is going, and don't mind if you break down in tears and babble on about how the next one isn't going so well ⟨in comfort, they'll hand you a tissue and hand-sell a book⟩ 19: it is where you arrive with your laptop not long after the doors open on July 5, 2012, to complete the final edits to this essay, a couple of hours before setting off on a road trip with your sons ⟨who are now 14 and 17⟩ You bring your twelve-ounce sugar-free hazelnut soy to one of the big round Doug fir tables ⟨the kind The Commoners preferred⟩, run a finger around the smoothed, curving, shiny edge, count a few closely spaced rings ⟨they could be the lines in fairy-ruled composition book⟩, realizing that the history of your life as told in this essay occupies only one and a quarter inches. A Chopin ballade is playing through the speakers. A shaft of sunlight illuminates seven middle-aged women gathered around a table beneath one of the skylights, knitting. The kiosk is now a flat-screen TV, but the content hasn't

> *17: it is where the Q&A is initiated when beloved author/buddy Jim Lynch stands up and asks: "How do you write with such authority about the dead?"*

changed: There are posted notices about Summer Story Times, invitations to join German and Spanish and French conversation groups, requests to consider donating your used musical instruments at the July Farmers' Market so that all children can play. You are a few days past the deadline, but the editor was understanding about the delay; and besides, it is so important to get this right, this ode, this *efharisto*, this love letter to the place that has nurtured, solaced, and challenged; the place that has forged connections far beyond those that can be measured on a road atlas; the place that has witnessed your growth into the contours of a grateful, full life, a life you always dreamed of **20**: on your way to bus your dishes, you notice two 11-year-old boys who have been sitting behind you as you write this: best friends out of school for the summer. They've ridden here on their bikes and are eating lunch at a low counter that encloses a small play area for young children. One boy is pale, freckled, shaped like an Idaho russet; the other is a pole bean with orthodontics. Pole bean is saying, "I said, 'Where?' and he said, 'Four hours ago.' I said, 'Where?' and he said, 'Four hours ago.'" They both throw back their heads and laugh. Pole bean repeats this exchange three more times before I am out of earshot, and they laugh hysterically every single time. *Why are they sitting there?* you wonder as you ride the escalator down to your car. *Why not at one of the other tables?* And then you realize that, of course, it's because they played in that play place as their folks looked on and chatted here, years ago, when they were still just little kids.

21: [insert your definition here]

STEPHANIE KALLOS spent 20 years in the theater as an actress and teacher before turning her full-time attention to writing. She has published several works of short fiction and two novels, *Broken for You* (chosen by Sue Monk Kidd for the *Today* show book club) and *Sing Them Home* (named by *Entertainment Weekly* as one of Top Ten Books of 2009). She lives in North Seattle with her husband and sons and is currently at work on her third novel.

Larry Kane

Chester County Book & Music Company

WEST CHESTER, PENNSYLVANIA

Before I begin this essay, a disclaimer. My favorite bookstore is forty miles from my home. I have purchased many books there, but I still frequent two Barnes & Noble stores within three miles of my home. I have sold four books at my favorite store: a biography of my career as a broadcast journalist, two best-selling books on my unique travels with the Beatles, and a newsroom murder mystery. A fifth, on the mystery of how the Beatles came about, is due next fall. I will sell the book there, as well as on a national tour. This essay will no doubt make me more popular at my favorite bookseller but perhaps create some controversy with all my friends in the book community.

When you read the name of my favorite bookstore, Chester County Book & Music Company, you may conjure up images of a lush green countryside, the smell of burning firewood, the evening sounds of owls hooting in the cool summer air, and the hues of green that makes Chester County, Pennsylvania, in the far suburbs of Philadelphia, a physically angelic masterpiece to the eye and a treat to the senses. Although that imagery may seem to fit the name, Chester County Book & Music Company is hardly anything of the above.

But it does fit a remarkably entertaining contemporary version of the extraordinary mix of old-fashioned values and modern technology, because the store's staff employs the first, and best, bookselling value: the art of the sale, performed not by lists or computer screens, but by face-to-face, person-to-person encounters that can be as exciting and fun as the book itself.

> *...the art of the sale, performed not by lists or computer screens, but by face-to-face, person-to-person encounters that can be as exciting and fun as the book itself.*

First off, Chester County is not located in the woods. It is nestled in a strip mall just off of Route 202 in West Chester, Pennsylvania, but no matter—this store could be located anywhere. Like all great institutions, the store thrives not on its physical structure, but on the force of its people.

People in the publishing business are facing some critical challenges, and the biggest of all are people in the publishing business. Retailers, whether they are in the two standout independents in the Philadelphia region—Chester County and The Doylestown Bookshop, where Shilough Hopwood manages a thriving, smaller independent—or the hard-working chain stores, are subject to a definitive lack of courage on the part of some major publishers in their selection of fiction. People with talent are often left out because publishers want guaranteed winners. The result is a "no-risk, no-reward" environment. Left holding the bag are retailers who are having a hard enough time selling paper books in the age of electronic wizardry. On that score, you've got to hand it to the people who are selling books by spoken word, and therein lies the special feeling of Chester County Book & Music. I've often told my good friends at Barnes & Noble to check out the selling techniques at Chester County. For it is the subtle and not so subtle that makes the book experience so special.

A little geography. When a reader walks through the door, there is a large, wood-paneled bookstore that transitions into another large store of music CDs and the resurgent vinyl. The music department gives you something that electronic services can never offer: atmosphere. If you like atmosphere, you'll love everything about Chester County's music department, including its children's section. While there are sections, sections that are actually marked, browsers are encouraged to work harder, to "feel free to browse" at their own speed.

As you walk back into the bookstore, when you glance to the right you will see an opening to a restaurant. Not a snack shop, but a real restaurant. This combination of books, beat, and food is hard to top, unless you are in the Borough of Doylestown and partake of the many restaurants within walking distance of the Doylestown Bookshop. The Chester County crew has its food and drink right there, and I must say, it's a terrific menu, with the chefs doing a fantastic job. This might sound a little silly, but I am a big fan of peanut butter and jelly sandwiches. Is it hard to mess up a PBJ? No. But it's also a great feeling to get what you want when you want it, even if it is on the children's menu.

Back in the main store, near the center, is the cash register and services desk, and that's where the shine comes through. There is a tradition at Chester County, a tradition that has launched so many good books and at the same time fulfilled the needs of the customers while filling their lives with joy, which I think is what a bookstore should be all about.

The tradition of R&R, or reading and recommending, began with Thea Kotroba, the current manager, some twenty-eight years ago, when she arrived at the store. It has continued into the next generation of booksellers. And it is largely a legacy of a man who may have been the most instrumental bookseller-reader in the northeast United States.

Joe Drabyak joined the store in the nineties. He took the art of R&R to new heights. Some customers would look at "Joe's List" and buy books by the bushel. Joe was *that* good. But he was also that good at fighting for the publication of great books. Joe, former president of the New Atlantic Independent Booksellers Association, probably did more to save independent bookstores in America than almost any individual in recent years. Authors and publishers were enamored of his ability to make a pick. Some of them, including this reporter, were indeed honored to speak and remember Joe at his funeral service on October 3, 2010. Joe had succumbed to cancer at the age of 60, but what he left at Chester County is still very much alive, in the store and in print. A record eight fictional characters are named for him in recently published books.

I could tell you a lot about Joe, but I think I'll leave that to Kathy Simoneaux, the owner of Chester County Book Company, who said right after his death, "Right now, I can't think of Joe as an employee, bookseller, NAIBA president, or pillar of the bookselling community, but as a fascinating, charming, and hilarious man I was lucky to know."

Hilarious was an understatement. Joe was so funny, alive. And inspirational to veteran and beginning authors. His personal impact on the store was monumental.

Thea Kotroba, who is a world-champion reader and picker in her own right, says she thinks of the "hole, the vacancy that remains, but there is the clear understanding that all of us want to continue the tradition."

The tradition includes personally recommended books, his own best-seller list, and a man brimming with eye contact, personal allure, and a determination to make the selling, buying, and reading of a book as exciting to the modern generation as the acquisition of a video game.

And Joe spread the word. During his life, and after, fellow booksellers got in the spirit. Everyone developed his or her own "picks." So, when you walk into Chester County Book & Music, the gang is ready. Joanne Fritz is on the kids' beat, and she knows her children's books. Michael Fortney is an artist that has eclectic tastes in fiction, but I've never left a recommended book unfinished. Julia Loving is a part-timer with a great track record. Tim Skipp has a flair for great books, and he loves reading books that were translated. *The Girl with the Dragon Tattoo* comes to mind. And Thea? Well, perfection has its moments, especially when you're aiming to please.

The difference? Dedicated readers. Diagnosing sellers, sellers who know their buyers. What a combination. You take these real-life talents and mix them with a deeply toned bookstore, a music palace, and some real American food thrown in, and you have a combination that draws you in like a magnet.

There is a downside. The place is so attractive and seductive that it provides a challenge. When you walk into the store and "feel" the presence, maybe have a bite of food and get lost in the books or just the browsing, time passes by, as it does when you are reading a great book. Suddenly, you look up, and you might be late, or missing an appointment. Going into a store like this could be dangerous to your schedule, if you want to have one. Shop at your own risk. And remember that Joe's presence is still there, lighting your path to the next great date with writing destiny.

Before I finish this little story, another disclaimer. I have been a "Joe's Pick" three times. It has not affected my view of my favorite bookstore, but it certainly was gratifying in a creative way. The fact is, selling a book there was my introduction to the store. If I had not written books, I probably would never have visited my favorite store, because it is forty miles from my home. Would you travel forty miles to buy a book?

LARRY KANE, known as the dean of Philadelphia television news anchors, has been one of the nation's most respected TV journalists for more than 43 years and has recently marked his 51st anniversary in broadcasting. Kane is current host of the Voice of Reason program on The Comcast Network. He is also a special contributor for CBS's KYW Newsradio and is a consultant for NBC Regional and National Sports. He is the author of four books, including *Larry Kane's Philadelphia*, a regional best-seller. As the only broadcast journalist to travel to every stop on the Beatles' 1964 and 1965 tours, Kane authored *Ticket to Ride*, with a foreword by Dick Clark, and *Lennon Revealed*, a *New York Times* and *Los Angeles Times* best-seller in 2005. His books have been printed in nine languages around the world. His most recent book is *Death by Deadline*, a murder mystery novel that examines the challenges facing local TV news.

Laurie R. King

Bookshop Santa Cruz, SANTA CRUZ, CALIFORNIA

B ooks run through the veins of any vibrant community. I knew
this long before I became a writer (can it be twenty-two books
ago?), but it came to me afresh recently as I sank into research for a
novel set in 1929 Paris.

After the Great War, American soldiers who had spent a leave in
Paris found that a part of their hearts and minds remained there—as
the song says, "How you gonna keep 'em down on the farm…?"

More pragmatically, these young men also discovered that the
exchange rate of the early twenties meant their dollars would support
them a lot longer—and a whole lot better—next to the Seine than

alongside the Hudson or the Ohio. Maybe even long enough to produce a novel, or a collection of poetry, or a roomful of paintings.

So the Lost Generation converged on the Left Bank, where rooms were cheap and wine was plentiful. And once there, it found its heartbeat in a bookstore.

A small American woman named Sylvia Beach had also fallen in love with Paris during the war and manufactured her own excuse to stay: The City of Light needed a shop selling English-language books. (Oh, the perennial optimism of the book-selling breed!) Shakespeare and Company, her bookshop/lending library, opened on the Left Bank—commercial rents being cheap there too—just in time for the trickle, then flood, of English-speaking expatriates. Customers both French and foreign came for the books and stayed for the talk. Ernest Hemingway and André Gide, T.S. Eliot and Ezra Pound, F. Scott Fitzgerald and Aleister Crowley, Man Ray and Gertrude Stein—all manner of odd pairings met and mingled among the stacks. They bought (or, more often, borrowed) the latest novel, they picked up their mail (those all-important checks from home!), they showed Sylvia their manuscripts. And of course, being artists, they also borrowed money from the bookseller, allowed her to feed them, and cadged stays in the apartment over the shop.

None went further than James Joyce, an unemployed English teacher with a wife, two children, and a book that wouldn't end. Shakespeare and Company supported him, emotionally, artistically, and above all, financially. Everyone agreed that *Ulysses* was a work of genius, but it was also a book so unwieldy—and judged so obscene—that no publisher dared touch it. So Sylvia Beach turned her hand to publishing, devoting years of her life to the novel and the author's endless emendations, bankrupting herself but for the donations of friends, left in the end with nothing except the knowledge that she had brought about one of the definitive works of English literature.

For her, that was enough.

Thankfully, not every bookstore is called to act as midwife to a *Ulysses*. Not all booksellers are quite so...let's call it "dedicated," although the word "nuts" does come to mind. However, all the bookstores I know stand foursquare in the support of literature, and foursquare at the core of a community.

Take Bookshop Santa Cruz.

I met Bookshop a few years after its 1966 opening, when I came to town as a student and wandered into this old brick building on the main street. Neal and Candy Coonerty owned it by then, a comfortable store with delightfully creaky wooden floors and a scattering of well-used armchairs, always occupied. It was the kind of building that seemed to have hidden passages and mysterious caves, like the hills around town. I suspected there were magicians living in the basement. Alchemists, maybe.

This was the first bookstore I had known, since my family, by nature and by the habits of chronic house-moving, almost exclusively patronized libraries. I bought my first hardback novel here when I was 23, James Clavell's *Shogun*: The library's edition was in two volumes, and I could find only Part One. Thank goodness, Bookshop Santa Cruz came to my rescue.

As it has any number of times over the years. This red-brick building was where the treasure of Santa Cruz was kept, where its entertainment waited, where knowledge lurked, where all the most interesting of its citizens were to be found.

Where the city's heartbeat lay.

I was a regular. I would buy a book and start it in the coffee house behind the store, listening to the wide-ranging, coffee-fueled discussions at the Penny University. I stopped in at the annual birthday party in early November. Over the years, a record of my purchases would trace the course of my changing life: from the world's religions to vegetable gardening and carpentry, then travel guides, followed by pregnancy manuals and children's picture books. (Unlike their mother, my kids grew up owning books.) For years, Bookshop was a part of my life, enriching and necessary.

Then came the Loma Prieta quake.

A fist smashed Santa Cruz. On October 17, 1989, at 5:04 in

the afternoon, people died, roads split, and buildings came to pieces, including the comfortable brick home of Bookshop Santa Cruz. Its walls trembled precariously. All the shop's glorious treasures lay in heaps, vomited off the shelves, unreachable behind the city's red-tag notices. Wrecking balls waited only for the highways to reopen. All around, the shocked community boiled its tap water, picked glass shards from its carpets, went to bed in the dark, and tasted fear with every aftershock.

The city's heartbeat faltered.

And Neal and Candy looked at each other, set their shoulders, and with that blessed, mad optimism of their breed, declared that Bookshop's annual birthday party would go ahead. It was the town's first glimmer of hope since the earth shook. Shortly after the party, when the temporary retail tents rose up in the downtown parking lots—the official name of "pavilions" never really caught on—hundreds of staunch and grateful friends turned up to rescue Bookshop's treasure, donning hard hats, carrying the books to safety, cleaning them of dust and wounds. By the end of the November, in a community hounded by unremitting chaos and dreary news, Booktent Santa Cruz opened for business.

Over the years, a record of my purchases would trace the course of my changing life: from the world's religions to vegetable gardening and carpentry, then travel guides, followed by pregnancy manuals and children's picture books.

We shopped in Booktent for three long years, scouring its sparse shelves for Christmas and birthday gifts, searching for kids' stories we didn't already have, investing in books on canning and cats—anything that would help Bookshop survive. And when the new store opened at last, again the community stepped forward, this time in triumph, to carry books from the dim, shabby tent to the startlingly bright, modern, and spacious new store.

Santa Cruz had its heartbeat again.

The second incarnation of Bookshop Santa Cruz opened two months before my first book was published. In the years since, I have done quite a few readings there, bought (and signed!) countless books, used the store as the site for any number of pre-dinner or pre-movie meetings, and downed gallons of latte in the adjoining coffee house. These days I shop the children's section with a small grandson, and although I've lost my interest in books on vegetable gardening and canning, I do buy plenty of hardback fiction.

Those of us who remember the original dark wood and creaky floors, who watched—and rejoiced—as Bookshop Santa Cruz rose from the rubble, do not take the place for granted. We value the store, we come to the events, we make it part of our lives. Where there was once devastation, there is now a vibrant community, filled with life and ideas, with books running through its veins.

Bookshop Santa Cruz: where people come for the books and stay for the energy.

Just like Shakespeare and Company, ninety years ago.

LAURIE R. KING is the author of *The Beekeeper's Apprentice*, *Pirate King*, and *Touchstone*.

Katrina Kittle

Saturn Booksellers, GAYLORD, MICHIGAN

My "hometown bookstore" is 437 miles away from my house. Saturn Booksellers in Gaylord, Michigan, is my go-to, all-time-favorite bookstore, the kind of bookstore I dream about as a book lover and as an author. It's the kind of bookstore I no longer have in my actual hometown of Dayton, Ohio. We have all the big chains in Dayton, where I can get any book in print, but not all the other essential things I crave in a bookstore.

What do I crave? Most important: passionate booksellers. Jill Miner and her crew are some of the most with-it, smart, spot-on hand-sellers I've ever encountered. And I should mention here that I lucked into experiencing Saturn Booksellers because Jill Miner nominated my third novel for the Great Lakes Book Award for Fiction in 2006. She introduced me for my acceptance of the award at the Great Lakes Independent Booksellers Association convention, and when we sat down for dinner, she said, "We need to get you to my store. How can we make that happen?" That's one of the (many) wonderful things about Jill—she makes things happen.

Within a year of that dinner, I walked into Saturn's embrace for the first time. From the sidewalk sign that demanded "GET IN HERE!" to the chalkboard walls and the coffee shop in the log cabin built inside the store, there was nothing cookie-cutter or chain about it. Jill showed me the press for my event and some fun marketing that included chocolate bars with my book cover on the wrappers (is that genius, or what? Not to mention one of my favorite combinations: books and chocolate). Jill said they'd all been hand-selling the book like crazy and they were confident of a crowd for my reading, but the rows and rows of waiting seats made me feel queasy. I wandered the aisles, the intriguing displays, the staff recommendations, checking periodically on those seats...which were not filling up. I thought, *Well, even if the event is a bust, I'll get some great shopping done.*

I took photos of the signs that threatened "Unattended children will be given an espresso and a free puppy" and "Be Nice or Leave" and of the "Insane Asylum Entrance" sign over the door to the Employees Only area...then obsessively checked my watch and those (empty!) chairs again. Every author has experienced the humbling three-people-in-the-chairs reading. I worried about being a disappointment to Jill after all her efforts to spread the word on my book. The store had a steady hum of customers, but they all bought their books and left, so I fought the impulse to hide in the bathroom and braced myself to give a good show to a handful of people.

At ten minutes before the event's start time, I got myself a drink in the log cabin coffee shop—and, by the way, that coffee shop? Di-vine. They'll customize your order there with the same skill they use to individualize book recommendations. The baristas happened to be experimenting with a smoothie and offered me a sample. I accepted a mango-coconut-rum concoction that seriously jeopardized my ability to form words.

When I turned around, wincing from my smoothie brain freeze, I blinked at the scene before me: Every seat was full. The booksellers were adding *more* seats. And more still. They packed so many readers into the bookstore that I could reach out and touch the front row—they were practically in my lap! People stood in the aisles, sat on the floor, and huddled shoulder to shoulder.

Jill Miner and her staff know how to throw a good author event. I say throw because the events feel like parties...and, as when you're in the hands of a great hostess, every last detail is taken care of—*such as stopping all coffee-shop orders during a reading*. Any author who's ever competed with the grinding of beans and the pounding of barista scoops knows what a thoughtful, gracious gesture this is.

The attendees of these events tell you a lot about Saturn Booksellers. Many of the people are loyal, die-hard fans of the store, willing to take a chance on whatever Jill and the Saturn booksellers recommend. The Q&A session after the reading was a rowdy, fun good time. Half of the audience had already read the book thanks to the store's buzz, so the discussion had real depth. I wanted to swoon, I was so smitten.

> *The attendees of these events tell you a lot about Saturn Booksellers. Many of the people are loyal, die-hard fans of the store, willing to take a chance on whatever Jill and the Saturn booksellers recommend.*

After the event, as I signed stock and kept laughing with the funny, smart booksellers (seriously funny—any one of these women could host *Saturday Night Live* with ease), I told Jill I needed her help. I'd finished my airplane book sooner than expected and was without anything to read at my hotel or on the plane the next day. The store went silent. All those booksellers turned to me with sharp, invigorating focus. I could tell in a heartbeat: They loved their jobs and they took my question seriously.

Jill asked, "What did you read lately that you loved?" She and the other booksellers listened, and, based on my answer, they made their brilliant suggestions. I left that night with *Whistling in the Dark* by Lesley Kagen and *Belong to Me* by Marisa de los Santos. I'd never read either of those authors before. Now, not only are they among my very favorites, they have also become my cherished friends. All because of Saturn.

I shouldn't have been so surprised. That's what good booksellers *do*. They should be knowledgable. Even if they haven't read it themselves, booksellers should have knowledge about current titles. But, alas, the following true experience from a chain store had become what I was used to. I once dashed into a so-big-it-feels-like-a-warehouse chain store to grab a copy of *Eat, Pray, Love* as a gift for a friend. I was on a tight schedule and didn't see the book up front, so I found a bookseller (no easy feat) and asked if she could point me in the right direction. The girl stared at me, blinked, and asked, "That's a cookbook, right?"

Um, that would *never* happen at Saturn.

I've done readings at Saturn Booksellers four times now. That standing-room-only crowd was no fluke. Every one of my events there has repeated it. I look forward to returning with the release of my new novel. I look forward to it the way I'd anticipate a reunion with old friends…which is exactly what it is.

KATRINA KITTLE is the author of four books for adults, most recently *The Kindness of Strangers* and *The Blessings of the Animals*. *Reasons to Be Happy*, her first book for tweens, was released in October 2011. She lives, runs, gardens, and teaches in Dayton, Ohio.

Scott Lasser

Explore Booksellers, ASPEN, COLORADO

S kiing, glamour, glitz, food, culture, natural beauty—there's plenty to love about Aspen, but nothing better than Explore. It is the town's crucial establishment, the store that feeds those hallmarks of the Aspen Idea: mind, body, and spirit. Put another way, you can't have a world-class town without a world-class bookstore.

I first visited the store in 1983, my first winter in Aspen. I was teaching skiing seven days a week, waiting tables another four nights. At least once a week, on a night off, I'd go to Explore. I was saving up money for college and usually couldn't buy anything, but stepping into the store was entering another world. It made Aspen a place where I could put down roots. Back in that pre-megastore era, Explore stood out for its inventory, a whole Victorian house filled with books, arranged with attitude. Categories like Literary Fiction, Nonfiction, and Children's Books got their own rooms, whereas Popular Fiction found itself crammed in a corner by the stairs, where until recently they sold coffee.

It was sitting on those steps that I gave my first public reading. (Climb those stairs today and you'll find Art, Music, Sports, and a restaurant with a liquor license—that is, heaven.) The reading occurred about a month after the issuance of the Rushdie fatwa, at an event organized at the store to support the author. I stood at the back of the room and listened to the organizer say that Mr. Rushdie and freedom of expression would be best served by reading briefly from his work. Then she picked me out of the crowd and said, "Scott, why don't you start us off?" I moved forward to the stairs, where I was handed a worn copy of *Midnight's Children*; I spent the next fifteen minutes mispronouncing Indian place names, though no one seemed to mind. The people were there for Rushdie.

At its heart, a bookstore should stand for what's best about a community. On that day, Explore did. On every day, in fact.

. . .

By now you're probably thinking it all sounds too good to be true. In these Web-based, electronic-reader times, surely this store has perished.

It has not, but the story, as you might guess, is complicated.

For decades Explore was owned and operated by Katherine

> *At least once a week, on a night off, I'd go to Explore. I was saving up money for college and usually couldn't buy anything, but stepping into the store was entering another world. It made Aspen a place where I could put down roots.*

Thalberg, who not only created this marvelous store but also was active in politics of the anti-meat, anti-fur, left-wing variety. (Her dogs were often found on the floor, chewing on carrots.) Ms. Thalberg died of cancer too young, and the store fell to her three daughters, who wanted to sell the building for market price and have it remain a bookstore. This being Aspen, market price was in the $4 million range. There was something close to a panic in town when everyone realized that Aspen might lose Explore. Without it, Aspen would no longer be, well, Aspen.

But four million bucks! Who would make such a crazy purchase? None other than billionaire Sam Wyly, the George W. Bush backer/ Swift Boat supporter. Only in Aspen. There is no way that Mr. Wyly bought Explore to make money; he must just like the bookstore. After all, he's changed almost nothing. To make the story just a bit stranger, the new manager's name is John Edwards, but not that John Edwards.

And so Explore endures, great as it ever was, catering to tourists and locals, and making the town worth living in. My advice: If you're ever asked to move to a new town, ask one simple question. Does it have a great bookstore?

SCOTT LASSER is the author of four novels, including *Say Nice Things About Detroit*. He currently lives in Aspen, Colorado, and Los Angeles California.

Ann Haywood Leal

Bank Square Books, MYSTIC, CONNECTICUT

He joined my classroom several weeks into the school year. The other first graders had long ago pushed aside the memories and excitement of their first days of school, but Raymond was having yet another first day. Five is a lot of schools when you're only in first grade. I found out from his caseworker that this was to be a special one for him. It was a no-more-foster-home first day. He was going to be living with a relative, and everyone hoped it would be different. Not another stopover, but a place where he might have his own pillow.

I brought him to the reading nook in the back of the room. He sat down across from me and scooted up to the table, his eyes wide and curious. When I set the book in front of him, he grabbed it roughly and rapped it on the table in a sharp, nervous rhythm, not bothering to open it.

"We'll read it together," I said. "You tap me when it's my turn."

He reached out and tapped me immediately, warm, sticky fingertips on the back of my hand. "You read." He pushed the book toward me, tipping back in his chair.

He wandered among the children later that morning during free reading time, hesitant to take a book down from a shelf, rummaging quickly through the colorful plastic bins, as if he were searching for something else in there. A stray Lego, maybe. Anything but books.

The other kids watched him warily as they settled in with their choices at their desks or on their bellies on the rug.

That was around when Raymond decided that free reading time wasn't on his agenda for the day. And he started to perform. He did his own spinning and tumbling version of break dancing on the carpet, wild, spindly legs catching a few kids in the process, trying to get them to pay attention to anything but their books.

The ever-helpful Jack decided to step in. "You can bring your own book from home if you want." He proudly held up his own copy of *Fantastic Mr. Fox*.

Raymond paused for a brief second, considering. He seemed suspicious of Jack, as if he was trying to give out the wrong rules for the game.

Jack narrowed his eyes at Raymond and marched over to me, followed by three or four other kids. Tattling is a team sport in first grade.

"He doesn't have one." Jack clutched his own book reverently in front of him. "The new kid doesn't have a book." His backup group nodded in agreement.

It turned out Raymond had never had one. None that actually belonged to him, anyway. He was used to light travel. When he left for the next foster home, his clothes had always needed to be packed first. There wouldn't be room for much of anything else in the plastic garbage bag.

I offered Raymond twenty different books, but he barely glanced at them. I needed to step up my game.

So after school I went to where I always go when I want to be swept away by a new story. I went across the bridge to Mystic, Connecticut, to Bank Square Books. I knew that Annie, Patience, and Leon would know how to find the perfect book for Raymond's hands.

Stepping through the front door of Bank Square Books always makes me feel as if I'm climbing down into the pages of a favorite story. Their Staff Picks are like carefully chosen guests at a lively party where everyone is interesting and gets along.

The owners and staff all share an expression. It's an understanding of sorts that each wears like an underground smile that emerges when someone loves something as much as they do. It's a silently stated recognition: *You're one of us.*

I spotted Leon Archibald in the Children's Section. He listened carefully to Raymond's story, nodding quietly. "Let's look," he said.

We wound slowly through the shelves, with Leon pausing and considering. *Ten Apples Up on Top* and some I Can Read books. With each book he pulled from the shelves, he was creating a connection for Raymond to another world, allowing him to add chapters to what he carried in his plastic garbage bag.

> *Stepping through the front door of Bank Square Books always makes me feel as if I'm climbing down into the pages of a favorite story. Their Staff Picks are like carefully chosen guests at a lively party where everyone is interesting and gets along.*

I planned on giving Raymond one book every week, and I decided to start the next morning with *Ten Apples Up on Top.*

"This is yours to keep." I held it out to him.

He gave me his whaddaya mean look, complete with narrow, suspicious eyebrows, as if I was trying to trick him into doing something wrong.

"It's yours," I said again. "It belongs to you now."

The book never went home. Each afternoon he stashed it away safely, inside his desk, among the wrappers from the special snacks that the teaching assistant, Linda, was always sneaking him. Then he brought it out again first thing each morning where it sat, reverently, in the upper right-hand corner of his desk. He opened it and read it constantly, his mouth moving slowly around each new sound, his body becoming more relaxed as the words became more familiar.

After he'd had the book for a couple of weeks, it started getting sticky from his snacks, taking on that worn favorite-teddy-bear look that all things get when they are fiercely loved.

I was searching for something on my desk one morning when I sensed someone at my side.

"I need to read this to you." Raymond was supposed to be at his desk, finishing his morning writing. But he stood next to me, his book clutched tightly in his hands. "I need to practice." His eyes nervously glanced from the book to me, and back again. "I'm going to read this to my mom." His breath caught on the way out. "It's going to be her favorite."

Raymond didn't get to see his mom often. She had never heard him read, and I knew this was important to him. So we practiced that book over and over again.

He nervously packed it into his backpack that afternoon, his eyes darting sideways at the other kids in the coat closet, as if he was mentally warning them not to touch his book.

He never did get to read the book to his mom that day. I hadn't realized that he wouldn't be able to bring it into the correctional facility where she was incarcerated. But he "read" it to her anyway, because my bookstore had found the perfect book for Raymond, and the words had made their way into his heart.

Finding a book a home in someone's heart is a talent. They may not know it, but Annie Philbrick, Patience Banister, Leon Archibald, and the staff of Bank Square Books are in the business of matchmaking.

ANN HAYWOOD LEAL is the author of two novels, *Also Known as Harper* and *A Finders-Keepers Place*. Originally from the Pacific Northwest, Ann now writes and teaches elementary school and writing workshops in southeastern Connecticut. *Also Known as Harper* was chosen by the Chicago Public Library for its Best of the Best 2009–2010 list and was an *ABC Good Morning America* Summer Reading Choice for 2009. It is currently on the Arkansas Charlie May Simon Master List, the Iowa Children's Choice Award Master List, and the South Carolina Children's Book Award Master List, and is a finalist for the William Allen White Children's Book Award.

Caroline Leavitt

McNally Jackson Books, NEW YORK, NEW YORK

For many years I lived in the heart of Manhattan, which really meant I lived in its bookstores. But when I fell in love, got married, and began yearning for a child, unfriendly Manhattan real estate made the price of the four-bedroom we needed (two home offices, a bedroom for us, and one for our child) as likely as a Martian appearing on 57th Street. So we were nudged to Hoboken, a seven-minute PATH ride away, a place where we could get a three-story 1865 brickstone for the price of a Manhattan studio, and where there were three indie bookstores just blocks away from our home!

Of course, Barnes & Noble came and gobbled the indie stores up. Of course Barnes & Noble then left a few years later, leaving Hoboken with just one used-books store, which wasn't enough. So we began to spend even more and more time in the city bookstores. When McNally Jackson (then McNally Robinson) opened in 2004 in Soho, I never wanted to leave. Splashed with light, filled with books (two stories!), it also had a café with a menu that had literary quotes right by the yogurt and banana entrée. I spent hours roaming the aisles, often with my son in tow. Part of the pleasure was browsing, never knowing what I'd find—but a larger part was watching my son become an expert and excited browser as well. McNally Robinson became my Valium when I was stressed (what's more calming than a great new read?), my pick-me-up when I was tired (people-watching is as much fun as book-browsing), and my inspiration.

But loving a bookstore as a reader is one thing (certainly a big thing), and loving it as an author is another. You notice different things. The whole bookstore feels and smells and looks like a different animal when you approach it as a writer. I've walked into McNally Jackson desperately worried about a manuscript or even my career, wondering if I'd have to give up writing and go to dental school instead, but seeing all the other novels made me more determined.

For a writer, readings are our way to connect with our readers and, hopefully, to sell books, but what writer hasn't had the experience of going to a reading only to find two people sitting there, and one of them came in just because he heard there was going to be free wine and cookies? McNally Jackson

> *I spent hours roaming the aisles, often with my son in tow. Part of the pleasure was browsing, never knowing what I'd find—but a larger part was watching my son become an expert and excited browser as well.*

was my launch for my ninth novel, *Pictures of You*, and when they said, "We want to do something different," I perked right up. They organized a conversation between me and the wonderful novelist Jennifer Gilmore, the two of us perched on stools, kicking back, laughing. The week before the reading, I had found the Twitter handles of a variety of A-list celebrities, and for fun, I invited them all. "It's at McNally Jackson," I wrote, because the name ramped up the cool factor. Tim Hutton didn't show up. Neither did Cher or Moby or Yoko Ono (I had high hopes for her), but a full house of readers did, and what I most remember is how even the air seemed charged that night.

McNally Jackson loves writers. All writers, in an equal-opportunity way. When a friend of ours couldn't get his book about world music published traditionally, he refused to give up and self-published it. Usually self-published books have a harder time getting shelf space and readings, but McNally Jackson gave him both, and two of the staff came down to listen to him read and even asked questions.

You want a sense of humor in a person, but it's even better when it's in a bookstore. McNally Jackson has a hilarious Twitter account and website. Plus, they have a great events coordinator.

Of course, McNally Jackson is a terrific bookstore. Of course, I want to be there in that store, among all the books, their covers like beacons. What more could I ask for?

Well, I'd really love a branch in Hoboken.

CAROLINE LEAVITT is the *New York Times* best-selling author of *Pictures of You*, which was on the 2011 Best Books of the Year list from the *San Francisco Chronicle*, *The Providence Journal*, *Bookmarks* magazine, and *Kirkus Reviews*. Her tenth novel, *Is It Tomorrow*, will be published by Algonquin Books in spring 2013. A book critic for *People* and *The Boston Globe* and a book columnist for Shoptopia online, she is also a senior writing instructor at UCLA Extension Writers' Program online. A recipient of a New York Foundation for the Arts Artist Fellowship and a Goldenberg Prize for Fiction Honorable Mention, as well as a Nickelodeon Writing Fellowship finalist and a Sundance Screenwriting Lab Fellowship first-round winner, she can be reached at www.carolineleavitt.com.

Mike Leonard

The Book Stall at Chestnut Court

WINNETKA, ILLINOIS

A Note to Roberta Rubin, owner of The Book Stall in Winnetka, Illinois:

I'm sorry, Roberta.

You asked me to write a simple essay about my thirty-year relationship with your wonderful bookstore, and I agreed.

That was a mistake.

I'm in over my head.

There wouldn't be a problem if I were writing about a hardware store. People interested in hammers or lawn sprinklers or mops usually don't come unglued over comma splices (whatever they are). But you're not peddling gardening tools or toilet brushes; you're in the brilliance business, with dozens of reminders on every shelf.

Tolstoy. Austen. Melville. Woolf. Rushdie.

How am I supposed to conjure up a clever phrase or a thought-provoking observation with The Bard staring me in the eye? And it's not just him. It's every name on every book jacket. Every novelist, memoirist, poet, and politician. Every celebrity chef, washed-up athlete, pop psychologist, and faded rock star. All intimidators overflowing with words. Words of wisdom. Words to live by. Beautiful words. Insightful words. Evocative words.

Crap!

I don't have those words.

Your bookstore is the heartbeat of our community—a gathering of great thinkers, a mindful meeting place. I stop in at least once a week, often just to wander the aisles or share a few words with your fine and funny staff. And I always leave with something. A new book. A shot of inspiration. A good feeling.

Emotional attachments, however, are difficult to put into words.

So, I found another way.

:-)

[Disclosure: This is my first experience typing a smiley-face emoticon. Upon completion of this essay, I vow never to type it again...or use the word *emoticon*.]

Perhaps an explanation would be helpful.

Go back to 1982, and your purchase of an existing but tired book-store on a tree-lined street just three blocks from my Winnetka, Illinois, home. From day one, you were a sight to behold, scooting joyously down the cramped aisles, a tilting pile of books in the crook of one arm, the other waving with televangelistic fervor about the importance of literature and the grand plans for your little store, re-named The Book Stall.

Meanwhile, 450 miles to the east, danger lurked.

Tap, tap, tap.

Big-time threats are often delivered in barely audible tones, like the dampened belly-growl of a seriously ticked-off dog.

Scott Fahlman, a computer scientist at Carnegie Mellon University, was neither ticked-off nor in any kind of threatening mood when he quietly tapped out his seemingly benign three-stroke message, a moment now viewed by some as the crucial first volley in what has become a grinding war of attrition against thoughtful, nuanced writing.

It was September 19, 1982, the same year you opened The Book Stall.

The message?

:-)

Scott Fahlman's intent was pure. The Internet was still in its embryonic, geek-only, hybrid phase—peopled by people moving to the algorithm of a beat totally beyond the register of everyday folk. From those primordial pools of programming logic came a new language, bubbling up bit by bit (or byte by byte) to flood the early computer bulletin boards with invented words, strange-looking acronyms, and weird symbols. There was humor, too. Or at least an attempt at humor.

Q: What's a Freudian virus?

A: Your computer becomes obsessed with marrying its own motherboard.

:-) :-) :-) :-) :-)

If a programmer's joke fell flat on a computer scientist's bulletin board, and nobody even noticed that it was a joke, did it really fall flat?

That, in short, was the issue Scott Fahlman was trying to address with the sideways smiley face.

It was a warning sign of sorts.

Beware—Joke Ahead!

Humor, sarcastic remarks, or ironic statements often go whistling past the intended mark, especially if the mark happens to be one of those laser-focused but worldly, oblivious, nose-to-the-ground Elmer Fudd types who, sadly, follow the rabbit tracks right off a cliff.

:-(

(Scott Fahlman came up with the frowny-face symbol as well.)

That was thirty years ago.

Since then, the birth of the Internet has given rise to email, which has morphed into text messaging, which has spawned a whole new vocabulary of computer-influenced shorthand designed to grease the whirling wheels of communication. Speed is the name of the game now. And simplification.

RU w me? RU perplexed?

I'll show you perplexed.

:-/

But doesn't the loss of nuance and subtlety diminish our standards of writing?

<:-)

(symbol for dumb question)

Sorry, Roberta. I'm wandering all over the place.

Maybe it's the ADD kicking in, or maybe it's something more basic like a lack of good old-fashioned, clear-thinking smarts. I do have a history of that. Five years of high school. Big trouble getting into college. A long list of menial jobs until a lucky break at the age of 30 got me going as a journalist. It's always been a struggle.

The slow thinker.

The late bloomer.

The 59-year-old debut author.

When my book came out five years ago, you put it in the front display window, organized a number of well-attended signing events, and talked me up to whomever would listen. It was a humbling experience, and something I thought would fade with time.

It hasn't because you won't let it.

You keep pushing, praising, promoting—day by day, book by book. Not being a numbers guy, I never thought of asking for a sales tally. Then last month, while doing research for this essay, I was astonished to learn that you have sold nearly 2,000 copies of my book.

One store.

Two thousand copies sold.

And you're not finished.

Since 1982, The Book Stall has more than doubled in size, the inventory growing to roughly 48,000 titles, the number of authors hosted and hailed somewhere in the tens of thousands. Impressive figures to be sure, but not the full measure of your value. And that's where the challenge lies for me—finding suitable words of praise for the stuff that can't be measured.

> *And that's where the challenge lies for me— finding suitable words of praise for the stuff that can't be measured.*

Your respect and compassion for my elderly, talkative father in the final years of his life.

Your genuine, eyes-to-eyes, on-bended-knee interest in the mumbled requests of my 4-year-old grandson.

Your unflagging belief in the merit of my words.

Where are those words? It would have been nice to close with a flourish of cleverly nuanced phrases, but they aren't coming and the deadline is.

So, Roberta, please accept my apology for failing to provide the flowery, literary bouquet you richly deserve. You have made our lives better, yet the only gift I can offer as an expression of thanks is embarrassingly simple to describe.

It's a smiling face.

But who would put that in writing?

MIKE LEONARD joined NBC News in October 1980 and, using the small town of Winnetka, Illinois as his base, has traveled across the country and around the world in search of stories that define our lives. In addition to his regular Today assignment, Mike's stories have appeared on NBC Nightly News, Dateline, NBC Sports, MSNBC, Showtime, and PBS. He is the author of *The Ride of Our Lives–Roadside Lessons of an American Family*.

Robert N. Macomber

The Muse Book Shop, DELAND, FLORIDA

I just had one of those odd mental moments. While folding underwear and socks into bizarre shapes so they'll fit into an already
crammed suitcase, Janet Bollum and The Muse popped into my
mind. Yes, I know that's a strange connection, but bear with me, because there is a cause and effect here. Or a more accurate description
would be "unanticipated consequences." Pretty nice unanticipated
consequences.

I'm packing for a six-week journey through the South Pacific,
my favorite region in the world. Beautiful islands, friendly people,
and fascinating cultures, all making the perfect grist for a novelist

like me. And best of all—this time I'm invited to see it in luxury, for a very exclusive private-condominium ship (160 ultra-comfy apartments circumnavigating the world each year) has asked me to be the guest author aboard for sixteen days as she steams through Fiji, the Cook Islands, Tonga, and the Society Islands of French Polynesia. After that, I'll be back on my own, living on Upolu Island in Samoa (close by Robert Louis Stevenson's house), then revisiting Pago Pago in American Samoa, and old-town Honolulu—all to research and finish writing my next novel.

Janet Bollum and The Muse had a role in this, for they are part of the reason for my success. The Muse is a quaint little bookshop located in the pleasant college town of DeLand, Florida. No chainstore glitz, hype, or come-ons; just a friendly oasis of 50,000 books, lovingly owned by Janet for thirty-two years, making it the state's second-longest-operating independent bookstore. Like every other author who signs there, I love the place. It's the sanctum sanctorum for bibliophiles who come a hundred miles to talk books, search the nooks and stacks for literary treasures, meet their favorite authors, and ask Janet or her helpers for their opinion on books.

It's the place where my readership in central Florida began, because Janet Bollum took a chance ten years ago on a new author from out of town and had him do a signing at The Muse for his third novel. She put the word out and readers came. They came because they trust her to understand what they like. Because of that they were already in the mood to like my books. For the next seven novels I've returned, and each time more and more people join me.

It's the place where my readership in central Florida began, because Janet Bollum took a chance ten years ago on a new author from out of town and had him do a signing at The Muse for his third novel.

Janet knows how to do a book signing right. Unlike the tired lines of sullen people silently enduring frustration at dreary chain-store book signings, Janet makes sure that readers coming to author signings at The Muse have fun! Music, snacks, drinks. Laughter. Buzzing conversation. Readers enjoying time with their favorite author. It builds readership, which builds success, for an author.

And successful authors get asked to do some unique things, like being guest writer aboard an ultra-comfy condo ship steaming through the South Pacific.

Thank you, Janet and The Muse, for helping to build my success, and for the pretty nice "unanticipated consequences."

ROBERT N. MACOMBER is an award-winning novelist, international lecturer, television commentator, and consultant. He lives at Matlacha Island, Florida. For more about the man and his work, visit www.robertmacomber.com.

Jill McCorkle

Flyleaf Books, CHAPEL HILL, NORTH CAROLINA

I magine the Bible Belt if you will, and then, at its center, place a shining, star-studded buckle; that's the Triangle area, and there in the very center of that buckle is Chapel Hill, site of the first public university in the United States and the place Senator Jesse Helms once suggested be fenced off and called the state zoo. Thanks to a thriving interest in the arts and higher education and independent thinking, the Triangle is an area that can rival any place in the country. And when it comes to successful independent booksellers, this state is one of the country's most exemplary, with thriving stores peppering the land from the mountains to the coast. At a time when other businesses are shutting down and when more and more people are resorting to the solitary path of online ebook buying, these are stores that are all about enhancing the community and preserving the history and business of real typeface-on-paper works of art, while also looking ahead to the transitions of the future. There is a lot of proof that people still love real bookstores and real books and those who read them, and you don't need to venture any further than the front door of Flyleaf Books in Chapel Hill to witness it. People, books, conversations about books, readings from books. Flyleaf being a common destination, I am one of many who make that regular pilgrimage, sometimes with something specific in mind, and other times just taking the opportunity to pause and browse and escape whatever else is going on in the day.

I have rolled in and out of this town since I graduated from the university in 1980, and the big wishes you hear expressed have consistently been for less-humid summers (impossible), more parking (nearly impossible), more NCAA titles (possible), and an easily accessed independent downtown bookstore (wish granted). Less than three years old, this store already has the good, comfortable feel of a long-loved and well-populated establishment.

Build it and we will come, the locals had said, and this is exactly what happened in 2009 when owners Jamie Fiocco, Land Arnold, and Sarah Carr joined forces and made it happen. This young and lively triumvirate—their talents and areas of expertise covering all corners of the book business—has taken the challenge and run headlong into success and beyond. Their names all run together may sound like the name of a prosperous law firm or accounting business, and the success of their endeavor may lead you to think they are just that, but then add passion—lots and lots of passion for the world of books and all people who share this love, from writers and publishers to readers and the community at large, and you've got the makings of what will prove to be as fixed and attached to this place as hot summers and ACC basketball and pride in having once summoned the wrath of the likes of Jesse Helms. Before the Christmas rush last year, they had already surpassed their sales of the year before. So now imagine that belt buckle getting bigger and shinier all the time. This is not a hold-your-pants-up kind of belt buckle, but one worthy of a heavyweight champion—a big, shining, powerful star.

Though I no longer live in Chapel Hill, Flyleaf is still my home-base store and easily reached on my daily paths to and fro. Sandwiched between two great places to eat, the store really does feel as if it's been there forever, people spilling from bookstore to the outdoor tables of Foster's Market, where they sit and read. Inside, the ceiling-to-floor shelves are fully stocked and there are big tables overflowing with the newly published and staff picks. There is an impressive used-books section and a large reading space that is now on the publicity radar of writers touring the country, so that each week there are scheduled readings and book-club programs and meetings that bring people into this amazing space. There are colorful posters and reminders about future events and memorabilia from the great events that have already happened. There is a terrific children's section, something that always thrilled me when I still had little ones in tow, because such a section immediately promises a little more browsing and shopping time, not to mention getting those new readers up and moving.

Before Flyleaf Books moved in, this was a gym, and I often imagine the sounds of iron pumping and hearts racing as bodies were transformed from flabby and weak into strong, sculpted pictures of good health. And so it continues. Flyleaf is the mecca for those seeking the ultimate workout program, only now the focus is that big gray muscle in the center of the skull as people get stronger and more flexible, the stamina of their own imaginations tripling and quadrupling, their hearts still racing with the sight of what's hot off the press and with jacket art and with the intoxicating smell of paper and ink. And, if you're like me and can't see anything without a pair of readers, they have a huge selection to insure that browsing is never interrupted. They also have beautiful jewelry and other creations from local artists. In fact, they have one of the best selections of purses and travel bags. I always find myself wanting to fill a bag with books and fly off to some quiet place to read for a month or two. But of course, what I actually do is also fine: buy a book or two, a new journal, some spare glasses, and head back home.

A flyleaf is that blank piece of paper at beginning and ending of a real *hold in your hand and turn the pages* book. That blank page is like a curtain rising, the promise of what is to come, and at end, it is the curtain closing, that collected pause before you face the slow return to the outer world. It's exactly what it feels like when you open the door to Flyleaf Books and step into that comfortable and stimulating world; when you leave, it's with the knowledge that you can always turn around and come right back, and chances are that Jamie or Land or Sarah will be there to greet you. For me, a visit to Flyleaf is like opening your favorite book—once-upon-a-time and happily-ever-after here in a great and thriving wonderland of independent booksellers. If anyone can keep that champion belt buckle all shined up and growing for generations to come, this is who I will bet on.

> *For me, a visit to Flyleaf is like opening your favorite book—once-upon-a-time and happily-ever-after here in a great and thriving wonderland of independent booksellers.*

JILL MCCORKLE is the author of four story collections and six novels including the forthcoming *Life After Life*. Her work has appeared in a variety of publications including *The Atlantic, The American Scholar, Ploughshares, Best American Short Stories* and *Best American Essays*. She lives in Hillsborough, North Carolina.

Mameve Medwed

Porter Square Books, CAMBRIDGE, MASSACHUSETTS

I once wrote a novel called *How Elizabeth Barrett Browning Saved My Life*; its launch took place around the corner from me at Porter Square Books, that home away from home where I now celebrate all my launches and those of my friends. That novel sprang from my imagination. In the real world, however, I can offer a nonfiction variation on that title: *Porter Square Books Saved My Life*. After all, a bookstore within two blocks of a writer and reader is mother's milk and a hot fudge sundae and a destination and a community and an antidote against both loneliness and—horrors!—having nothing to read. This bookstore is the best thing that ever happened to my

221

neighborhood and one of the best things that happened to me.

Let me backtrack. In Bangor, Maine, where I grew up, the single bookstore that sold current books was tiny and three miles downtown; its secondhand cousin occupied a dank basement that smelled of mildew and old age. At home, the classics stuffed our shelves. Our encyclopedias were as antique as our furniture. We didn't buy books. Like the Boston Brahmin's hats, we simply had them. Anything suspiciously new, we could borrow from the library. Just as long-distance calls were considered a luxury (my husband's father stuck a clock next to the phone when his son dialed from Skowhegan to set up our first date), you never bought books that weren't self-improving dictionaries or SAT preps.

When I moved to Cambridge, our first apartment was two steps from the library's main branch. Since we lived on a student's budget, I resisted the bookstores in Harvard Square. Still, the waiting list at the Cambridge Public Library seemed endless, a testament to an active (and competitive) readership. I remember the thrill of the self-addressed, self-stamped postcard announcing that my request had reached the top of the queue. But I wanted to own the book, not be obliged to return it.

Our next apartment was a manageable hike to Harvard Square. Having both jobs and brand-new bookcases to fill, we began to indulge ourselves for birthdays or the blahs. Back then, the Harvard Book Store boasted a window seat, ostensibly for children, with a sock monkey and a collection of well-thumbed Dr. Seusses. But if no kids lounged against the cushions, you could curl up with the new Anne Tyler and monitor the line for Bartley's Burgers. We knew we'd achieved status as regulars when Frank Kramer, the owner, said *hi*.

After a movie, we would head around the corner to WordsWorth Books, which stayed open until eleven. Though there was no cozy window seat—or even a single chair—no one bothered you if, sitting on the floor between aisles, you started a novel before the movie and returned to finish it afterward.

On a rainy day, we'd wait out the weather flipping through magazines at Reading International. John, behind his desk, didn't seem to mind our indiscriminate perusal of both *People* and *Ploughshares*. When guests appeared, Reading International was where we rendezvoused. From the large front windows, we could spot our visitors bounding down Brattle Street while we caught up on poetry and celebrity.

Such indie havens, alas, did not survive. All too soon the volumes on the shelves thinned. The piles flattened. The once narrow aisles widened and emptied. "Oh, no," my husband and I whispered. WordsWorth closed. Reading International became a health food shop, then an American Apparel. Barnes & Noble took over the Coop. The Harvard Book Store, its window seat sacrificed for more display, was the lone voice crying out in the increasingly book-pruned wilderness.

Soon enough, we moved again. Though we were not far from a firehouse, a gas station, a Chinese restaurant, a psychic, a soda shop, our most valued public utility was missing; we had planted ourselves in bookstore-bereft territory. Though not for long. When, in 2004, Porter Square Books opened a five-minute walk away, we uncorked the Champagne. We cheered. We danced. "Now that we have our own literary refuge, we never again have to trudge to Harvard Square," my friend Steve pointed out. What a plus for our neighborhood. What a boon for local writers. Our books festoon Porter Square Books' windows. Our launches in the store's well-lighted room are celebrated with wine and cheese. The attached café is a meeting place and community center. We bump into our neighbors in the aisles and by the latte machine. On stools tucked under counters, writers pound their laptops, revise paragraphs, share book-jacket JPEGs.

And, oh, the staff! Knowledgeable, funny, smart, they sprint halfway across the store to find the volume that you've missed or to recommend a treasure you shouldn't miss. What's more, sometimes they take you into that back room where the galleys are stored and where, with a sweeping gesture, they pronounce the magic words *Help yourself.* They are our bookstore family, our private book club. Carol advises us on children's lit; Ellen plans upcoming author appearances and joins us for her coffee break. We laugh with Josh and Gary, chat with the two Janes and Dale, gossip with Nathan. We bring children and grandchildren and houseguests. In the evenings, we attend bookstore events. Almost every night there seems to be yet another wonderful writer standing behind the podium. We arrive early, get a coffee, find a seat. Later, we skip home, enlightened, entertained, challenged, and more often than not, with a crisp,

> *And, oh, the staff! Knowledgeable, funny, smart, they sprint halfway across the store to find the volume that you've missed or to recommend a treasure you shouldn't miss.*

new, just-signed book under our arm. Recently, our own son traveled across the country to launch his first book inside these doors, in front of these shelves, in this place that, to all of us, feels so much like home.

After a lonely morning of writing, I call a neighbor. "Want to take a walk?" I ask. "Sure," she says, knowing that what I'm saying is *let's head for the bookstore.*

Porter Square Books is our Café de Flore, our Les Deux Magots. We linger at the outdoor tables. We keep our biscotti away from pristine pages. We make impulse purchases and place advance orders. The shelves and aisles, card racks, and benches are as familiar to us as our own rooms. Every so often an email pings—*Haven't seen you for a while,* Ellen will point out. Nathan will write, *Coming tonight? It's going to be good.*

It *is* good. That Porter Square Books not only endures but also flourishes is the gift that keeps on giving. No Kindle or Amazon or national chain will ever substitute for this place where everybody knows your name. We shop local. We are local. We're proud to call ourselves regulars.

MAMEVE MEDWED is the author of five novels: *Mail*, *Host Family*, *The End of an Error*, *How Elizabeth Barrett Browning Saved My Life*, and *Of Men and Their Mothers*. Her essays and reviews have appeared in, among others, *The New York Times*, *The Boston Globe*, *The Washington Post*, *Gourmet*, and *Redbook*.

Wendell and Florence Minor
The Hickory Stick Bookshop
WASHINGTON DEPOT, CONNECTICUT

Wendell's View

Try to imagine the perfect independent bookshop in one of the most beautiful little towns in America. Perhaps you could imagine a Norman Rockwell *Saturday Evening Post* cover depicting a busy weekend in a small village center, and the focus in Mr. Rockwell's composition would be people arriving at the town's bookshop for a signing by their favorite author. That bookshop would definitely be the Hickory Stick!

The Hickory Stick has been the center and anchor of Washington Depot, Connecticut, for more than sixty years. For all of its long history, it has had only four owners, and the current owner is the incredible Fran Keilty. If ever there was the perfect owner and book person, it is none other than Fran. In this digital age of constant change, independent bookstores across America have been challenged to adapt and remain viable for their customers. Thanks to Fran Keilty, the Hickory Stick not only continues to amaze in its ability to remain relevant, but continues to serve the community better than ever.

These kudos may seem a bit much if you haven't had the opportunity to visit the Hickory. As an author/illustrator team, Florence and I have done countless book signings at independent bookstores across the country. None have ever been better than those at the Hickory Stick. Fran and her wonderful staff make every effort to promote and advertise all of their author and illustrator appearances. The Litchfield Hills have been blessed with an abundance of creative talent, with writers of all stripes and numerous children's-book authors and illustrators. And what history! Famous authors who have topped the list of signings at the Hickory are Tom Brokaw, Frank Delaney, Francine du Plessix Gray, Ann Hodgman, Ann Leary, Frank McCourt, Dani Shapiro, and Rose Styron, and the list goes on. Authors from outside Litchfield County who have done signings at the Hickory are Mary Higgins Clark, Jean Craighead George, Bruce McCall, William Martin, and Stuart Woods, to name but a few.

Local children's-book authors and illustrators, such as Barry Blitt, Kinuko Craft, Mercer Mayer, Marilyn Singer, Lane Smith, Nancy Tafuri, and Mo Willems, among others, have the good fortune to be represented in the Hickory's terrific children's-book section and have all had many well-attended, successful book signings there.

Florence's View

Fran is that very rare combination of professional bookseller and warm and engaging friend who immediately makes you feel at home at the Hickory and creates an atmosphere that makes a visit to the store the kind of experience you want to repeat again and again. She and her knowledgeable and friendly staff help you find any book you are looking for, promptly order it if it is not in stock, and also recommend other books in the same vein that might be of interest.

Her outreach in the community is widely known and respected, and Wendell and I cannot count the number of times that Fran has graciously (often with her husband, Michael Keilty) provided books for signings in conjunction with various appearances off-site: at area schools, libraries, galleries, etc. Books are obviously the mainstay, but knowing that we can find cards and gifts as well, seven days a week, is an added bonus. And at holiday time, the Hickory outdoes itself. Each December, the town of Washington designates one night as "Holiday in the Depot." It is a festive time when all the stores remain open through the evening, providing people an opportunity to shop for the holidays while enjoying the companionship of friends and neighbors. On that evening, the Hickory Stick provides generous amounts of warmth and good cheer, serving eggnog, cookies, and music, presided over by Michael. It is a family affair and one more way in which the Hickory is an integral part of the family of Washington.

Being in the Hickory Stick is, for me, a bit like being the proverbial kid in a candy store. I cannot begin to imagine living in a town that does not have a bookstore, and Wendell and I feel so very fortunate that, having left New York, we find ourselves living in a town that is not only uniquely beautiful but also home to the uniquely wonderful Hickory Stick, which exemplifies everything a bookstore should be… and then some.

Our View into the Future

We often hear the term "bricks-and-mortar stores" used as if such stores have been relegated to the dustbin of history. Who needs an old-fashioned bookshop when it's so easy to shop in cyberspace? The more our culture becomes disconnected by the age of "instant digital communication," the more we feel the loss of the personal, the human-contact

> *Many of us are beginning to realize what a great loss it would be not to have a place like the Hickory Stick.*

experience. Many of us are beginning to realize what a great loss it would be not to have a place like the Hickory Stick. The use of mobile reading devices has become a fact of modern life, and they certainly have their place.

But we believe that the book as a tactile object with beautiful graphics, binding, color, and deckle-edged paper will be with us for some time to come. A bookstore like the Hickory Stick is also a thing of beauty to behold, with its intelligent, friendly staff and a wonderful display of inviting books of all kinds. The bricks-and-mortar bookstore continues to be an irreplaceable part of what makes life better for us all. We can't image a world without our beloved Hickory Stick.

WENDELL MINOR has illustrated more than 50 award-winning picture books for children, including *The Seashore Book* by Charlotte Zolotow; numerous books about the outdoors, most recently *The Eagles Are Back* with Newbery Medal–winning author Jean Craighead George; and *New York Times* best sellers *Reaching for the Moon* by Buzz Aldrin and *Ghost Ship* by Mary Higgins Clark.

FLORENCE MINOR is a former film editor for ABC news and the coeditor of *Wendell Minor: Art for the Written Word*. She currently collaborates with her husband, Wendell, on picture books, among them *If You Were a Penguin*, which was selected as Pennsylvania's choice for its "One Book, Every Young Child" program in 2009. Their third collaboration, *If You Were a Panda Bear*, will be published in 2013.

WENDELL AND FLORENCE are dedicated to creating books that will entertain, teach, and inspire children. They live in Connecticut with their two cats, Sofie and Cinder, and you can visit them at www.minorart.com or at the Minor Art fan page on Facebook.

Barry Moser

Lemuria, JACKSON, MISSISSIPPI

I would be most content if my children grew up to be the kind of people who think decorating consists mostly of building enough bookshelves.
—Anna Quindlen

A few years ago I was writing a speech and wanted to quote a line that Lt. Col. "Bull" Meacham says in the film *The Great Santini*. I had not read Pat Conroy's book at that time and wanted to know that what I was about to quote was in the book, not just in the movie. Now understand that I live in one of the most bookish places in the country, home to Smith College, Amherst College, Hampshire

231

College, Mt. Holyoke College, and the main campus of the University of Massachusetts, all within ten miles of each other. But when I started looking around the area for a copy of Conroy's book, I couldn't find one. Nary a single copy was in any bookstore—new or used, big box or independent—in the valley. So I decided to call John Evans. John owns one of the finest bookstores in America: Lemuria Books in Jackson, Mississippi, which specializes in books by Southern writers and all manner of things Southern. I called Johnny and asked if he had a copy. His response?

"Yeah, Barry, sure I do. You want it in paperback, hardback, or signed first edition?"

This kind of response you don't get from Books-a-Million or any big-box chain bookstores, much less from an online behemoth like Amazon. This manner of service is strictly the domain of the independent bookseller.

I've known Johnny for a long time now. We met at an American Booksellers Association party in Dallas, Texas, in 1983, the year my newly illustrated edition of *Alice's Adventures in Wonderland* was published. He asked me to sign a poster for his daughter Saramel. I am something of a collector of names and this was a new one for me, so I signed it "For Saramel." Johnny went his way, probably to the closest bar, as did I, probably to a different bar.

Two years later ABA was in San Francisco and Johnny and I ran into each other again, this time on the marble staircase of one of the city's municipal buildings. There was a big party under way and some loud jazz was playing. We had not been in contact since Dallas and when I asked about Saramel, Johnny was surprised and impressed that I remembered her name two years later. We talked for a while and during the conversation I told him, over the loud jazz, that I had just finished reading a book written by a neighbor of his, and that I felt it was one of the most influential books I'd ever read.

"What book is that?" he asked.

"Eudora Welty's *One Writer's Beginnings*," I replied.

"Oh. *Oh.*" Johnny said excitedly. "She's a big fan of your work!"

I looked behind me to see who he was talking to, certain that he surely must have been talking to somebody other than me. But he was, in fact, talking to me. I said, "What? You kidding me?"

"No." he said. "She loves your *Huckleberry Finn*. I'm going to have to get you two together. Do a project or something."

A year or so later I flew down to Jackson, Mississippi. True to his word, he introduced us. It was a sunny afternoon and Miss Welty welcomed us into her home with the graciousness you might imagine. We stayed a good part of the afternoon, enough time to put away a good bit of some bourbon whiskey I brought Miss Welty as a present. It was also enough time for us to lay down some preliminary plans for a collaboration: the Pennyroyal Press edition of *The Robber Bridegroom*, which we published in 1987.

From then on Lemuria was always on the itinerary when I went on the road to promote a new book—that is, until my publishers stopped spending the money to send me on tour. But until that happened I always had Lemuria scheduled—and scheduled last. In case you don't know, Johnny Evans has a soft spot for good bourbon whiskey, as do I. In fact, I am fairly sure that we might just enjoy it a tad too much, and that's why I always want to end my travels in Jackson so that all I'll have to do in my hurt state is to go home. Nobody wants to promote a book while nursing a two-day hangover.

Johnny and his wife, Mel, and I became friends, good friends. I saw little Saramel grow up to be a fine young woman with a bent toward the arts, and I saw Austin, Saramel's little brother, grow up to be a strapping young man who, with business partner Richard Patrick, makes some mighty fine (and legal) Cathead vodka over in Gluckstadt, Mississippi. That makes his daddy proud. Me too.

John introduced me to Willie Morris, too. I think that was in 1994. And that introduction led to yet another collaboration. At that time Johnny was coaching the North Jackson Little League team. Young Austin Evans was on the team. Johnny had been after Willie for some time to write a prayer for the opening of the Little League season, but Willie had not been forthcoming, and I am fairly certain that the delay was not a result of Willie's respect for federal laws prohibiting public displays of religion. I think it may have been that it was going to be the last season Johnny was going to be coaching, but regardless, Willie finally wrote the prayer. Johnny was very happy with it and sent it on for me to read. I liked it too and showed it to my business partner, Jeff Dwyer, who immediately recognized it as a book for kids…or, more likely, for the parents and grandparents of Little Leaguers. We pitched the idea to Ruben Pfeffer at Harcourt Brace, and he bought it (Ruben himself was a Little League coach).

I set about designing *A Prayer for the Opening of the Little League Season* and doing sketches. To do the sketches properly and accurately, I, of course, had to fly down to Jackson to attend practices and games, photographing the field, the equipment, the players, the grandparents, the coaches, the umpires, and Mr. Morris his ownself. When I got the book laid out and some of the sketches in place, it was four pages too short to make a proper thirty-two-page picture book—despite my having put in as many functional extra pages as I could think up. So I called Willie and asked him if he would be amenable to writing one more verse to take up the slack, and he said that he'd be happy to. He asked me if I had something particular in mind. I said something like: "Yeah. You know, Willie, I tried to play baseball when I was a kid. But I didn't know that I needed glasses to see, so I never connected with a single pitch. Not one. I might have been the only kid in the history of the game who had a zero batting average." Willie thought this was funnier than hell and thus he wrote the extra verse:

> *Comfort the smallest of the ballplayers, who have never gotten*
> *a hit, and those who strike out time and time again or languish*
> *on the benches day after livelong day, for their moment, too, is*
> *destined to be.*

When the book was published, Harcourt Brace sent Willie and me on the road to promote it. All around Dixie we went, from Jackson to Chapel Hill, from Atlanta to New Orleans. From Memphis to

Blytheville. We did a live radio show on public radio at the Research Triangle outside Chapel Hill. And never, ever did Mr. Willie Morris pass up an opportunity to tell an audience the very funny story about Moser, the nearsighted kid who had a zero batting average.

The dedication of *A Prayer for the Opening of the Little League Season* reads:

> For our friend, John Evans: who is either a literary man who loves baseball, or a baseball man who loves literature, or both.
> —W.M & B.M.

I could keep on telling such stories, at least the ones I can remember. But I am afraid that my readers' patience might run short, so I'll tell just one more.

From 1995 till 1999 I was hard at work illustrating what happens to be the first and only fully illustrated King James Bible of the twentieth century. It was a pretty big deal in certain specialized corners of the book world, especially the world of the limited edition. Viking Studio picked it up and published it as a trade hardback that appeared simultaneously with the Pennyroyal Press edition. Viking sent me on a nationwide tour in the autumn of 1999—twenty cities, I believe it was. And, as always, I asked that they set up an appearance at Lemuria at the very end of the tour, which would be in early December.

And that happened.

When I got to the store to sign stock, Johnny gave this really cute woman the chore of helping me sign box after box of these big, heavy books. I didn't catch her name right off, but that did not dampen my urge to flirt with her. And, though modesty forbids, she returned the attention, though in a sassy, smart-ass kind of way. She was the first person I ever signed books with who could keep up with me—as a printmaker, I have learned to sign my name really, really fast. When I

> *"You're not so fast. John Grisham's a lot faster than you are."*

mentioned this little bit of information, she looked me straight in the eye, one eyebrow raised, and said, "You're not so fast. John Grisham's a lot faster than you are." Well, shut my mouth. And it did. I did ask her name, though, and was told that it was Emily.

A few weeks later, Johnny called to do an interview with me for the store's newsletter. He asked Miss Emily to listen in, take notes, and write it up. I asked her to kindly send it to me so I could thoughtfully reconsider my responses to Johnny's questions.

And so she did.

The story from here is far too long and complicated to tell, but the capsulated version is that within six months Emily and I had nearly two thousand pages of email correspondence. Some letters were a couple of lines long. Others several pages. Alas, we fell in love in the old-fashioned epistolary manner. At one time I had to confess to her that I did not know her last name and that somehow it seemed important that I do. "Crowe," she said. "Emily Crowe."

The next year, January of 2001, I stole her away from her beloved Johnny, from her beloved Lemuria, and her beloved Dixie and brought her up here to "the Kingdom of the Yankee," as Willie Morris once called the northeast. Two years later we were married. At sundown on the island of Antigua in the British West Indies, seventeen and a half degrees off the equator, on the summer solstice. And we've been living happily ever after in a big house in Western Massachusetts with rooms full of books, big mastiff dogs, and a couple of neurotic cats that made the trip north.

So, you see, how could Lemuria *not* be my bookstore?

BARRY MOSER is the prizewinning illustrator and designer of nearly 300 books for children and adults. He is widely celebrated for his dramatic wood engravings for the only 20th-century edition of the entire King James Bible illustrated by a single artist. He is the Printer to the College at Smith College, where he is the Irwin and Pauline Alper Glass Professor of Art. His work can be found in the National Gallery of Art in Washington, D.C., the Metropolitan Museum in New York, and The Victoria and Albert Museum in London, among scores of other libraries and collections. He lives in Western Massachusetts.

Howard Frank Mosher

Galaxy Bookshop, HARDWICK, VERMONT

Five years ago I embarked—in my falling-apart 1987 Chevy with 280,000 miles on the odometer—from my home in Vermont's Northeast Kingdom on an inspiring, if somewhat crazed, 100-city book tour. Three months, 20,000 more miles, and nearly 200 independent bookstores later, on the day after I got home, a reporter from our local newspaper called with a question. Could I, he asked, from my coast-to-coast and border-to-border odyssey, select a favorite bookseller, a favorite bookstore, and a favorite town or city?

"Absolutely," I said. "My longtime personal bookseller, Linda Ramsdell. Linda's Galaxy Bookshop. And Hardwick, Vermont, at the

237

southern gateway of the Northeast Kingdom, because that's where the Galaxy is located."

But wait. Just where in the world, you may well be wondering, is the Northeast Kingdom? And how did it get its name? "The Kingdom," as it's often referred to, comprises the three northeasternmost counties of Vermont: Essex, Orleans, and Caledonia. Named by Governor (later U.S. Senator) George Aiken in the 1950s while he was fishing a wilderness pond near the Vermont-Canada border, the Kingdom is a spectacularly gorgeous enclave of glacial lakes, icy trout rivers, jumbled mountains, and heavily wooded hills interspersed with dairy farms and tiny villages. At the same time, Vermont's "last best place," as the Northeast Kingdom is sometimes referred to, is an economically depressed northern fragment of Appalachia, with interminable winters, few decent-paying jobs, desperately underfunded schools, and the highest incidence of rural poverty in New England.

As for Hardwick—well, as the Kingdom poet, playwright, and novelist David Budbill put it, "Hardwick is tough and has always been tough. It was tough one hundred years ago when it was the center of a huge granite industry, and was referred to as 'Little Chicago,' and it's tough today when it is the center of nothing."

Let's face it. The Northeast Kingdom in general and, for all of its gritty authenticity as one of those rare, "true places" Melville mentioned in *Moby-Dick*, Hardwick in particular are about the last spots on earth where you'd expect a nationally renowned bookseller with a small but marvelously eclectic bookshop to survive for six months.

Yet as Linda once said to me, "A bookshop in Hardwick is not an oxymoron." Point taken. Still, how under the sun, in this era of Amazon.com, big-box chain bookstores, and dwindling numbers of readers for literary fiction and nonfiction, has the Galaxy Bookshop managed to flourish for nearly a quarter of a century in a community that, to this day, looks more like a hardworking western cow town than a quaint New England village?

It all comes down to the vision and determination of a trim, attractive, entirely unpretentious, delightfully humorous, and remarkably friendly Northeast Kingdom woman and world-class bibliophile and bookseller named Linda Ramsdell.

If I were asked to describe, in a single word, Linda's personal vision for the Galaxy, I think I'd say "connected." As independent-minded as Vermonters—especially Northeast Kingdom Vermonters—have been since the beginning, citizens of the Green Mountain State have also, perhaps necessarily, been deeply connected to the natural world of the fields they've tilled, the forests where they've cut their firewood and tapped their maple trees, and the communities where they live and work. They're connected to Vermont's long and unique history as a bastion of grassroots, town-meeting democracy. Most of all, they're connected to their immediate and extended families and to their neighbors. Linda Ramsdell and the Galaxy Bookshop exemplify the tradition.

For starters, there's Linda's impeccable pedigree as a native Vermonter, born and raised in the Northeast Kingdom. After graduating from Craftsbury Academy, just a dozen or so miles north of Hardwick, Linda did her undergraduate work at Brown University. In 1988, a year after completing college, she returned to the Kingdom—which, unlike Thomas Wolfe's Great Smokies at the other end of the Appalachians, seems very much a place to which people can and frequently do "go home again"—and established a bookstore in Hardwick's old firehouse.

"I didn't have anything else to do," Linda said. "I opened the Galaxy before I could even think about it." That's a Vermonter's way of saying that she did what her heart told her to do, bookselling being, most decidedly, a labor of love. No doubt Kingdom natives are drawn back to their hardscrabble hills and granite mountains for the same reason. An avid cross-country skier, hiker, horseback rider, and cyclist, Linda lives on a dirt road in a farmhouse built in 1830 that overlooks a rural prospect as varied and lovely as any in these United States—the sort of place visitors from New York and Boston would, and do, toil fifty weeks a year to enjoy a few days in. In the Kingdom, geography still shapes character. It's hard for me, at least, to imagine

> *"I opened the Galaxy before I could even think about it." That's a Vermonter's way of saying that she did what her heart told her to do, bookselling being, most decidedly, a labor of love."*

Linda living anywhere else.

In many ways, the Galaxy is both a reflection and an extension of Linda's personal connection to the Kingdom. After shifting quarters three times since 1988—once to a former bank, where the Galaxy had the distinction of being the only bookstore in the country to sell books out of a drive-through window—the store now occupies a former local grocery. In fact, the Galaxy still has the feel of a welcoming country store, where Kingdom residents and visitors alike gather at "the table" on which Linda displays her favorite books each month, instead of around a potbelly stove.

The Galaxy's Northeast Kingdom and Vermont section is a trove of regional literature and information. You can find poems set in the Kingdom by Robert Frost (who loved to botanize at Lake Willoughby, the "Lake Luzerne of Vermont"), Galway Kinnell, and Leland Kinsey; browse through essay collections on local country fairs, railroads, and old-time woodsmen by Edward Hoagland; pick up a memoir by Garret Keizer about teaching in the Kingdom, or buy the kids a stack of children's and young-adult stories by award-winning Kingdom author Natalie Kinsey-Warnock, who grew up on a seventh-generation farm nearby.

Over the years, Linda has hosted scores of local and nationally acclaimed authors at some of the best and most inclusive readings I've ever attended. In the company of Northeast Kingdom farmers, teachers, business owners, horse loggers, high school and college students, seasonal visitors, and retirees, I've had the pleasure of hearing and meeting such distinguished writers as Wallace Stegner, Howard Norman, Richard Russo, Jodi Picoult, Chris Bohjalian, Jeffrey Lent, and Gish Jen, among many others.

At the heart of Linda's own philosophy of bookselling is her unwavering belief in our constitutional right to read whatever we wish to read. A former president of the New England Independent Booksellers Association and board member of the American Booksellers Association, Linda worked with librarians and other booksellers to petition Vermont's Congressional delegation to sponsor legislation to repeal Section 215 of the abominable (and abominably named) "USA PATRIOT Act," which requires booksellers and librarians to turn over their purchasing and borrowing records to federal agents. In a 2002 press conference in Washington, D.C., with then Representative (now U.S. Senator) Bernie Sanders, Linda declared, on behalf of all readers, writers, and booksellers, "We celebrate the freedom of expression that brings us books with stunningly divergent points of view. We open our doors to welcome all customers and celebrate their freedom to read exactly what they choose without threat of government intrusion."

At home in the Kingdom, Linda and her longtime, knowledgeable bookseller colleague at the Galaxy, Sandy Scott, have also fostered the bookstore's ties to the region by cosponsoring book events with, or donating books to, local schools, libraries, churches, and nonprofit arts and social-service organizations such as the Northeast Kingdom Learning Services, the Hardwick Area Food Pantry, Head Start, and AWARE (Aid to Women in Abuse and Rape Emergencies).

So. How about that 100-city, 200-bookstore junket of mine? What's that got to do with the place Kingdom residents regard as "the greatest indie bookshop in the galaxy?" On the last day of my trip, very early in the morning, as I drove back into the Kingdom through Hardwick, I glanced down Main Street and glimpsed the colorful and distinctive Galaxy Bookshop sign, under which, some months earlier, I'd had the jacket photo taken for my own latest book.

I don't know if I've ever had a true epiphany. But suddenly I realized, with almost transformative clarity and force, that I was home. Not just home in Vermont and the Northeast Kingdom. But back in the place that has for twenty-five years provided me with the books that are my truest home of all.

To my dear friend and neighbor Linda Ramsdell, then—Ivy League graduate, Kingdom native through and through, and bookseller par excellence, whose Galaxy Bookshop is the heart and soul and home of readers throughout the Northeast Kingdom and far beyond—on behalf of book lovers everywhere, thank you.

HOWARD FRANK MOSHER is the author of 10 novels and two memoirs. He has lived all his adult life in Vermont's Northeast Kingdom.

Arthur Nersesian

St. Mark's Bookshop, NEW YORK, NEW YORK

Greenwich Village always had a great tradition of independent bookstores, from Frank Shay's Bookshop on Christopher Street back in the 1920s, which invited every major and minor writer of the day to sign its front door (including Theodore Dreiser and Sherwood Anderson) to the legendary Eighth Street Bookshop owned by the Wilentz brothers near MacDougal that finally closed, some say because of their refusal to allow their employees to unionize.

They lasted thirty-two years, officially making the St. Mark's Bookshop, at thirty-five years, the oldest indie bookstore ever to exist in the Village. Spring Street Books in Soho and old Marloff Bookstore in the West Village, both long gone, are examples of how bookstores sometimes are the canaries in their financial/cultural coal mine. By the time the Spring Street Bookstore went under—in a neighborhood once known for its rich art community—most of the artists were gone as well. When the Marloff in the West Village turned into a bar, the neighborhood, too, became…different. These were just a few of the countless bookstores that came and went through the area over the years. They are not to be confused with the many book re-sellers, such as those that made up the infamous Book Row. In its heyday, it had used-book shops side by side all the way up Fourth Avenue from 8th to 14th streets—now more or less consolidated into the mighty Strand.

New bookstores sometimes sprout out of old ones. Both Roger Jescha and Charles Dudley started out at the old Eighth Street Bookshop before they joined the staff at the St. Mark's in 1977. In fact, Robert Contant and Terry McCoy, the two owners of the St. Mark's, met and got their initial experience at the old East Side Book Store, a store that lasted about ten years. When they opened the first St. Mark's Bookshop at 13 Saint Mark's Place—they're currently on their third location—the neighborhood was still feral, febrile, and, by today's standards, dirt cheap.

Whether they knew it or not, the store was launched at the right place and perfect time, just as the East Village was coming into its own as the new artistic center of Lower Manhattan. In the relatively tight grid of as-yet-ungentrified and therefore affordable streets that made up the area, over the course of the next three decades there were vibrant movements in film, theater, and literature, as well as the visual and performance arts. Although the area had its share of crime and grime, you still felt the possibilities and the sense that your future was before you. During that time, before the age of laptops and cyber cafes, St. Mark's Bookshop was the Internet. If you wanted to know about a writer or artist or anything, you stopped at the bookstore. It simply held the finest selection of books and journals that one could find. In this age, when the future of bricks-and-mortar stores seems uncertain, this store illustrates precisely how the Internet fails. Never, while Googling someone or purchasing some obscure work, did I meet another writer or editor or learn about some new journal or anthology soliciting for submissions. The St. Mark's Bookshop is a crossroads for the serendipitous and the unplanned, where you can meet older authors— and frequently find why the best parts of them are in their books.

> *The St. Mark's Bookshop is a crossroads for the serendipitous and the unplanned.*

For fledgling writers and poets, the consignment shelf at the shop offers a chance to display their work and earn an audience. Likewise, editors of local literary journals, like *The National Poetry Magazine of the Lower East Side* and *Untitled* and *Between C & D* and *The Portable Lower East Side* and so many others, can come in with a sweaty armful of their latest issues and have a chance alongside the tweed-jacketed members of the literary establishment. Modern counterparts of these journals now live online, but in fairness you simply can't hope to hijack the attention of readers who came in for genre best sellers and the "it" books of the day. The St. Mark's Bookshop is meritocracy in action, where a browser might pick up an unknown novel, read through a few pages, get hooked, and become a loyal reader for life.

Although I've always appreciated the chain stores, whenever I'd ask for their small-press buyers I was usually given an extension of their corporate headquarters, frequently in another state.

Back in the late 1980s, when I finished my first novel and secured an agent, he sent the manuscript around and a year later it was roundly rejected. After years spent on it, I defiantly decided to self-publish it and let it be my headstone to the futility of writing. After every major house had passed on it, I really had no expectations of sales.

Susan Wilmarth, one of the buyers at St. Mark's at the time, took my little offering and gave it front-shelf ranking side by side with the big presses. Over the ensuing weeks, every time I'd stop by, she'd ask for more copies. Soon I had run out and ended up going back to the printers. Eventually I reprinted the book three times before I finally received a solicitation from an indie press that was just starting out, Akashic Books. The editor asked if they could make my book their maiden novel. Afterwards a large corporate press secured the rights. It has since sold more than 120,000 copies and has been translated into over a dozen languages. Currently my tenth novel is going to press, and I couldn't imagine any of it without the St. Mark's Bookshop.

This might sound like a spectacular example of how a bookstore gave one author his big break, but a more realistic picture is the million little breaks that occur each and every day. Smaller authors gradually become bigger ones, starting out at little literary journals and tiny presses before getting picked up by large corporate publishers. For years, aside from being booksellers, the St. Mark's Bookshop had been the prime downtown location where established writers found a market and young writers were given a chance. I find it hard to imagine how the Internet, which focuses on specialty websites, can offer these eclectic services to the future of literature.

ARTHUR NERSESIAN was born and raised in New York City. His tenth novel, *Gladyss of the Hunt* will be published in the fall of 2013 by Verse Chorus Press.

Kate Niles

Maria's Bookshop, DURANGO, COLORADO

Old snowshoes serve as decor on the high walls above book displays at Maria's Bookshop. So do Navajo rugs and local artists. The Southwest oozes through the store, because the mountains and deserts we all live here for are our muse and deserve a place in this haven of bookdom.

I have read about the demise of the independent bookstore and think: Not Here. One thing about living on the Western Slope of Colorado is the feeling that you are somewhat impervious to trends elsewhere, that the housing collapse or gangland murders or Amazonia's huge Kindled tentacles can't and won't happen here.

> *I have read about the demise of the independent bookstore and think: Not Here.*

This feeling is of course somewhat of a myth; I am good friends with Maria's book buyer and I know she's seeing all the same handwriting on the wall that other booksellers are. But if Denver's Tattered Cover is down to one store (reduced! Such a shame), Maria's keeps on shinin' on.

I gave my first reading here as a published novelist. More than forty people showed up, and when one of the bookstore personnel told me that this was their largest reading as far as she could remember, it gave me a belief in myself as a writer that the store has nurtured for me ever since. If no one else is buying my books, someone at Maria's finds mine and purchases a copy or two every so often. I get little checks out of this, a trickle of *Keep Going. It's OK.*

I once had a dream in which Virginia Woolf gave me six brown-paper-wrapped books and said, "These are yours." I've written three of the six so far. In this lull of mine at age 50, this middle-age transition place where my past has wrung itself out on the page and future writing is struggling to commence, I have to trust dreams like this. I have to trust, too, Maria's staff, who still value me as a writer, who whisper, after someone famous does a reading, *Was that you who asked that question?* Because, I mean, why doesn't she just get a therapist? And we chuckle and I feel a bit redeemed even as I admire, greatly, the other author's writing.

Another packed house: The Ed Abbey Memorial Reading, sponsored by a now-defunct magazine I used to write for. Me and a bunch of guys. Me and Art Goodtimes, the mushroom-hunting, Green Party County Commissioner helluva poet from Telluride. Me and B. Frank, M. Michael Fahey, Ken Wright, Dave Feela. Most of them the drink-beer-and-regale-ourselves-in-writing-with-the-latest-river-running-adventure crowd. I love their outlaw reverence for the land. I love Art's tie-dyed bard-dom, Dave's droll poetry. But I hardly fit in. That's why I was there. To read my little essay, 1,200 words straight from the hip and shaped perfectly, as it had sat there, inside, editing itself for twenty years over Cactus Ed's misogyny, his brash mid-20th-century male bravado that split the feminine and the family from adventures in the wild. I could be wrong, but I think I saw the snowshoes nod their toes ever so slightly in approval as I read.

Another reading. Watching Karl Marlantes read from Matterhorn. Watching that crowd. That aching audience of aging men, Vietnam vets all of them. I see a former colleague in the crowd, a few other men I knew who pitched a fit when John McCain, in a desperate act, came to town to campaign; who attend each Memorial Day with a patriotic fury at what was done to them and what should never be done to anyone again. Karl Marlantes reading, talking, too, about process, about that Endless Book his family joked would never see the light of day. The writer in me appreciated that.

I made a midlife career switch from teaching to psychotherapy for my day job not long ago. In a job interview for a therapy position, one of my interviewers asked me whether I was OK with starting low-ish again, giving up what I'd gained elsewhere. I answered in some professional tone then, but later I realized that no job switch, no low woman on the totem pole, was as deeply a trial by fire as being a bona fide writer in an era of rampantly dysfunctional Big House publishing. I was lucky to have been published at all. I know this. I have won a prestigious award or two. I have a small, small, but very loyal fan club. I will never, I doubt, see an advance above a grand, which I will promptly spend on book promotion. I could weep about this if I wanted to. All those Grand Dreams! That false myth of Making It!

I usually stop myself. Seems so self-pitying. Dumb. Not snowshoe-approved, as they are so hearty and have never been self-indulgent. Yet when another award-winning author, who is one published book ahead of me, comes to another of my readings in another brick-and-mortar blessed beacon of community enlightenment in another Four Corners state, I ask her what's she's doing now. Her lip curls, the despair trying so hard not to slide into bitterness. She says, "I'm waiting to see what New York does. I have six unpublished novels.

I just fired my agent because she wants me to write trash. Unless your name is Jonathan and you are from Brooklyn, forget it."

Amen, Sister of the Four Corners. Amen. Just as we do not understand Brooklyn, Brooklyn will never understand why there are snowshoes—those symbols of local perseverance—hanging in a bookstore in Durango.

I think those snowshoes in Maria's are the luckiest alive. They are the old-fashioned kind, the kind lashed to feet of miners in 1890, or mail carriers in 1910, or mule skinners. Webbed, made of curved wood and sinew woven into flat baskets. They have stories to tell themselves. And they've heard so many in Maria's. So many writers and readers and questioners and lovers of split bindings and falling-apart paperbacks and the chance to reserve a book in your own name behind the counter.

And that's the point, isn't it? The indie bookstore is what's left of The Commons. It's the one place people can still come with journals in hand and not feel self-conscious. The one place where veterans and punk college students and extreme sports fanatics and broken-hearted writers all mingle under the same roof, unafraid to discuss ideas. Jesus. What kind of country have we become that this is it? That this is what remains? No Amazonia of the Kindled tentacle can possibly take that place.

Maria's stays open till 9 p.m. Around here, that's late. So if you're walking Main in Durango on, say, an average Wednesday, you will hear faint laughter from the restaurants, maybe a raucous hoot from the El Rancho Bar because that is what the El Rancho is for, the whoosh of a car or two. Not a whole lot else. And the light shining out, the one that matters, is in the middle of the block between 9th and 10th, with the discount rack out front.

KATE NILES is the award-winning author of the novel *The Basket Maker*. Her second novel, *The Book of John*, was published in 2010. She also has a book of poetry, *Geographies of the Heart*, and is widely published in several genres. She is the recipient of ForeWord Review's Book of the Year Award for

Fiction in 2004 and a Colorado Council on the Arts Individual Artist Fellowship. She was nominated for a Mountains and Plains Booksellers Award in 2004. A former archaeologist and teacher, she now makes her living in the social-work field. She lives in Durango, Colorado, with her family.

Ann Packer

The Capitola Book Café, CAPITOLA, CALIFORNIA

The Capitola Book Café is tucked into the corner of an unprepossessing shopping center, hard to find unless you know it's next to the pizza place and catty-corner to the sewing machine repair shop. It's one of the finest independent bookstores in northern California, but more to the point, it's a haven for writers on tour to promote their books. I should know—they've hosted me for every book I've published.

Which is kind of amazing, given my first visit.

It was 1994, and I was promoting *Mendocino and Other Stories*, a collection of short fiction. It had been six years since I'd finished my MFA at the Iowa Writers' Workshop and four years since I'd left a fellowship at the University of Wisconsin, and so I'd been out of the academy for a long time. Yet it was the academy model that I envisioned for my maiden bookstore appearance.

I should explain. At a university reading an eminent writer, or even a not-so-eminent writer, reads for quite a while, choosing either a longish chunk of a novel or a full-length short story. It is a Literary Event. At a bookstore, an author reads for twenty minutes and then signs books. This is a promotional event. Unfortunately, I had not spent enough time contemplating the difference between a writer and an author, and for my first visit to the Capitola Book Café—which was also my first appearance at any bookstore anywhere—I read an entire short story, taking at least forty-five minutes. When I finished there was a rush for the exit—or maybe that's just how I recall it, memory making sure I got my just desserts. In any case, it was very clear that I had gone on for far too long. (Years later, an author escort—a category of being I didn't know existed until my second book tour, when I flew around the country from strange city to strange city and was met by kind people in clean cars who drove me from radio stations to bookstores to hotels—anyway, an author escort told me his bookstore appearance guidelines: twenty minutes is good, thirty minutes is pushing it, forty minutes is a hostage situation.)

And yet...the wonderful people at the Capitola Book Café invited me back. Again and again. They invited me when I'd written a best seller, and they invited me when I'd written a not-so-best seller. They set up a taped interview in their back room so a local radio journalist could talk to me while I was in town. They scheduled a book-group event on one visit, and my reading/signing was preceded by a delightful round-table discussion with a dozen avid readers. When I made a stop at a nearby bookstore for the paperback publication of one of my novels, a Capitola Book Café employee was in the audience because she'd missed my appearance for the hardcover publica-

> *When I made a stop at a nearby bookstore for the paperback publication of one of my novels, a Capitola Book Café employee was in the audience.*

tion of the same book a year earlier. In other words: wonderful, welcoming people.

And the store! It's big enough that there are corners and aisles to get lost in, small enough to feel intimate. The selection of fiction reflects the sensibilities of the staff, who love to share new discoveries and old favorites, to lead a customer into the interesting backlist of an author whose early books may not have received the attention they should have. Then there's the café—this is, after all, the Capitola Book Café—where visitors can have coffee or a snack while thumbing through a book still under consideration: It's as close to homey as any retail establishment can be. Located at least an hour away from where I live, the Capitola Book Café is one of my hometown bookstores, and my gratitude to its book-loving staff and owners is deep and abiding.

ANN PACKER is the author of *Songs Without Words*, *The Dive from Clausen's Pier*, and *Mendocino and Other Stories*. Her most recent book is *Swim Back to Me*, a novella and five short stories. She lives in San Carlos, California.

Chuck Palahniuk

Powell's City of Books, PORTLAND, OREGON

When your novel is first published all the book snobs ask: "Are you reading at the Tattered Cover? At Dark Delicacies? How about Cody's? Or Barbara's? Or Powell's?"

A book tour is just as exhausting as doing old-time vaudeville on, say, the Schubert circuit. It includes appearing at the Strand in New York...Books & Books in Miami...Lemuria in Jackson. It's a long series of one-night engagements sandwiched between early-morning flights and train rides. Left Bank Books in St. Louis...Rainy Day Books in Kansas City...Malaprops in Asheville. Late in life Mark Twain lost most of his fortune and was forced to pay the bills by almost constant tours of this sort. That's how he died: The stress killed him. Vroman's in Pasadena...Booksmith in San Francisco... Elliot Bay Books in Seattle.

In Portland, Oregon, Powell's City of Books is the equivalent of playing the Palace.

Each room of the city-block-sized building is named for a different color. Please understand, each of these rooms is the size of most independent bookstores. The Green Room, for example, is the store's main entrance. For years Powell's staged book events in the Purple Room. The drinking fountain in the adjacent Rose Room is legendary because longtime employees swear that the ghost of the store's founder, Walter Powell, occasionally appears there, almost always on Tuesday nights. The Orange Room is where the store buys used books, and insider sources report that surly, less-socially-apt staffers are relegated to work there. The Orange Room is the Alba of Powell's. For years a canister of ashes moved around the store, bumped from shelf to shelf. These were the cremated remains of a book lover who wanted to spend eternity at this, his favorite place. In the street entrance to the Orange Room is a column sculpted to look like a stack of books, and it's sealed inside this stone column that those ashes found their final resting place.

The Pearl Room is on the third floor, where the Rare Book Room occupies one corner and the rest is given over to art, architecture, film, and erotica books. My insider sources swear the Pearl Room is the store's cruisey sexual pick-up spot. Otherwise, it's a gallery, a wonderfully big, empty space where authors present their work almost every night.

The trouble is: Nobody teaches you how to do a book event. A publisher might send you on a tour to promote a book, but they don't coach you about what to actually do while standing in front of real-live readers. It's theater, but—usually, for the audience— inconceivably boring.

Go look for yourself. Check out a few nights at Powell's. It's one train wreck after another. But they're wonderful train wrecks. In the interest of full disclosure, I studied writing with Joanna Rose, the person who for many years organized author events and publicity at Powell's. She and I were students in Tom Spanbauer's weekly workshop, and our respective debut novels—mine, *Fight Club*, hers, *Little Miss Strange*—were published within a few months of each other. She was succeeded by Steve Fidel who coordinated author appearances until he joined the Peace Corps and went to work in Budapest. Both worked with hundreds of authors.

Through my friends at Powell's I learned that Amy Tan doesn't like to touch people, or books. It's for some reason having to do with germs or viruses, and most of her autographing consisted of people sliding their open books past her while she leaned over them and wrote her name at arm's length. The game changer was the tour when she hurt her leg boarding her flight and had to be taken to the emergency room upon arrival. With the help of painkillers she did the Powell's event that night, transformed. She touched the books. She hugged her fans. Giddy, she laughed and juggled her two tiny Yorkies, to everyone's delight.

At Powell's you see the literary gods at their not-best. Exhausted from weeks of sleeping in a different hotel bed every night. Starved. Lonely for family. Hung over. Here they are. When Bret Easton Ellis came to promote his story collection, *The Informers*, his novel *American Psycho* was still freshly stuck in everyone's craw. So many politically outraged people telephoned the store, threatening to plant bombs, to throw pies, to splash red paint on him, that Ellis spent the evening in a scrum of bodyguards.

When Jonathan Franzen appeared to promote *The Corrections*, he told what seemed like wry, funny stories about the local publicist who was escorting him around town. Unknown to him, everyone in Portland adores this woman, Hallie. To date, the Portland literati still spit on the ground when his name is mentioned. Hell hath no fury like an audience of Portland book snobs.

Few stores manage author events as well as does Powell's. There are seats for everyone. The microphone works. There's no competition from any loud espresso machine, and they even cease overhead announcements. The exception was when Diana Abu-Jabar launched her lovely novel *Birds of Paradise*. Her reading there was inspired. Spellbinding. Listeners were enthralled as Diana built dramatic tension. Nothing existed outside of the sound of her voice until—

"Attention, Powell's employees…" the PA speakers blared, "Does anyone have a copy of *The Catcher in the Rye?*"

The narrative spell was broken. There were a few nervous laughs. Still, Diana forged on. Reading clearly, enchantingly, she built to a new climax, and just at the cusp of her payoff—

"Attention, all Powell's employees…Does anyone have a copy of *The Catcher in the Rye?*"

Twice more she pushed on past the interruption, and twice more the announcement drowned her out. By the Q&A session, she was almost in frustrated tears.

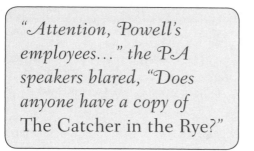

"Attention, Powell's employees…" the PA speakers blared, "Does anyone have a copy of The Catcher in the Rye?*"*

What no one knew was that a larger drama was taking place. When anyone loses a child at Powell's the store goes into lockdown. *The Catcher in the Rye* is the coded cue for staff members to block all exterior doors and prevent the lost or kidnapped kid from leaving the building. There are other book titles, representing other crisis situations, but really, you should read *Birds of Paradise*. It's a wonderful book.

More important than seeing a seamless, perfect show, the magic of Powell's is that you see these authors in the flesh. Tired or grumpy—especially tired and grumpy or loaded on painkillers—they're living proof that actual human beings write books. It's a kind of reverse miracle to see that this profound story came from this profane source. Authors, even brilliant ones, get flustered, act badly, but at Powell's you can shake their hands. Yes, the same hands that wrote

The Joy Luck Club and *Infinite Jest.* It's amazing.

This brings us to David Sedaris's appearance in Portland. David is the only person who's ever given me good advice on what to do at a public reading. Glorious advice.

In the interest of fuller disclosure, David gave me this advice in Barcelona where he and I were spending a week. We were there with Jonathan Lethem, Michael Chabon, and Heidi Julavits, doing a week of public readings and media interviews at something called "The Institute of North American Culture." Rather a deep-pockets project that prompted Michael to the conclusion that the CIA was funding the whole shebang and our real agenda was to promote goodwill for America, not an unlikely idea after September 11, 2001. Anyway, it was in Barcelona that David and I went shopping one afternoon.

At an open-air flea market, I was perusing a box filled with antique chandelier crystals, silently debating whether or not to spend 200 euros on a deck of swastika-emblazoned playing cards issued by the Nazis—were they an eternal totem of everlasting evil, or just in poor taste?—when apropos of nothing, David said, "I can't believe you're really gay."

In response, I pointed out the fact that I was wearing pleated pants and a pink silk shirt. I was in Barcelona with my partner of many years—as was he. And I was haggling over eighteenth-century chandelier crystals to hang on my Christmas tree. I said, "The only thing that could make me more gay at this moment would be a cock in my mouth." And David laughed. And not just a polite laugh, he brayed.

I still marvel at that moment: *I made David Sedaris laugh!*

Beyond that, while we shopped, he told me to never read from the current book while on tour. Always read from the next one. Doing so builds reader awareness of your upcoming work. It rewards the audience members by giving them something exclusive. And it beta-tests the new material to see if it's actually as funny as you imagined.

As if to illustrate the last point, the next time I saw David was in Portland. He was telling an anecdote at a public reading. In front of hundreds of rapt listeners he described sitting in the lunchroom of a medical examiner's office, at a table of people eating food. Talking shop, cramming sandwiches and potato chips into their mouths, they were watching an autopsy in the next room through a large window. The subject was a dead boy, 8 or 9 years old. At the book event David worked his audience, describing the dead child's blonde hair and unmarked body. The boy looked perfect, as if he were just asleep. He'd fallen on his bicycle, and now he was dead. Among the readers present, you could've heard a pin drop as David described in slow-motion detail how the attending physician cut across the child's forehead and peeled aside that lovely face the way you'd peel an orange.

Among the lunchroom observers, someone pointed out the stripped skull and the exposed, magenta-colored musculature. His mouth still full of half-chewed tuna sandwich, this man said, "See that, there? That color of red? That's the color I want to paint our rec room."

Everything about the story should've worked. The setup, the pacing, the payoff. David Sedaris is a brilliant storyteller. But this was Portland, Oregon, the capital of Earnest Empathetic Sincerity. At the punch line, no one laughed. Hundreds of faces just stared, their eyes brimming with tears. A few sniffed loudly. OK, one person laughed. I laughed. Give me a break—it was a hideously funny story, but the beta test had failed. Needless to say it did not go into his next book. And at the insensitive braying those hundreds of weeping heads swiveled to glare at me.

David had laughed at my joke in Barcelona. I'd laughed at his in Portland. And now all those readers who loved him had someone safe they could hate.

And, no, I didn't buy the Nazi poker deck.

Powell's City of Books is located at 1005 West Burnside Street in Portland, Oregon.

CHUCK PALAHNIUK is the author of *Fight Club* as well as 12 other novels and two books of nonfiction, all of them national bestsellers. He lives in the Pacific Northwest.

Ann Patchett

McLean & Eakin Booksellers, PETOSKEY, MICHIGAN

Imagine there are plenty of people who travel around the country going to baseball games, and that those people can tell you everything there is to know about the motels near the various stadiums and the quality of the chili dogs. What they know of America's cities they know insofar as it relates to the game: the convenience of the parking, the freshness of the popcorn. Over time the things that make us travel can also give us a certain kind of expertise. It could be amusement parks, Civil War battlefields, marinas, museums.

For me it's independent bookstores.

Most of my travel is bookstore-based. I am a novelist, and when

I'm not at home writing a book I tend to be sitting at a small table in the back of a bookstore trying to sell it. I can tell you who has the best selection of birthday cards, who is still serious about poetry, who's got unusual coffee-table books. It isn't just that I dip in and out of bookstores. I stay there for hours looking at the inventory. At the end of the night I'll go to some hotel I won't remember, eat dinner alone at the bar, and then the next morning I'll fly to another city to see another bookstore. I can remember the fiction sections, the new-releases table; I just can't remember which store was in which town. Like the baseball fan, the details of anything outside the parking lot kind of blur together. Except in this particular story.

The first time I was sent to Petoskey, Michigan, was in 2001. I wasn't happy about it. It was sandwiched into my itinerary among cities like New York, Boston, Chicago, L.A. For this store I would have to fly to Detroit, take another flight to Traverse City, rent a car, and drive an hour and a half, give a reading, sign some books, get back in the rental car and do the whole thing in reverse. It was such a tight trip I wasn't even going to get the dinner at the bar. "It's supposed to be a really great bookstore," my publicist said. I said that I didn't care. I had already seen really great bookstores, loads of them. She told me I was going anyway.

Here's a universal truth: The really great places are often the ones that are a drag to get to, and they have been able to remain great places for exactly that reason. Try going to the Spear-O-Wigwam ranch in the Big Horn Mountains of Wyoming (rutted dirt road, straight up) or Isle au Haut off the coast of Maine (you arrive on the mail boat). Petoskey isn't that challenging, but it's certainly off the beaten path. I drove my rental car down two-lane highways that were riddled with fruit stands, vegetable stands, pie stands, all of them nestled in orchards. I thought it was the loveliest drive I had ever been on, and then I was in Petoskey. The houses were wide of porch and steep of gable, many of them painted in the colors favored by seventh-grade girls. Petunias dangled from window boxes. Below the town the sun spread its diamond light over Lake Michigan, over the boats and the swimmers and the shore. The small downtown was a throwback to some simpler idea of American vacations, a couple of ice cream stores that sold taffy and fudge, a gift shop with T-shirts in the window that said LAKE. The world was leafy and dappled, quiet and cool. Within ten minutes I started to wonder how I could spend the rest of my life in Petoskey.

Say that you've fallen in love both unexpectedly and hard, only to discover that the object of your affection is a graduate of the Cordon Bleu and plays all the Chopin Nocturnes from memory and has a trust fund the size of Harvard's endowment. Just when you thought that nothing could be better, it got so much better. I walked into the bookstore of this dreamy little town and at that moment all the other bookstores I'd known in my life fell away.

> *I walked into the bookstore of this dreamy little town and at that moment all the other bookstores I'd known in my life fell away.*

Julie Norcross founded McLean & Eakin Booksellers in 1992, naming it for her two grandmothers. Like the town she came from, I imagined she had a long history of people falling in love with her at first sight. She was one of those supremely competent individuals who would have made an excellent pioneer. She could have built a sod house in a pinch, but she could also tell a joke, drink a martini, run a business. Her son Matt Norcross worked at the store as well, a fellow as charming and book-savvy as his mother. A family business named for family members—what's not to like about that? The disposition of the store was one of warmth and comfortable intelligence. It was the favorite sweater of bookstores. The books at McLean & Eakin were arranged to beckon, and there were plenty of big chairs to fall into once you heeded their call. It was the kind of store where I could happily spend a summer.

But on that particular day I only had minutes before I had to get back in the car. Back at the Traverse City airport I bought a paper cup full of cherries (in the airport!) and ate them while I waited for the plane. I cursed the world that would come between me and the place I loved, and I swore an oath on my cup of cherries that I would return. I'm a big one for keeping my oaths. With every book I wrote after that, I said to my publicist that McLean & Eakin was at the top of my personal wish list. (For anyone who thinks that authors get to decide where they're going on book tour, think again. Writers are more like soldiers: We get our marching orders and we go.) The next time I went back to my favorite bookstore, there was a wonderful new girl working there named Jessilynn. I was crazy about Jessilynn, and I wasn't the only one. With my next novel, Matt and Jessilynn were dating. The last time I went back, they were married. Julie had retired and they now owned the store.

Which is all to say that life marches on, and yet at the same time I can't help but feel that in Petoskey, some essential decency, some beauty, found a way to stand still. Julie Norcross made a brilliant bookstore, Matt and Jessilynn Norcross burnished it to something even brighter. Every customer shaped the terrain with their own interests, taking books away, requesting what was missing. The tourists come all summer long, wanting books to read on the shores of the lake, and the regulars come in all winter, wanting books to read in front of the fire as the snow banks up against the windows. The Norcrosses are there to help them all.

The best bookstores I can think of are the ones based in communities of readers. Petoskey is that sort of town, and it makes McLean & Eakin that kind of store. Or maybe it's the other way around, and the store has made the town. It seems possible. Frankly, it is enough of a bookstore to make the place a destination all by itself; without the lake or the pie or the gabled houses, I would go to Petoskey just to buy books (and I say that as someone who owns her own bookstore now). It is just so thrilling to be around people who read, people who will pull a book off the shelf and say, "This is the one you want." People who want to know what I'm reading and will tell me what they're reading so that while we talk, stacks of books begin to form around us. It's my own personal idea of heaven. It is also, in this age of the overnighted electronic handheld, a bit of Americana you aren't going to see everywhere. Like the town of Petoskey itself, a very good bookstore feels a little nostalgic, a place out of time. Look at all those people looking at books! It is at once both rare and beautifully ordinary. I can get choked up just thinking about it. But then, that's my job, the reason I go out to see this country in the first place. Books and bookstores are really the only things I can speak to with authority. And so I say to you absolutely: McLean & Eakin, Petoskey, Michigan—go.

ANN PATCHETT is the author of six novels and two works of nonfiction, including *Bel Canto, Truth & Beauty,* and *State of Wonder.* She lives in Nashville, Tennesee, where she is the co-owner of Parnassus Books.

Edith Pearlman

Brookline Booksmith, BROOKLINE, MASSACHUSETTS

Despite the claims of the righteous, reading is not a virtue—
"a commendable quality or trait," as Webster would have it,
or "conformity to a standard of right." It's not a vice, either, though
teachers urging children toward books might profitably suggest that
it is the favorite hobby of pirates and lion tamers. But, really, reading
is a simple addiction, curable only by death—ours, or the world's.
Those of us in its grip turn our attention away from truly virtuous
activities—writing thank-you notes, for instance, or washing the
kitchen floor. It is, in Philip Roth's words, a "deep and singular pleasure"—and we damn well won't give it up.

My bookstore, Brookline Booksmith in Brookline, Massachusetts, caters to our habit. The Booksmith stands in the center of town among other pleasure palaces (sports bars, delis serving chopped liver to die from, cigar stores, vendors of dubious videos). The place is full of light—sunlight on a good day, fluorescence on a gloomy one; the enlightenment of scholarship in the Philosophy section, lighthouses in Travel, stars in Cosmology. Its generous hours accommodate those who need a late-night fix. There is a children's section where some old party is usually sitting on a rocker provided by the Booksmith, reading to kids on the floor and kids on her lap. Most of them she's never met before.

> ...*reading is a simple addiction, curable only by death—ours, or the world's.*

There's a used-book cellar downstairs. You clamber down in search of a particular volume, fail to find it, and instead encounter four other books you've been meaning to tackle for years. There's a mini lecture space where visiting writers read sometimes to overflowing crowds, sometimes to half a dozen fans and one slightly malodorous local who dropped in for forty winks. Brookline Booksmith tolerates this variety of audiences; it realizes that the popularity of a book does not necessarily indicate its worth. Its salespeople, addicts themselves, can direct you to the book you crave or order it for you if it's not on hand. Patrons are diverse. Diversity is not the Booksmith's mission; it just happens—the town is home to people of all ages, ethnic groups, skin colors, degrees of education, degrees of craziness. All are welcome here, as long as they keep their voices reasonably low and their clothing mostly on.

I have been a patron for decades. I walk in, glance at the newspaper rack near the door, and learn from its headlines that the world, though a little worse than yesterday, is still spinning. Off to the bookshelves I wander, to sniff familiar substances or try new ones, all in grave solitude. Oh, I can greet people if I'm feeling friendly (rarely); if I'm feeling reclusive (often), I can slide behind a rack of H.G. Wells novels and achieve instant invisibility.

But if the blessed bookstore itself ever disappears, I will know without the aid of newspapers that the world has finally come to an end.

EDITH PEARLMAN has published four collections of short stories. The latest, *Binocular Vision*, won the 2011 PEN/Malamud Award for excellence in the art of the short story and the 2012 National Book Critics Circle Award for Fiction.

Jack Pendarvis

Square Books, OXFORD, MISSISSIPPI

One night my wife and I walked into the City Grocery restaurant and there was D-Day from *Animal House* having dinner. Naturally, we sent over a drink.

After he finished eating, the actor came over to our table. He was graceful and courtly, especially for a man I knew mainly for driving his motorcycle up the stairs and playing the overture from *William Tell* on his Adam's apple.

He said he was passing through town.

"I've been enjoying your apricot-colored bookstore," he said.

That threw me for a second. Did he mean Square Books?

He had to mean Square Books. It's the heart of Oxford, Mississippi. It's the only game in town. If something happened to it, everything else would tumble into the hole.

But I don't know what color Square Books is. I vaguely associate it with marshmallow circus peanuts, but walking home after dinner (Square Books is right up the block from City Grocery), I had to admit that D-Day from *Animal House* was closer to the truth. Maybe. Yes, the surface of Square Books is considerably darker than the disagreeable candy in question, and imbued with a rich, mysterious glow, but I still maintain there is a hint of circus peanut in the soft and bumpy texture of the building, so cool and refreshing to the touch, not that I've ever hugged or kissed it or tried to make sweet respectful love to it, not sober I haven't.

I'd like to take a bite out of Square Books. It's nutritious and delicious.

How do I tell you about it? A writer needs a little detachment. William Wordsworth would not approve of my desire to eat my subject, but he's dead. I have no "emotion recollected in tranquility" when it comes to Square Books.

It is my tranquility, that's the problem. I live there. I can't write about my internal organs either. If my brain stopped working my legs would automatically walk up the street to Square Books. If I miss a day I start feeling shaky. When I die my fleshly body will appear levitating among the paperbacks, dotted with stigmata and exuding a pleasant fragrance.

What's so great about Square Books?

> *If my brain stopped working my legs would automatically walk up the street to Square Books.*

There are books. That's always nice, especially in a bookstore.

What else can I say with certainty? It's two stories tall. But that's wrong. Between the ground floor and the second level is a strange half-space where all the spirituality and erotica in Mississippi has been shelved in case of emergency.

I teach a few classes at the local university and I have my office hours on the top floor of Square Books, a charming area that mitigates the grotesque prospect of listening to the thoughts and feelings of young people. There are tables and chairs. You can get coffee or even a scoop of ice cream. On my birthday one year the owner Richard Howorth voluntarily made me a root beer float and would accept no payment in return. I don't expect he'll do the same for you. He didn't get where he is today by giving away free root beer floats.

Where is he today? He used to be the mayor of the town. That's how much our townspeople love books, and how much Richard has done for us in return. President Obama appointed him to the Tennessee Valley Authority, but I don't know what that proves. It's a bit out of our orbit. Once you walk in the door of Square Books, you're in a self-contained cosmos with its own government and physical laws. One day I saw Lyn, the manager, sorting through a pile of tiny, broken doll arms.

"What are you doing?" I asked.

"I'm going to put these in a gum machine," she said.

I must have looked confused.

"Don't worry, there's a sign on the gum machine that says it's not for children," Lyn said.

Step out on the breezy, sun-dappled balcony and you will likely see a writer, although smoking isn't allowed anymore and boy do writers love to smoke. I hear stories about the days when Barry Hannah, Willie Morris, John Grisham, Donna Tartt, and Larry Brown used to congregate on the balcony together, and I imagine that most of them—especially the ones who are dead now—were smoking like chimneys.

Tom Waits was spotted lurking in the "Mississippi Writers" section. We all wanted to know what he bought. Probably some Larry Brown, everyone decided. This is the kind of speculation that Richard discourages. Discourages? Once an innocent clerk asked me whether on a previous visit I had really purchased Jung's *The Red Book*, an enormous facsimile of his twisted dream journal it would take two people to carry. I was happily responding when Richard appeared in a puff of smoke and scared the poor kid so bad his skeleton jumped out of his body.

"We don't discuss our customers' purchases," Richard said.

He was serious, too. He's a zealot. He's a priest. He doesn't joke around, not about books. Well, I take that back. You know how thriller writers usually have a full-color portrait of themselves taking up the entire rear side of their dust jackets? Once I saw Richard go to the table where those books were displayed and turn them all around until there was nothing but a big, terrifyingly cheerful pyramid of author photos staring and grinning insanely at the world.

"Let's see how long it takes anybody to notice," he said.

In the old days Richard talked books with Larry Brown. Square Books was Brown's alma mater. There and the public library were the places he learned to write.

I didn't know him.

I ran into Barry Hannah a lot at Square Books, though. I saw him in the store just a couple of days before he died. He talked the way he wrote. Once he told me, "Everybody wants to go to the Baptist heaven but nobody wants to do the Baptist time."

A lot of good writers have gone to Baptist heaven recently, including Lewis Nordan and William Gay, both of whom I used to see at the store. Our neighbor Dean Faulkner Wells passed away. She was Faulkner's niece and he raised her like his own daughter. You go over and take the tour of Rowan Oak, his home, and the only picture of William Faulkner smiling was taken at Dean's wedding.

The last time I saw her was at Square Books too.

Even Michael Bible, the nosy young clerk whom Richard scared, is gone. Not dead, though a pixie-like representative of Hollywood came into the store and literally snatched him away to the coast in a chariot of gold. That makes Michael the Lana Turner of Oxford, Mississippi, and Square Books our Schwab's. He's out there working on an adaptation of *Light in August*. One of my great joys used to be bugging him while he tried to work.

You walk around town and things aren't the same. We leftover writers are fine, but we're not fooling ourselves.

Thankfully, when you walk into Square Books, feeling comes back strong. Nobody's dead. Everybody's at the party.

It's the books, stupid.

One New Year's morning Square Books was giving away free Bloody Marys but I guess somehow the word didn't get around because it ended up being just me and the *New York Times* columnist John T. Edge on the quiet balcony over the empty square, sipping our drinks and thinking about how nice it all was.

Sooner or later we had to go home but I guess we could have sat there all day.

JACK PENDARVIS is the author of two story collections and a novel. He is a columnist for *Oxford American* and *The Believer*.

Francine Prose

Strand Book Store, NEW YORK, NEW YORK

For as long as I can remember, "18 Miles of Books" had been the slogan of the Strand Book Store. To the passionate reader and the writer—or in any case, to me—this sounds like a description or a map of the Kingdom of Heaven or the Emerald City of Oz.

When I was in high school, in the early 1960s, the few blocks that now constitute Fourth Avenue in Manhattan were lined with secondhand-book stores. These stores were treasure troves, crammed full not only with books but also with prints and photographs, postcards, and God knows what else.

Perhaps the most famous customer of these places was the artist

Joseph Cornell, who combed the Fourth Avenue bookstores for the images and objects he used in his beautiful and otherworldly shadow boxes. I often wondered if my path ever crossed that of Joseph Cornell when I went to the stores with my friends, as we did almost every Saturday morning.

> *It's the kind of bookstore to which I go when I want a specific book, but also when I don't know what I want, or when there's nothing I want, in particular, except to be in a bookstore.*

The Strand is the last remaining survivor of these destination bookstores. It's the kind of bookstore to which I go when I want a specific book, but also when I don't know what I want, or when there's nothing I want, in particular, except to be in a bookstore. It's the ultimate place to browse: that thing one can't do when one orders books online.

At the Strand, I can allow serendipity to pull me from table to table, all the while discovering interests I never knew I had—a fascination with medieval medicine or Scythian gold, with the poetry of Philip Larkin, with the novels of Ivy Compton-Burnett, or with Walter Benjamin's recollections of his Berlin childhood. It's easy to spend hours there, and easy to buy books at the end of those hours. In this way, like so many others, it is different from bookstores that somehow manage to make me feel that I've overstayed, or that the time I've spent there has been wasted. Eventually, I rush out of such stores as quickly as possible, which may be why I see so few customers at the registers and so many, like myself, hurrying out the door.

I feel extremely fortunate to live very near the Strand. Quite often, it's where I go when I want to take a break from writing. I can go there in every season and during most waking hours and clear my head, much in the way a healthier person might go to the gym or an unhealthier person might step outside for a cigarette. By now I have friends who work there, whose advice and conversation I value, and who I am very glad to know.

The Strand's rare-book room is astonishing: a wonder of the world. One of my proudest possessions is a first edition of the fiction of Jane Bowles. My students chipped in and bought it for me as a gift at the end of a semester during which we'd read her work together.

I fear I would not be telling the entire true story of my relationship with the Strand without mentioning the fact that it not only sells but also buys books, including used books and review copies. I've often sold it books I have enjoyed but simply have no room to keep. I live in a New York apartment! Were it not for the Strand, and its proximity, I would have had to move out of my apartment years and years ago. There would have been no room for me.

So that is yet another way in which those 18 miles of books are the description not simply of a bookstore but of an institution that, in many ways, makes it not merely more pleasurable but possible for me to read and write—and live.

FRANCINE PROSE is a novelist and critic whose latest book, the novel *My New American Life*, was published by Harper in May 2011. Her previous books include the novels *Goldengrove*, *A Changed Man*, and *Blue Angel*, which was a finalist for the 2001 National Book Award, and the nonfiction *New York Times* best seller *Reading Like A Writer: A Guide for People Who Love Books and for Those Who Want to Write Them* and *Anne Frank: The Book, the Life, the Afterlife*. Her articles and essays have appeared in *The New Yorker*, *Harper's*, *The Atlantic*, *Condé Nast Traveler*, *ARTnews*, *Parkett*, *Modern Painters*, and *The New York Times Magazine*. She is the recipient of numerous grants and awards, among them the Dayton Literary Peace Prize, the Edith Wharton Achievement Award for Literature, and Guggenheim and Fulbright fellowships, and is a past president of PEN American Center. She is a member of both the American Academy of Arts and Sciences and the American Academy of Arts and Letters. She lives in New York City.

Ron Rash

City Lights Bookstore, SYLVA, NORTH CAROLINA

Buying an independent bookstore is a risky venture in the best of times, but when Chris Wilcox bought City Lights Bookstore in 2009, it was an especially risky venture. With the economy in shambles, how could a small-town bookstore survive? But booksellers, like book authors, tend to be a dreamy yet determined lot, and when Chris took over he managed to persevere when many other independents went under. Hard work (Chris always seems to be at the store) and frequent readings and signings are certainly part of why City Lights has continued to be successful, as is a whole room devoted to books about Appalachia. The store itself is pleasing, with a layout, including a fireplace, that allows the customer to feel relaxed, even reflective. But the staff is what makes City Lights such a delightful store. Chris is incredibly well read, and so are his employees. In a country where reading is less and less valued, City Lights is a literary oasis. Books are important here, and so are their readers. Every time I enter the store, Chris or one of his staff is able to suggest a book specifically for me. City Lights knows its customers, and that, to me, is what makes an independent bookstore great. So the next time you are in Western North Carolina, stop by City Lights. Maybe there will be a fire burning, but even if not, you will find this bookstore warm and welcoming.

> *City Lights is a literary oasis. Books are important here, and so are their readers.*

RON RASH is the author of the 2009 PEN/Faulkner finalist and *New York Times* best-selling novel *Serena*, in addition to three other prizewinning novels, *One Foot in Eden*, *Saints at the River*, and *The World Made Straight*; four collections of poems; and four collections of stories, among them Burning Bright, which won the 2010 Frank O'Connor International Short Story Award, and *Chemistry and Other Stories*, which was a finalist for the 2007 PEN/Faulkner Award. Twice the recipient of the O. Henry Prize, he teaches at Western Carolina University.

Tom Robbins

Village Books, BELLINGHAM, WASHINGTON

Baptized in ink and swaddled in a dust jacket, I'm one of those cats for whom a good bookshop serves as a temple, a cathedral, a holy shrine, a sacred grove, a gypsy caravan, a Tijuana nightclub, an amusement park, a mental health spa, a safari camp, a space station, and an indoor field of dreams. Over the years, Village Books of Bellingham has functioned as all of those things for me, most memorably the last, because a few years ago the store quite literally made one of my wildest dreams come true.

It was while on tour to flog *Wild Ducks Flying Backward*, a collection of my short writings, that I was asked by an interviewer if at that stage of my life and career there was anything missing, anything that I still wanted badly but didn't have. My answer was spontaneous yet honest. "Yeah," I said. "Backup singers."

The more I thought about it, the more the idea appealed to me. What if there were a trio of singers—sexy girls in long, slinky dresses—who'd follow me everywhere I went and harmonize and scat and *ooh wah wah wah*, riffing on whatever I said in any situation? They'd stand behind the dental chair, for example, if I was undergoing a root canal, just swaying, smiling, seamlessly improvising on my gurgles, my grunts of pain. At the bank, the supermarket, the IRS office arguing about taxes, there the ladies would be, over my shoulder, turning my utterances, however mundane, into improvised three-part harmony, vamping all the while like fallen angels from Motown heaven.

From a hotel room in Denver or Minneapolis or Ann Arbor, I can't remember where, exactly, I telephoned Chuck Robinson, the enlightened owner of Village Books, and asked if he'd mind if I brought along backup singers to the reading I was to do in his store the following week. There was a long pause on the other end. Then, a dry, cautious chuckle. "Go for it," he said. That's the kind of guy Chuck is.

My next call was to the salon where I get my hair cut. I pitched the idea to the gorgeous young stylists who work there. Jennifer, Susan, and Michelle are by no means aspiring vocalists, but they're stand-up, extroverted girls with an appetite for fun, and all three rather quickly agreed. We were able, unfortunately, to manage only one brief rehearsal. Then, it was showtime.

As adept at promotion as it is exhaustive in its inventory, Village

> *I telephoned Chuck Robinson, the enlightened owner of Village Books, and asked if he'd mind if I brought along backup singers to the reading I was to do in his store the following week.*

Books has always provided big crowds for my events, and that night it was literally SRO. I read a few passages from *Wild Ducks*, then called for "my backup singers" to join me at the podium. The audience assumed I was joking, but minutes later the girls were undulating and *da da dee da-ing* behind me as I read lines in that flat, funky voice of mine that sounds so much like a can of cheap dog food if a can of cheap dog food could speak. The crowd seemed quite entertained by the novelty of it all, although I don't recall many shouts for an encore.

In the end, whatever else it might have meant for me personally, the event proved that Village Books is a store apart, a store with nerve, a store with heart; a three-dimensional literary supercollider where fantasy can fuse with reality at the speed of a turning page.

TOM ROBBINS is the author of nine offbeat but popular novels and a collection of stories, poems, and essays. His books have been published in 22 foreign countries, have topped best-seller lists in Australia, and have been adapted for stage and film. A Southerner by birth, he lives in a small town north of Seattle.

Adam Ross

Parnassus Books, NASHVILLE, TENNESSEE

It's an unseasonably warm, early spring evening, and I'm at Nashville's new independent bookstore, Parnassus, where former Rolling Stones saxophonist Bobby Keys is launching the tour for his memoir, *Every Night's a Saturday Night*. Not surprisingly, half the crowd is composed of session players, touring musicians, and songwriters, mostly men in their late forties and early fifties who've come out on a Wednesday night to see a legend of the rock 'n' roll wars. After a brief introduction by cowriter Bill Ditenhafer, Keyes gets up and, in a style that's best described as wry, high, and dry, describes his childhood in Texas, his fateful failure as a football player that led to him playing sax in the marching band; he tells a few bawdy anecdotes about Keith and Mick (including the famous bathtub-full-of-champagne incident) and bemoans life as a saxophonist in a country-music town. In short, listening to him is a blast. After the Q&A and signing, I run into several friends I haven't seen in a while, another of the evening's pleasures, and one of them is about to go on vacation. She asks for some reading suggestions, so I pull down Edward St. Aubyn's *The Patrick Melrose Novels* and James Salter's *Light Years*. I've heard nothing but great things about the former; the latter rocked my world. She thanks me, promises to report back, and heads to the register.

Nothing out of the ordinary at a great local bookstore; however, on such a night, the ordinary seems extraordinary, because at this time last year, Nashville was a major American city without one.

The coverage attending Parnassus's opening has been jaw-dropping: stories in *The New York Times* (on the front page!), *Publishers Weekly*, *Garden & Gun*, *The Christian Science Monitor*, *Southern Living*, *Salon*, and *USA Today*; *Time* magazine naming co-owner Ann Patchett one of the 100 Most Influential People in the World; her appearances on NPR's Marketplace and Fresh Air; and then, to top it all off, her guest slot on *The Colbert Report*—as a bookseller. That's just a sampling, and even though Patchett's no stranger to celebrity, hers is literary celebrity, and while she's enjoyed what she likes to call "media-heavy" moments in the past, the attention focused on her decision to open a 2,500-square-foot bookstore in a Green Hills mall was as colossal as it was unexpected, the sort of heat normally reserved for a star like, well, Nashvillian Nicole Kidman or Taylor Swift. The upshot: Parnassus might be only six months old, but it's not a stretch to say that it's currently America's most famous bookstore.

Why that's the case has something to do with its owner, of course. Timing is everything, so the saying goes, and Patchett's business venture with partner Karen Hayes coincided with the release of her sixth novel, *State of Wonder*, considered by many fans and critics the best since her Orange Prize– and PEN/Faulkner Award–winning international best seller *Bel Canto*. Throw into the mix the turbulent state of publishing, questions about the future of print, the looming specter of Amazon, the rise of e-books, the locavore movement, Occupy Wall Street, the destruction wrought on independent bookstores by both the big-box retail wars and the Great Recession, and so it was that Parnassus, like Batman, became more than just a store: It became a symbol. Of what, exactly, has been mulled over by so many journalists and pundits that any interpretation I'd add to the mix is guaranteed to be redundant.

Still, I'd urge book lovers to keep this in mind: After Nashville's thirty-year-old quasi-independent bookstore Davis-Kidd Booksellers shuttered its doors in December 2010, and before the news broke that Ann Patchett would be opening Parnassus, ours was a city cut off from America's literary life—a city of no choices whatsoever when it came to the humane and meaningful pleasures associated with

> *...and so it was that Parnassus, like Batman, became more than just a store: It became a symbol.*

buying books, and that makes for a very grim place indeed. Borders had also closed down, mind you. The nearest Barnes & Noble was twenty miles out of town. Our terrific used bookstores like McKay, Elder's Bookstore, and BookManBookWoman are wonderful for a certain kind of experience, but they aren't particularly vital *destinations*. You don't take your kids there to play with toys and pick out a book; they're not on the map as tour stops for widely recognized authors; their staff doesn't get you excited about what's coming soon or put in your hand the one book you didn't know you needed to read until right now.

"I love being able to press books on people," says Patchett about the thrill of being a bookseller. "I don't know why I never anticipated what a pleasure it would be to corner people and say, 'You *must* read this book.' I've been forcing books on friends and family my whole life, and now my scope of recommending is much wider. It's a real joy."

Joy is a great word to associate with Parnassus, because Nashville's book lovers were without that emotion for a year—our *annus mirabilis*, a year lost to us, never to be recovered, and hopefully never forgotten. This served as a wake-up call to the Athens of the South, at least in the near term, and Parnassus's subsequent success (business is booming) demonstrates how grateful our print consumers are that this gaping void has been filled. But our fellow enthusiasts in other cities beware: Unless you protect your local bookstores with your pocketbooks, they could easily suffer a fate similar to what did Davis-Kidd in; and unlike Nashville, those cities might not enjoy such a happy ending.

ADAM ROSS lives in Nashville with his wife and two daughters. His debut novel, *Mr. Peanut*, a 2010 *New York Times Notable Book*, was also named one of the best books of the year by *The New Yorker*, *The Philadelphia Inquirer*, *The New Republic*, and *The Economist*. *Ladies and Gentlemen*, his short-story collection, was included in *Kirkus Reviews* Best Books of 2011. His nonfiction has been published in *The New York Times Book Review*, *The Daily Beast*, *The Wall Street Journal*, *GQ*, and *The Nashville Scene*. His fiction has appeared in *The Carolina Quarterly* and *FiveChapters*.

Carrie Ryan

Park Road Books, CHARLOTTE, NORTH CAROLINA

Here's what I remember about The Open Book, the local independent bookstore in my town growing up: The kids' section was in the back, where the oddly shaped store narrowed to a point. It was a destination, not a thoroughfare, and so once you found yourself back there, you could settle into the nook between shelves and your world became nothing but books and words. The air smelled like deckled edges, the dust that sometimes collects on old spines, and rhymes. It felt like its own little fort, a secret sort of place filled with promises of undiscovered worlds and adventure.

In my memory, the rest of the store barely exists. There must have been other sections full of adult-minded tomes, but the treasure always lay squeezed into that point in the back. I remember the white metal spin rack with the latest Nancy Drews, the ordered row of Sweet Valley Twins and Highs, the classics nestled among Christopher Pikes and R.L. Stines.

On Saturday mornings, this was my home and I could spend hours sliding through the pages before choosing one or two or three to take with me to keep me company late into the weekend nights. I'm sure if I'd have asked, one of the booksellers would have helped me narrow my selections by pointing out the new arrivals, but I chose to discover these things myself. It was like an Easter egg hunt, finding the latest releases among the old familiars.

And to me, every book on the shelf eventually became an old familiar. Whether I'd read them or not, I spent enough time among them to recognize spines and covers the same way I would later, as an adult, learn to recognize faces waiting at the elevator banks for work every morning.

> *The thing I came to learn as I grew older is that I wasn't the only girl who found dreams tucked away on the shelves.*

The thing I came to learn as I grew older is that I wasn't the only girl who found dreams tucked away on the shelves at The Open Book. It was a place of connection for many people, the booksellers knew us by name, and when a book came in they thought one of us would love, they'd set it aside, knowing they'd see us in a week or two.

This was what I missed when I left for college and moved from town to town. What I never realized is that, while I rarely asked a bookseller at The Open Book for suggestions, they were curating a selection for me regardless. Every time they placed an order, they were keeping me, and all their other readers, in mind. Not as nameless droves, but as individuals whose tastes they knew by heart.

There was no corporate office telling them what to buy and how to shelve it. There was no one asking them to push a certain book because the corporation or publisher had decreed it become a "make book." They stocked titles because they loved them and they knew their customers would as well.

This is what I often fear we've lost over the years: the bookseller who knows her customers by name. Who can tell you their reading history and who can, almost at a glance, pick a title from a catalogue and say, "You know who would love this?" The bookseller who is involved in the community in a deep and personal way—who is a part of the community in ways few of us would ever realize until it's gone.

That's what happened to The Open Book. That nook where I fell in love with reading…is gone. The owners who shaped the literary lives of my community are no longer behind the counter. I'd already moved to a new city but still I felt its loss, like hearing a friend you've gone to school with, but subsequently lost touch with, has passed away.

By then I'd found a new indie, Park Road Books in Charlotte, North Carolina, that welcomed me to the community with open arms. Every time I step inside, someone behind the counter smiles and says, "Hey, Carrie!" Not a visit goes by when we don't discuss the latest releases or what's coming out in the next season. I stand at the counter and swap stories as other patrons get called by name, get asked how their families are, have books recommended to them.

There are algorithms that can predict what books we might enjoy, what brand of cereal we're likely to buy, what kind of music we want to listen to. There are stores built like warehouses with wide aisles and anonymous cashiers. But how can that replace what it's like to walk into a store like Park Road Books and have Yola, the store dog, greet you with tail wagging? To have Sally Brewster, owner and bookseller, lean across the counter with a wide smile and say, "You know what I just read that I think you'll love?" To hear the customer ahead in line chat about a recent review in the local paper and wonder if her book club would like it (and Sally would know!). To have Sherri

Smith, kids'-book buyer, call up to say a fan just ordered a book and if I'll come down and sign it, they'll take care of shipping it out.

Independent bookstores like Park Road Books are so much more than a place to buy books. They're a place for gathering, for sharing, for learning, for meeting new people. They are a home. There have been times I've been far away traveling and I've become homesick and walked into an independent bookstore because that's something they all have in common: a feeling of coming home.

This is how I fell in love with reading: sitting in that narrow point, tucked away from everything, deciding what worlds I wanted to explore. And when my first novel came out, this is where I held my release party: at The Open Book, where I saw my own book tucked among the others. I wondered if any other young girls like I had been would find it there one day, take it home, and build dreams on those foundations.

Now, every time I run down the street to Park Road Books I sneak back to the kids' section. Sometimes it's just to see what's new on the shelves, sometimes it's to close my eyes and remember the smell and feel of being a kid. But most often it's because I'm able to catch glimpses of readers, ones like I used to be, trailing fingers over spines and wondering which world they'll take home with them today.

CARRIE RYAN is the *New York Times* best-selling author of the critically acclaimed *Forest of Hands and Teeth* trilogy and *Infinity Ring: Divide and Conquer*, the second book in Scholastic's new multi-author/multi-platform series for middle grade readers. She is also the editor of the anthology *Foretold: 14 Tales of Prophecy and Prediction*. A former litigator, she now writes full time from her home in Charlotte, North Carolina, where she lives with her writer-lawyer husband, two fat cats, and one rather large rescue mutt. You can find her online at www.carrieryan.com.

Lisa See

Vroman's Bookstore, PASADENA, CALIFORNIA

When my first book, *On Gold Mountain*, came out in 1995, I had two launch parties. One was at Dutton's Bookstore very near where I live in Los Angeles; the other was at Vroman's Bookstore in Pasadena. Both parties would have cheese, crackers, and wine. At both parties I would read. That's where the similarities ended. The party at Dutton's was outside on a patio; the party at Vroman's was inside and upstairs. The party at Dutton's was for friends; the one at Vroman's was for family. (I didn't have fans back then, so I didn't factor them into the equation when I made my plans.) For some authors of first books a family party might not have been a big deal, but

On Gold Mountain was about the Chinese side of my family, so that event seemed daunting—a potential disaster.

For *On Gold Mountain*, I spent five years interviewing my family's business associates, friends, and enemies. I went to the home village in South China, where my great-grandfather was from. I found over 500 pages of interrogations, boarding passes, health certificates, and photographs concerning my family at the National Archives. I also weeded through my relatives' closets, basements, attics, and garages, looking for anything that would help me tell the story of the Chinese in America and my family in particular. Most important, I got my relatives to talk. This isn't easy to do in any circumstance, but I was asking my parents, grandmother, aunts, uncles, and cousins to relive moments of great sorrow, embarrassment, shame, and sadness. No one wants to go over the details of being kidnapped, finding out your husband was fooling around, experiencing different forms of racism, or losing a beloved parent, child, or other loved one. They also weren't too keen on talking about things that were either borderline illegal or full-on, out-there illegal, such as multiple marriages (known in this country as bigamy), smuggling, circumventing miscegenation laws, and the like. I knew that getting people to talk about these things would be difficult, and it was, but somehow I had the sense—even though it was my first book—to get everyone to sign releases. I believe my relatives signed them because they never thought I would actually write the book.

While *On Gold Mountain* wasn't a memoir in the sense that those weren't my memories, it was a memoir of my family. Memoirs, as we all know, are fraught. There are things that people don't want to remember, things they remember differently, and things they'd rather keep a secret. And at some point the book is going to come out, and those people are going to read it.

. . .

I don't know if my great-grandparents knew the Vromans, but it wouldn't surprise me if their paths had crossed at some point. In 1895, a year after Adam Clark Vroman opened his bookstore on

Colorado Boulevard in Pasadena, my great-grandparents arrived in Los Angeles and opened a Chinese antiques store called the F. Suie One Company. In 1901, my great-grandparents opened a branch of the store not far from Vroman's. My family then had a presence in Pasadena on and off over the next eighty years. In 1981, the F. Suie One Company moved permanently to Colorado Boulevard just east of Vroman's. Today Vroman's and the F. Suie One Company are two of the oldest independently owned family businesses not only in Pasadena but in the state. Having my launch party at Vroman's was not a matter of convenience or a business decision based on the fact that the store reported its sales to *The New York Times*. (Believe me, I absolutely wasn't thinking about the latter. Reporting store? What was that?) Rather, it just felt right—like circling the wagons. I knew I would feel protected and safe.

Although I was a nervous wreck, everyone at the store made me feel welcome. There were huge stacks of books—more than could ever be sold—but they told me not to worry about it, because they could keep some and return the rest. They suggested that they write down people's names before they came though the signing line, in case I happened to get brain freeze and forget the name of one of my 400 relatives (whose names are hard to spell even on a good day). They suggested I just talk instead of read—something I've continued to do to this day. So I spoke for a bit, and I'll admit it, I cried. Then people got in line to buy a book. Let me say this: My relatives were not what you'd call book buyers or readers. Some of them may not have read a book since high school, but they were good sports and they love me so they dutifully did their duty.

Pretty soon I started to hear snippets of conversation as people gathered in corners and opened their books. "Look, here's a photo of my mom! We never had a picture of her." "Here I am as a baby! I thought my first photo was when I joined the army." At the National Archives I had found immigration photographs of my family that no one knew existed. They hadn't read the book yet, but through those photos I had brought back people and history that my family thought had disappeared for good. Now they came through the line again, this time with stacks of three, four, ten books. Vroman's sold every single copy of *On Gold Mountain* that day.

. . .

So here we are seventeen years later. Dutton's Bookstore, where I had my other launch party, closed a couple of years ago, as have so many other bookstores here in Southern California. Happily, Vroman's has continued to thrive. One of the things that I've always admired about the store—and even more so in this hard economic climate—is the Vroman's Gives Back program, which allows customers to donate a portion of their purchases to a local organization of their choice, including public radio stations, arts centers, family services, and programs supporting literacy, the homeless, and animal welfare. To date, Vroman's has donated an amazing $530,000 on behalf of its customers. The store serves as the heart of the community, hosting food and gift drives, free HIV testing, and pet adoption days, and making donations to charity raffles and school book fairs. Not only has Vroman's continued as the oldest and largest independent bookstore in Southern California, but three years ago the store stepped in and bought Book Soup in West Hollywood when the owner died and that store was in danger of closing. The folks at Vroman's are book-selling heroes!

> *The store serves as the heart of the community, hosting food and gift drives, free HIV testing, and pet adoption days, and making donations to charity raffles and school book fairs.*

On a more personal level, I've done a launch event at Vroman's for every book I've written. Over the years, I've stood at the podium and seen my relatives, who were once vital and strong, begin to rely on canes, walkers, and wheelchairs. I've watched great-uncles lose their hair and great-aunts go gray. I've seen shoulders weaken and feet begin to shuffle. These people, who I loved, who made me the person I am, have disappeared one by one. As they've passed away, fans have come to fill their seats. But I still see my relatives in those chairs or huddling together in a corner. I still hear them whispering to each other, "Look, here's a photo of my mom!" And I still feel them in the stacks, in the shelves, along the walls of this beautiful, loved, and well-cared-for and curated bookstore in Pasadena. Vroman's Bookstore may not be my neighborhood bookstore, but it is my family bookstore, for which I will always be grateful. I will always be loyal to Vroman's, and I believe Vroman's will always be loyal to me.

LISA SEE is the *New York Times* #1 best-selling author of *Dreams of Joy* and the *New York Times* best-selling author of the novels *Snow Flower and the Secret Fan*, *Peony in Love*, *Shanghai Girls*, and the critically acclaimed memoir *On Gold Mountain*. The Organization of Chinese American Women named her the 2001 National Woman of the Year. She lives in Los Angeles.

Brian Selznick

Warwick's, LA JOLLA, CALIFORNIA

I didn't really want to move to California. But my boyfriend was offered a great teaching position at U.C. San Diego, so off we went.
He found an apartment for us in La Jolla, a block from the beach and
two blocks from a bookstore, so I figured things wouldn't be that bad.
The bookstore, Warwick's, has been around for over a century, and I
felt right at home the moment I walked through the doors.

La Jolla is a beach town. Surfers abound, and everyone gathers
on the beaches. Dr. Seuss lived here. All the trees look as if they
were drawn by him. But there is an incredible intellectual and artistic
life amid the sunshine and the sand. There are great theaters here,

and music and museums. And bookstores. Warwick's, like most great bookstores, is the beating heart of its community. It holds readings and signings and events throughout the year. The staff has not only read everything, it seems, but they have an opinion about everything as well.

Independent bookstores like Warwick's feel like home to me. In the early 1990s I worked at Eeyore's, a children's bookstore in New York City. I learned all about books and bookmaking while I worked there. That's where I came to understand and appreciate the picture book as a beautiful art form, and where I studied the history of children's books by reading as many books as I could under the careful guidance of my boss, Steve Geck. I also used to love it when authors came to the store. We'd always ask them to sign stock, and some of the authors became friends. Paula Danziger, who wrote the *Amber Brown* books and *The Cat Ate My Gymsuit*, among many others, took me under her wing before my first book was published. Now, many years later, walking into Warwick's, I am the author and it is fun to feel connected to both sides.

I first started visiting Warwick's in 2004, about the same time I started working on *The Invention of Hugo Cabret*. I'd bring little sketches to show the staff to get their feedback. At the time I didn't know if anyone would want to read a book about French silent movies for kids, so it was great to get their positive feedback. When I was working on my most recent book, *Wonderstruck*, I reached an impasse with my publisher over the cover design. Jan Iverson, the store's buyer for children's books, and the rest of the staff gave me excellent feedback that helped me create the final cover. I couldn't have done it without them, and when *Wonderstruck* was complete, I invited the entire staff over to my house for a celebration. We drank wine, ate cheese, listened to music, and looked at all of the 250 drawings that I had hung up on my studio wall.

I'm so grateful for all of Warwick's support over the nearly nine years we've lived in the neighborhood. They have hosted readings for me, including a spectacular book event for *Wonderstruck* at the San

Diego Natural History Museum in Balboa Park. My favorite times at Warwick's, though, are when I simply stop by the bookstore to shop and say hi. I knock on the swinging doors of the back office, and soon I'm caught up in a conversation to find out what books various staff members are reading and which ones they want to recommend. We gossip and catch up with our lives and talk about whatever it is we are all reading. A few months ago I began reading Edith Wharton's works for the first time, and as I was buying *Old New York* after having finished *The Age of Innocence* and *The House of Mirth*, members of the staff and I got into a very heated debate about which of Wharton's books was the best and why oh why Lily Bart made all those terrible choices.

> *Members of the staff and I got into a very heated debate about which of Wharton's books was the best and why oh why Lily Bart made all those terrible choices.*

Thank God for bookstores and booksellers.

It's been over twenty years since I actually worked in a bookstore, but I still feel very much like a bookseller at heart. Of course, when I actually was a bookseller, I was tired all the time. I hated reshelving books, and there were customers who drove me crazy. There were authors we didn't like who would sneak into the store and put their book covers face out on the shelves. There were thieves to deal with, and late shipments, and grandmothers who were never satisfied with any of my suggestions for gifts for their grandchildren. It was hard work. But I was able to read everything I wanted and was surrounded by people I could talk about all those books with. There were the regular customers who loved the books we gave them and wanted more. There were the kids who would curl up and sit on the floor, eager to start reading before they got home. There were the cartons of books, freshly arrived from the publisher, filled with good-smelling volumes of some new thing that no one else had seen or read yet.

There was a lot of pleasure and satisfaction among the difficulties. And now, all these years later, it's only gotten more difficult for bookstores. Bookstores survive, though, and the ones that really reach out to their community, that make themselves indispensable, not only survive, but thrive. A bookstore is only as good as its staff, of course, and Warwick's is among the best.

BRIAN SELZNICK is the author/illustrator of the *New York Times* #1 best-selling novels *The Invention of Hugo Cabret* and *Wonderstruck*. *Hugo*, the 3-D major motion picture directed by Martin Scorsese and based on *The Invention of Hugo Cabret*, won five Academy Awards. His books have received many awards and distinctions, including a Caldecott Medal for *The Invention of Hugo Cabret* and a Caldecott Honor for *The Dinosaurs of Waterhouse Hawkins*. He divides his time between Brooklyn, New York, and La Jolla, California.

Mahbod Seraji

Kepler's Books, MENLO PARK, CALIFORNIA

B ookstores have always been a source of wonder and intrigue to
me. I grew up in Iran, and as a child every day on my way to
school I stood outside a tiny bookstore near my home and stared at
the titles placed in the windows, thick books with fancy names and
big-name authors—*White Fang* by Jack London, *Crime and Punish-
ment* by Fyodor Dostoyevsky, *Germinal* by Émile Zola, *The Blind Owl*
by Sadegh Hedayat.

*How long did it take for each of those masters to write their
stunning stories? I wondered. Did they know how many lives their books
had touched?*

Even at that age I couldn't imagine a feeling greater than that of seeing your name on the cover of a book for the first time. With a secret desire to be a writer someday, I surreptitiously envied my favorite authors with respect and longing.

I left Iran when I was 19, and as life went on, one thing never changed: my fascination with books and bookstores.

Fast-forward thirty-plus years; I moved from Chicago to the Bay Area, working a few doors down from Kepler's Books in Menlo Park, California. Unbeknownst to me, Kepler's had been a landmark and a community hub for readers and nonreaders alike for many years. Standing outside its window and staring at the books on its shelves instantly reminded me of the cozy bookstore in my childhood neighborhood. And from that moment on, Kepler's became my lunchtime Mecca; my daily visits there a daily pilgrimage home to the innocent fantasy worlds of my childhood.

> *Kepler's became my lunchtime Mecca; my daily visits there a daily pilgrimage home to the innocent fantasy worlds of my childhood.*

It was in June of 2009, a month after the release of my first novel, *Rooftops of Tehran*, that I received an invitation from this prestigious cultural center to do a reading there. The thought of walking through the same doors as I had done so many times before, but this time as an author, was beyond invigorating to me. It was also nerve-racking. Despite my career in management consulting and public speaking, I knew that this experience would be nothing like standing in front of a room full of Silicon Valley executives. This was Kepler's and its audience was far more sophisticated than the average business executive who mostly cared about quarter-end results, Wall Street expectations, or earning-per-share ratios! This was where people came together to feel the sense of community, to be a part of a larger whole, to belong….and I was the guest speaker.

The experience was extraordinary. The staff was gracious and kind and mindful of every detail in preparation for my visit. The large audience, well informed, welcoming, and ready to ask insightful questions, embraced me with enthusiasm and awareness. I could not believe that the same boy who longingly gazed at the titles in the windows of that small bookseller in Tehran so many years earlier was now in Menlo Park, California, at Kepler's Books.

In our travels and along our paths we all come across places, havens, that stay with us and feel like home, a place of belonging. As an author, as a reader, or simply a fiercely loyal supporter, Kepler's has always been that place for me. A wonderful reminder of my childhood dreams and all that I had to do to achieve them.

MAHBOD SERAJI was born in Iran and moved to the United States in 1976 at the age of 19. He attended the University of Iowa where he received an M.A. in Film and Broadcasting and a Ph.D. in Instructional Design and Technology. He currently works as a management consultant, and lives in the San Francisco Bay area.

Nancy Shaw

Nicola's Books, ANN ARBOR, MICHIGAN

I shop at Nicola's Books, in Ann Arbor, Michigan. I love having a store that respects its customers and that brings mega-sellers and literati, as well as hopeful authors with new projects, in front of audiences and lets them have a conversation. *Nox* played here, and Laurie King, and Dava Sobel, and *Speed Bump* cartoons.

Nicola Rooney and her staff read and recommend. If I want a book, they find it fast. I can browse art-museum cards here without trekking to the museums. My friends' books are here, and so are mine, and I like feeling that we are more than sales units.

I can sit on the sofa by the fireplace, where travel guides transport

> *My sheep went shopping once, in a country store. I think they'd like to come to Nicola's to enjoy the customer service.*

me to Edinburgh or Guatemala; and David Wiesner and Eric Rohmann take me other places entirely—or I can look up at the fairy door crafted in the paneling above the mantel, its frame incorporating fairy-tale book spines. The tiny door is a portal into a world of stories, as is every alcove here.

My own characters are on the shelves in the children's section. My sheep went shopping once, in a country store. I think they'd like to come to Nicola's to enjoy the customer service. Here's what might happen if they came upon a smartphone, tried it out, and then visited the Westgate Shopping Center to ship back the disappointing results.

SHEEP PHONE IT IN

What's this lying in the grass?
A rectangle with screen of glass.
Sheep explore it. What's that tone?
Do they hear a ringing phone?
Something's showing on the screen:
Icons, hot links—what's it mean?
Sheep try apps.
Sheep take snaps.
Sheep text.
What's next?
Sheep tap screen and go online.
Cyber-shopping—how divine!
Items land in shopping cart.
Wow! This phone is really smart!

. . .

The UPS man brings a box—
Glenn Beck, *Quantum Physics*, *Vox*,
Da Vinci Code, and *Picking Stocks*.
Oops! These books are not their type.
What to do? Sheep gripe.
Sheep repack
To send them back.
Returning from their shipping chore,
Sheep espy a special store.
At Nicola's, their spirits soar:
Picture books and so much more!
Folks who help, with such rapport!
Sheep choose titles, all tip-top,
And satisfied, they leave the shop.
Sheep traipse back and drop the phone.
It's in the pasture, all alone.
Bleating praises, loudly vocal,
Sheep are pleased with shopping local.

NANCY SHAW is the author of *Elena's Story*, *Raccoon Tune*, *Sheep in a Jeep*, *Sheep in a Shop*, and five other sheep books. She holds degrees from the University of Michigan and Harvard University. Her website is nancyshawbooks.com.

Jeff Smith

The Book Loft of German Village, COLUMBUS, OHIO

W hich do you love more: books or bookstores? That's something to contemplate these days, as the resources for both appear to be receding from us. They go together for me; starting back when I was a kid, a bookstore was the first place I experienced freedom—the ability to wander about the rows and sections, discovering my own tastes and interests. Of course, at that age, science fiction and fantasy were my favorites, but still, what were all these other books about? History, science, classics. I remember well the day I discovered Penguin Books!

But I want to tell you about *my* bookstore, The Book Loft in Columbus, Ohio. Not just any independent bookstore, but a masterpiece of warmth and retailing that winds and sprawls throughout a number of connected old

Which do you love more: books or bookstores?

Victorian-era brick buildings that once housed a general store, a saloon, and a nickelodeon on a quaint little street in historic German Village.

On foot, as you turn off Third Street and enter the open iron gates, a worn brick path leads you away from the bustle into another world, through a small garden to the entrance, where books are piled on tables outside by a fountain. Inside, doorways and staircases immediately lead off in multiple directions, all the nooks and crannies stuffed with books—everything from expensive Taschen tomes to paperbacks, note cards, calendars, best sellers, out-of-print books, audio, and more, all at good discount prices that a starving young artist can appreciate. It's a place where your imagination can have free rein. You know, I don't think I've ever not found what I was looking for in the thirty years I've shopped there. I write graphic novels about medieval landscapes and ancient religions, as well as modern physics, war, nature, art, and tons of things that I need reference and inspiration for, so my searches swing pretty far afield sometimes. Not only that, but as a Herman Melville fan, I have five editions of *Moby-Dick*, and four of them still have The Book Loft's little removable orange sticker on them.

Each room or hallway is filled with different categories and is accompanied by its own soundtrack provided by little speakers up in the corners. The place is clean, never dusty, but it has that old-bookstore feel, and smells like print. If you love bookstores, you know what I mean. You can get lost here, in every sense of the word. It's old-school, and people come from out of town just to visit it. There's also a great coffee shop next door.

After all this time, there are still a few rooms I haven't sufficiently explored. Categories, genres, and topics that I haven't gotten to yet, but I will.

The Book Loft was one of the first bookstores I know of to get hip to the new wave of comics and graphic novels. That might not be a big deal to you, but the day I saw *BONE* on the shelf there was more important to me than the owners will ever know. So thank you, Book Loft, for being there, and here's wishing you a healthy and prosperous future!

JEFF SMITH is a co-founder of the 90's self-publishing movement and an early adopter of the graphic novel format. He is best known as the writer and artist of *BONE*, an award winning adventure about three cartoon cousins lost in a world of myth and ancient mysteries. In 2009, Smith was the subject of a documentary called *The Cartoonist: Jeff Smith, BONE, and the Changing Face of Comics*. Along with *BONE* and *RASL*, his other books include *Shazam: The Monster Society of Evil* and *Little Mouse Gets Ready!*

Lee Smith

Purple Crow Books, HILLSBOROUGH, NORTH CAROLINA

"It saved my life," Sharon Wheeler says, thinking back to that day in April 2003 when she literally walked into the bookstore business. She was still reeling from the news that her beloved husband, Joe, had been given a dire diagnosis—brain tumors and kidney cancer. Sharon had just taken an early retirement from her teaching job in Burlington, North Carolina, but was finding that she "didn't have enough to do" on that day when she and a friend went window-shopping in nearby Hillsborough.

"I walked into the bookstore and said, 'Oh, I would give anything to work in a bookstore like this!'"

And the owner said, "You're hired!"

Thus it began, a few days a week. Joe died two years later. And later still, when that bookstore closed, Sharon realized, "I knew I was ready to open my own."

In 2009, Sharon Wheeler moved to Hillsborough and opened Purple Crow Books in a tiny storefront on King Street, smack in the middle of the historic town.

At first, her grown daughters were not happy with the move. But now her daughter Ashton says, "I think you have become who you were meant to be."

"Any time you have something to do—somebody who depends on you—that gives your life purpose," Sharon explains. "Back in Burlington, my husband knew everybody. But when I came to Hillsborough, I was just me. So I am indebted to the whole community—it allowed me to find my wings on my own."

The Purple Crow has been flying high ever since.

"The fact that I can have a bookstore and pay the bills in a town of this size, despite Amazon and Kindle, is amazing! I think we read because we want to be connected—and that's one service of the independent bookstore. People do love to make a personal connection with a book—and this is a place to connect. Also, I try to get to know the people. This bookstore reminds me of the bar in *Cheers*—we all want to be where somebody knows our name. That's what makes it work—it's a place where people know your name. I think that we are all on the short end of actually communicating with people the way we used to—all this electronic stuff, tweeting and email, gets in the way. I like to really connect," Sharon emphasizes.

"The people who come in here on a regular basis love to read and also love to support bricks-and-mortar bookstores—and real books. They have a dedication to shopping local, too. They cherish tradition."

Nancy Vest, who works in the store, interrupts: "I think they come to see Sharon! They want to talk to Sharon!"

"I'm astounded at what people come in here and tell me," Sharon admits, laughing. "But I love stories—I just love their stories!"

She also has a master's degree in counseling. "I worked in a very poor school," she says. "And I always used books to help my children. There's nothing more important for a child than reading a book and realizing that other people have fathers who go to prison, other people have mothers who are on drugs....Books can give you other worlds and other possibilities, too. All the stories, all the places, can be yours. That's the gift of books."

Sharon also used books to develop a prizewinning curriculum for character education. "Everything meaningful and good in life you can find in children's literature. All the questions of the universe can be answered in children's lit," she says. At my prompting she lists some of her favorites: *Charlotte's Web*; *Teammates, a true story of Jackie Robinson and Pee Wee Reese*; *Baseball Saved Us*; and "anything by Patricia Polacco"—holding up a Civil War book titled *Pink and Say*.

An old claw-footed bathtub in the Purple Crow has been filled with bright pillows and stuffed animals so children can snuggle down to read a book...or bored husbands can catch a little snooze!

I love to hang out in the Purple Crow myself trying out the new books, soaking up the peaceful atmosphere, and waiting to see who's going to come in the door next, announced by the little bell.

> *An old claw-footed bathtub in the Purple Crow has been filled with bright pillows and stuffed animals so children can snuggle down to read a book...*

"It's good to see you all again," Sharon says to her many repeat customers, including one visitor who has driven down from Virginia. She listens carefully as this woman describes her granddaughter's love of reading: "She's into Greek and Egyptian mythology, she loves series books...."

Sharon doesn't have to go far afield for a suggestion, recommending local phenom John Claude Bemis, a middle-school teacher turned author of the popular "Clockwork Dark" trilogy, which he describes as "American Harry Potters." John's new book, *The Prince Who Fell from the Sky*, came out in June, 2012, and the Purple Crow planned a big release party in a larger space—our local farmers' market, complete with entertainment. John's a musician, too!

Sharon directs a new customer to her "Local" bookcase. "These books are all by Hillsborough authors—we have over thirty Hillsborough authors. Yes, that's right—in this tiny little town!" Authors include Michael Malone, Frances Mayes, Allan Gurganus, Jill McCorkle, Zelda Lockhart, Hal Crowther, Craig Nova...the list goes on and on. Elizabeth Woodman's new Eno Publishers recently published *27 Views of Hillsborough*, with selections by many of us."

In fact, Hillsborough was picked by *Garden and Gun* magazine as "the most literary small town in the South," beating out Oxford, Mississippi, and Milledgeville, Georgia. I am not so sure about that!

Hillsborough authors are not exactly "retiring" either, but very civic: Each Christmastime, for instance, Michael Malone and Allan Gurganus don their top hats to present Dickens's *A Christmas Carol* with Allan Gurganus as Scrooge and Michael Malone as all the other characters! This show is so popular that they have to have two performances, all to benefit local charities. A yearly storytelling festival brings writers out too—and somebody can always be found writing a novel or a poem at local hangout Cup A Joe, right across the street from the Purple Crow.

This little section of King Street is actually a microcosm of the "New South." The Dual Supply hardware store next door has looked "pretty much the same" ever since proprietor Wesley Woods started working there when he was "8 or 9 years old, putting up stock, sweeping...." There's still no computer. Across the street is Evelyn Lloyd's little family pharmacy, which she took over from her father in the '80's; and the Carolina Game and Fish selling hunting bows and fishing tackle and offering seasonal prizes for deer and turkeys. Their carcasses are weighed on the sidewalk right next to the sophisticated Cup A Joe with its latte, cappuccino, and multiply pierced baristas, doing a thriving business.

With her old-fashioned friendliness and the latest books, Sharon navigates both worlds with ease. "There is a peaceful rhythm to life in downtown Hillsborough, which is unique to this town. I have always felt the spirit of Hillsborough encouraging me to succeed. We all cheer for each other. I think Joe feels it too, right now in heaven."

Ring! Here comes a forthright old gentleman looking for an unabridged copy of *The Count of Monte Cristo*. No luck on that one. Ring! A woman whispers her request for *Fifty Shades of Grey*, but no luck on that one, either—Sharon just sold them all at Ladies Night Out. She takes the order, then grins at me when the woman leaves. "I think everybody has a right to read whatever they want, don't you?" Absolutely!

Ring! Some tourists come in. "Look!" they cry. "It's a real bookstore!" *Flash!* They take a picture.

LEE SMITH is the author of 15 works of fiction, including *Oral History, Fair and Tender Ladies*, and her recent collection, *Mrs. Darcy and the Blue-Eyed Stranger*. Her novel *The Last Girls* was a 2002 *New York Times* best seller as well as winner of the Southern Book Critics Circle Award. A retired professor of English at North Carolina State University, she has received many awards, including the North Carolina Award for Literature and an Academy Award in Fiction from the American Academy of Arts and Letters.

Les Standiford

Books & Books, CORAL GABLES, FLORIDA

It was close to five, and time for a drink, I thought. Another sultry summer afternoon in Miami, circa 1981. Thunderheads boiled over the Everglades a few miles west, promising a downpour any minute. No point in hanging around the office any longer. Business was lousy. Who needed a private eye in a town where everything is public?

And that is when she came in.

"I'm sorry," she said as she appeared in the doorway. She was a trim brunette with curls and the kind of figure that makes men want to write sonnets. "I knocked," she said, "but it looks like your girl is gone for the day."

313

Gone for the year, I wanted to tell her, and still wanting her last two weeks' pay, but why shake a client's confidence? I pointed to a chair. She sat down and crossed her legs. I admired the process. "How can I help you?"

She dabbed at her eyes with a tissue. "It's my boyfriend," she began.

"There's always a boyfriend," I muttered.

She looked at me plaintively. "His affections have been alienated."

I nodded. "So he's fooling around, and you want me to find out who with?"

She shook her head. "It's worse than that," she said. "He wants to open up a bookstore. It's all he thinks about."

I leaned back absorbing it all. "So you want to have him Baker Acted. Why didn't you just say so?"

She dropped her gaze. "It's all so shameful," she said. Out on the street a klaxon sounded. *What's a klaxon?* I wondered.

"He'd been going to law school," she was saying. "And then, when that didn't work out, he started teaching high school English. But I know that was only because he got to read books and talk about them." She looked up, shaking her head. "Now he wants to *sell* them. He's in love with books." Tears were running down her cheeks. "Books and books," she said helplessly.

I came around my desk and put a hand on her shoulder, "Listen," I said. "I'm just a fictional character, so I'm prejudiced. But your boyfriend...what's his name?"

"Kaplan," she said. "Mitchell Kaplan."

"Right," I told her. "What this Kaplan's doing is important. Books are important."

"But this is Miami," she said. "People fish. They drive fast boats. They commit fantastical crimes. They don't *read*."

"That could change," I said. "This Kaplan's a smart guy."

"How would you know that?" she said.

"Well, he picked you, didn't he?"

. . .

You don't need me to tell you how it worked out. Kaplan did go into the bookstore business, all right. He leased a 1920s building in Coral Gables, on Aragon, a block east of LeJeune, and filled its rabbit warren of rooms, upstairs and down, with artwork and books, most new, some rare. And people parked their boats and came. They liked the books, sure, but they liked the atmosphere just as much. They could browse and talk to this Kaplan about what he thought was worth reading—including all the books about crime in Miami—and no actual gunfire ever blew out any windows.

Though the store's biggest room was about the size of a shoebox, Kaplan started bringing in authors to read from their books. At first the publishers in New York only wanted to send down people who had written manuals on better geriatric living and how to crime-proof your condo, but Kaplan kept at them, bringing in the local desperadoes all the while. Before long, no book tour worth its salt failed to list Books & Books as a destination.

Kaplan wasn't satisfied with just bringing people into his store, though. He teamed up with Eduardo Padrón, president of Miami Dade College, to create the Miami Book Fair. The idea was to close the streets of downtown Miami and set up tents where people could buy and sell books and listen to writers of every stripe, 500 or more of them over the course of a week. Good thing the girlfriend hadn't shared that plan the day she came into my office, or I might have gone along with the Baker Acting. The funny thing is, the Miami Book Fair—in pretty much the form Kaplan described it—has become this smashing success.

. . .

For a dozen years or more, Kaplan had it pretty good. He was inching back toward the level of luxury he'd enjoyed as a high school teacher and had even opened up a second store in Miami Beach, on Lincoln Road, which at the time had one shop that sold used vacuums and another that refurbished buggy whips, and that was about it. Kaplan had grown up on Miami Beach, though. As amazing as it sounds, he wanted to give people there access to books, and once again he was proved a visionary. The store on Lincoln Road—where he added one of the best sidewalk cafés around—has thrived.

It was not until the early '90s that things got a little dicey. During the prior decade, entrepreneurs in the U.S. had been making out like bandits, creating chain and franchise stores for shoes and vitamins and fishing tackle and ladies' underwear, so it was only a matter of time until someone figured out that there was a fortune to be made by getting people to buy stock in bookstore chains. Before you knew it, there were as many bookstores being opened around the country as there were doughnut shops, driving a bunch of the independent stores out of business. This is also the point at which my author got involved with Kaplan in a way that threatened to end things between us forever.

. . .

"Yo, Mr. Big Shot," I said, when my author finally picked up. I'd been calling him for days. But that is a character's lot in life.

"What is it, Exley?"

"What's this I hear you're going to write a novel about the Kaplan guy?" I said.

"You hear correctly," my author said. "Mitchell was saying he thought there'd be a good thriller in the so-called bookstore wars, and I thought he was right. I told him he would have to die in the book, of course, but he was cool with that, so I'm going to do it."

"How about me?" I said. "Do I get in the story this go-round?"

"I'm sorry," my author said. "It's going to be a John Deal book. You're just not right for the part. Maybe we'll get you into something another time."

. . .

It hurt, but when you are just a figment of imagination, what are you going to do? Besides, the book did get published (though why they called it *Deal on Ice* instead of *Book Deal*, I'll never know) and my author got to read from it at Kaplan's store. Everybody seemed to like it, even the part where the bookstore owner gets offed. I figure some of the people laughing were probably criminals themselves.

What makes for a really amazing story, though, is the fact that in real life this Kaplan not only doesn't die, he keeps on chugging like the Energizer Bunny. A few years back, he finally outgrew the original store and moved up the block on Aragon to a new set of digs that my author likes to call "The Temple to the Book." It is a big place with two wings and a cozy central courtyard cafe where combos jam on weekends, and it has the same old-timey charm that the first store had. On moving day, a couple hundred customers showed up to form a book brigade, and they passed the books from the old place to the new, hand to hand, section by section. It's the kind of thing people would accuse you of making up if you put it in fiction.

The new place has also gone gangbusters and draws people from everywhere—presidents have signed books there and you can find celebs and famous writers skulking around the stacks all the time. Kaplan has gone on to open another spot in Bal Harbour and to partner in more Books & Books stores in the Miami International Airport, Fort Lauderdale, Grand Cayman, and Westhampton Beach, and this is at a time when a lot of independents and even a bunch of those chain bookshops are closing up.

If you want to know how he's managed it, I figure it this way: Just like I told that bombshell who came in the office all those years ago, this Kaplan understands that books are important in a way that safari shirts and whole-grain cupcakes are not. Anybody who walks into one of his stores—they are more like destinations, really—can tell that the guy who set the place up knows and cares about what he has for sale; and if you ever doubted it, all you would have to do is spend a few minutes talking with him, or any of the dyed-in-the-wool book people he has working with him.

So, how this ends is, my author and I go up to New York not so long ago to see Kaplan get the Literarian Award for Outstanding Service to the American Literary Community at the National Book Awards ceremony. It was a black-tie affair, but because I am barely apparent unless my author seems to be mumbling to himself, I went in my dressing gown and slippers. Being unseen, I could take as many glasses of champagne from the trays circulating as I wanted, and I will admit that I was a little hammered by the time Kaplan walked up to get his kudos and talk about his devotion to what he described as a "very fragile literary ecology."

But I remember very clearly watching and thinking, *Forget about fiction—in real life, sometimes good guys do finish first.* And, by the way, the real-life bombshell who was sitting by Kaplan in his glory that night had this uncanny resemblance to the gal who came so worried to my office all those years ago. Like I keep telling my author, this would make a hell of a story.

LES STANDIFORD is the author of 20 books and novels, including the John Deal mystery series and the *New York Times* best seller *Bringing Adam Home: The Abduction that Changed America.* He is the director of the creative writing program at Florida International University in Miami, where he lives with his wife, Kimberly. He met his pal Mitchell Kaplan, former ABA president, more than 30 years ago, when Books & Books was still just a gleam in Kaplan's eye.

> *If you want to know how he's managed it, I figure it this way: Just like I told that bombshell who came in the office all those years ago, this Kaplan understands that books are important in a way that safari shirts and whole-grain cupcakes are not.*

Nancy Thayer

Mitchell's Book Corner, NANTUCKET, MASSACHUSETTS

One day you wake up and everything has changed. The electric typewriter is passé. The computer rules the world. A new children's wing is built onto the island library. The fast ferry arrives in Nantucket in just one hour. But I thought I'd have Mimi with me all my life.

Mimi Beman owned Mitchell's Book Corner, on the corner of Main Street in Nantucket. The first time I met her, in 1986, she terrified me. The bookshop owners I'd known before were demure and hesitant. Mimi came at me like a great powerful righteous force. She was opinionated and loud. I'd enter Mitchell's, and she'd bellow, "We've got the new Elizabeth George!" Other times she'd slip me a reader's copy of a brand-new first-time author. "I think you'll like it. Try it," she'd say, out of the side of her mouth, like a spy. She was always right.

She did this with all her regular customers.

Mimi had enormous amounts of energy. She rose at four or five in the morning and read until eight, when she had to go open her store. It seemed she'd read every book ever printed, and she had the remarkable facility of remembering each person and which author they favored. She loved matching people with books. She loved this island. She loved the young people who were her staff, and I know she was a mentor in many ways to so many young women who worked for her, my daughter among them.

> *The bookshop owners I'd known before were demure and hesitant. Mimi came at me like a great powerful righteous force. She was opinionated and loud. I'd enter Mitchell's, and she'd bellow, "We've got the new Elizabeth George!"*

For an author, she was a godsend. She gave fabulous book signings, treating the author like a star. She always had a book-themed bouquet of flowers on the table, along with fresh water and a small box of exquisite chocolates. She was wonderful with consolation; she was magnificent at celebration. Whenever the library presented a speaker, Mimi was always there with a big box of the writer's books and cheerful, encouraging words for the writer after the talk, whether the writer sold ten books or none at all. New writers came into her store and Mimi took the time to read their work and provide her judgment and expertise. And, always, her honesty.

If you wanted an opinion from Mimi about anything, you'd get it, and you'd get it loud and clear. Once a person who thought he was a celebrity wanted the newest Harry Potter book the night before it was officially out. When Mimi refused, he said, "Do you know who I am?" Mimi said, "Yes, I know who you are, and you're not getting the book until tomorrow morning."

Mimi was not an electronic blip on a computer or a voice on a machine. Mimi was a friend right there in her store, ready to listen to you rave about a new writer, or to tell you in no uncertain terms why you wouldn't like a certain writer. She boomed, "I'm so glad you're back! How was your winter? Did your son get into Harvard? Did your knee operation work out?" She listened to your answer, and she cared. She truly cared. She knew all the town news and she couldn't wait to share it with you.

Mimi was the high school teacher who turned our lives around with a few choice words of advice. She was the Brant Point lighthouse guiding us toward pleasure on a gloomy afternoon. She was the mother who introduced us to Beatrix Potter and the old-timer at the bar who told us an outrageous off-color joke. She was a neighbor walking down a small-town street on a summer's afternoon, glad to stop and take time to chat with rich and poor, old and young. She was a wholehearted welcome on our loneliest day. She was *there*, and we knew we could go into Mitchell's and find her there, a reliable provider of comfort, wisdom, humor, and happiness, every day of our lives.

Mimi died in March 2010 at the age of 62. She was an iconic literary champion, a touchstone to reading, and as we enter into a faster, electronic, less personal world, we are at a loss without her.

NANCY THAYER is the *New York Times* bestselling author of *Summer Breeze, Heat Wave, Beachcombers, Summer House, Moon Shell Beach, The Hot Flash Club, The Hot Flash Club Strikes Again, Hot Flash Holidays,* and *The Hot Flash Club Chills Out*. She lives on Nantucket.

Michael Tisserand

Octavia Books, NEW ORLEANS, LOUISIANA

A day or so into the New Orleans Flood of 2005, I found myself on the phone with my wife's father. He's not somebody I normally would choose for unburdening, but it was no time for choosiness. My voice breaking, I cataloged the losses: jobs, schools, the chance to see our friends' faces. "It's all gone," I said, fighting back panic. "It's not all gone," he replied, speaking with the matter-of-fact tone of a scientist, which he is, and of a Latvian immigrant with childhood memories of displaced persons camps, which he has.

It was both the shortest and most reassuring conversation I remember from those days. Still, in the weeks when the road home was a closed highway off-ramp, despair remained a threat. Anxieties multiplied. The future involved more guesswork than planning.

I recall this now in an attempt to explain just what it felt like to walk through the door of Octavia Books on a Saturday evening in November 2005, just shy of three months after the frightful storm and the criminal levee collapse that we call "Katrina." Octavia was the first bookstore in New Orleans to reopen, and on this night there were hundreds of people crowded into a small, rectangular, shelf-lined room. The occasion was a reading for *Why New Orleans Matters*, a book-length treatise that was written in a white heat by my friend Tom Piazza.

There were reunions that night, both planned and unexpected. Tears poured even more copiously than the wine. My primary memory of the reading itself was a blistering passage about former first lady Barbara Bush, who had visited a shelter in Houston and commented that the evacuees on the cots "were underprivileged anyway," so it was all "working very well for them." I will never forget, nor will I ever want to forget, the feeling of standing together in that packed, humid, book-filled room, at one in that moment in our grief and anger.

That same night, I also met up with Bruce Raeburn, a Tulane University jazz historian. At Octavia, we hatched a scheme to dive into the flooded house of the jazz musician (and underappreciated author) Danny Barker. Although Barker had died several years earlier, his family had kept the house and its belongings intact, and we knew it was filled with priceless mementos and papers, now rotting in the Katrina muck. As we made our plans, I could hear other rescue missions being plotted all around us. Some, like ours, involved houses. More were about identifying and trying to save fragile psyches.

Nights like these would be repeated in the weeks and months to come, often with similar intensity. As more Katrina-related books appeared, readings at Octavia became something of a ritual. Chris Rose, Douglas Brinkley, Jed Horne, Josh Neufeld, Anderson Cooper, Dave Eggers, writers with the Neighborhood Story Project, and dozens more made their way to the wooden podium in front of short rows of folding chairs, and each took a turn leading the service. That Louis Armstrong song, the one with the line about friends shaking hands and really saying "I love you"? That was our hymn.

This is why Octavia Books is my bookstore.

Octavia is a relatively recent addition to a city where, I'm happy to report, independent bookstores are the rule, not the exception. The husband-and-wife team of Tom Lowenburg and Judith Lafitte opened their shop in 2000. I knew of Tom from his years with the local activist organization The Alliance for Affordable Energy, and although he and Judith are sweet and soft-spoken booksellers—complete with a shop dog bearing the musical-theater name of Pippin—there is an unmistakable aura of activism around the place. I've been at after-hours community meetings at Octavia, and Tom recently helped defeat a ridiculous piece of censorship-related state legislation. He's also a self-taught expert on the survival of local businesses in a big-box world.

Octavia is by no means the only New Orleans bookstore to recommend. I'm also partial to Maple Street Book Shop, where I once danced with the owner during my first-ever book release party; to Garden District Book Shop, especially for hosting an inspiring evening with George McGovern; and for Faulkner House Books, which occupies the same room where William Faulkner hashed out his early career with his neighbor Sherwood Anderson. Faulkner House is also home to the Pirate's Alley Faulkner Society, which sponsors the local Words & Music festival and much more. Also essential is Vera Warren-Williams's wonderful Community Book Center, where I once picked up a copy of the biography of Civil Rights pioneer Ruby Bridges. I gave it to my daughter, then in first grade. She wrote to Bridges, and Bridges replied with a letter that now is a family treasure.

We also have more than our deserved share of wonderful used-book stores, from musty French Quarter shops to the newer Blue Cypress Books. There's also a place I can't name, because my kids just call it "books, books, books" after a sign in its window. It stands across the street from Hansen's Sno-Bliz, which for more than seventy years has purveyed the city's finest sno-balls (shaved ice drenched in syrup). Our family tradition is that I wait in line for the sno-balls while the kids get to peruse the books, books, books. On a recent trip, my 10-year-old ended up with a strawberry sno-ball layered "lasagna-style" with condensed milk, and a book claiming scientific proof that space aliens exist. That was a very good afternoon.

New Orleans is a city of neighborhoods, and Octavia Books is named for the street on which it resides, which in turn is named for Octavine Ricker, the daughter of one of the many nineteenth-century scoundrels whose names still tag our city (nearby Leontine Street is named for Octavine's sister). The store is surrounded by mostly modest shotgun houses; one house around the corner offers a blinding lights display each Christmas. (Rick Bragg once opened a reading by noting that the lights display is the most impressive neighborhood institution, bumping Octavia Books to second place.) The neighborhood surrounding Octavia contains numerous bars, a yoga studio or two, and food joints like Hansen's (twelve blocks away), the tile-walled oyster palace Casemento's Restaurant (sixteen blocks away), and Domilise's Po-Boy and Bar (just five blocks away).

The mood at Octavia has changed in recent years. There used to be a Katrina table at the front of the store. I would habitually stop and check out each new title. I don't even know if it's still there, or if it has been reconstituted back to "books of local interest" or some such thing. Lately, I've noticed that more than one local author has started out a reading there with the sort-of disclaimer, "This isn't really a Katrina book."

> *We no longer cry when we step into the store. We buy books; we don't plot rescue missions.*

We no longer cry when we step into the store. We buy books; we don't plot rescue missions.

Yet it is impossible to forget what Tom and Judith gave us when we needed it the most. I was reminded of this at another reading at Octavia, this one on August 28, 2008. Just a few days earlier, Hurricane Gustav had formed off Haiti, and it was making its way across Cuba and into the Gulf of Mexico. We expected to evacuate the next day, but that evening I called Octavia to find out if a scheduled appearance by Tony DiTerlizzi, who cocreated *The Spiderwick Chronicles*, was still on. It was. While my wife packed our suitcases, I brought our two kids to the store. DiTerlizzi presented a master class on how to differentiate between dragons of Asian mythologies and those of European mythologies. My own kids took their turns at the easels to imagine their own dragons. The symbolism was not lost on the parents in the room, as we prepared to flee another monster storm of yet-unknown proportions.

That evacuation was, thankfully, brief. I don't know when the next one will take place, or how long it will last. We live in New Orleans, and so does Octavia Books. Whatever happens, I fully expect that we'll go through it together.

MICHAEL TISSERAND is the author of *The Kingdom of Zydeco* and *Sugarcane Academy: How a New Orleans Teacher and His Storm-Struck Students Created a School to Remember*, as well as a forthcoming biography of the cartoonist George Herriman, the creator of Krazy Kat.

Luis Alberto Urrea

Anderson's Bookshops, NAPERVILLE, ILLINOIS

I didn't get to grow up with a local bookstore. But my daughter did. When I was a kid, there was not only no bookstore in the 'hood, but no library, either. It wasn't until we left the barrio close to the border and got to a little dull suburb that I found the joy of a regular bookstore.

It was one of those little storefront shops behind the supermarket. Down from the barbershop where the old barbers were ignored by the hippies and trimmed the same granddads' crew cuts every week. Next to the coin-op laundry.

The bookstore was one of those shops with a cute name—Book

Nook or Second Time Around or Sally's Re-Readers. It was chock-full of used paperbacks, and you could buy them for a few cents, or you could trade Sally two books for one unread one. Heaven! My mom unloaded so many unwanted paperbacks there that we had a card full of credit in the little plastic box. I discovered John D. MacDonald's Travis McGee books there, thank you very much. And Elmore Leonard.

Nothing fancy, but magic in every dusty sneeze-inducing coffee-stained moldy section. Sally even had a raggedy shelf of profoundly unwanted poems. Yevtushenko! I tell you, this was a revolution to have a Russian lurking around behind Von's market.

I moved to the Boston area in 1982, and it was an orgy of bookstores. I went from zero to sixty in four seconds flat. Bookstores in Cambridge, Somerville, Waltham, Boston. I went two hours on the Red Line and the Green Line just to get to a bookstore off the beaten track. I was making up for lost time, I guess.

No wonder, then, that I became a writer. Everything about books was sacred and fun and self-indulgent—and every book was a new addition to my own self-made Ph.D. I had a Ph.D. in basement shelves.

It came to pass that I published a bunch of books, and they ended up in other peoples' favorite bookstores. I went on tour, visiting these great shops all over the country. I realized even then, when some people in Indiana knew of this new book awesomeness called Borders, that it was the independent booksellers selling my work. These smaller stores in neighborhoods were the only way a guy like me could connect with readers who did not know me or care all that much about my subject matter. I learned this new phrase they used: "Hand-selling."

I got better at it. My original one-client or zero-client book signings started to generate, oh, six, seven, even eight rabid fans. Stampedes, I tell you! And the hand-sellers acted as if it was a great evening and gave me tea and sold me haiku books and weird European books about talking fish. But they always invited me back. We have come a long way, those of us who have survived these hard years. A lot of those cherished spaces are empty now, and I wish everybody had grown up in a book desert so they would have cared for their neighborhood stores better.

And then I moved to Chi-town. It wasn't part of my life plan. My family was like a fairy-tale gone sideways. I was trying to get us all back up to the Rockies, where I had lived among some sweet bookstores and sweeter mountains. But my attention was caught by the University of Illinois, which offered me tenure if I would bring my writin' ways to the city. Yowza! A job they can't fire me from? I'm *there*.

We gravitated to Naperville. Thirty miles closer to the Rockies. (I'm doing things more gradually now.) It's a little gem of a town—a river, as they say, runs through it. A fat wild turkey seems to think itself sheriff of our street and patrols the houses, scolding parked cars that irritate its pin-sized mind. And downtown, that cool little downtown I never had, with old cowboy buildings and sparkling lights in the trees on the main street, there was this bookstore. Anderson's.

Went in. Loved it. Hung out there a lot. Was deeply proud when it won awards for general awesomeness. Hung out with Becky Anderson at various literary events around the country. Got to go to the thousands of book signings they sponsor and use my evil influence to go down to the basement to meet the literary heroes hiding down there before their readings. Thank you, Becky.

But this story is not about me. This story is about my daughter. She first entered Anderson's as a toddler. Can you imagine what that meant to me? My baby girl stumbling around, chewing on books and playing with the wooden train set they had in the front of the store.

It began at Anderson's. It didn't take long for our girl to turn from the huge stuffed animals and trains to the bright shelves. *Books!* She found books. She liked scary monster books, though she called them "cary mongers." And, at 18 months, had the bug bad enough that she'd listen to us read the stories, memorize them, and then hold the book and make believe she was reading them back to us. Out loud. Perfectly. Thank you, Becky.

Our daughter is now 12 years old. She has spent her entire child-

> *Our daughter is now 12 years old. She has spent her entire childhood among the turkeys and the trees and the shelves of Anderson's. I can chart the seasons of her life by the section of shelves we enter.*

hood among the turkeys and the trees and the shelves of Anderson's. I can chart the seasons of her life by the section of shelves we enter. Cary monger books followed by *Mr. Putter* and pop-up and *Goodnight Moon* books. And first chapter books: that series about the nutty little girl in fourth grade who always gets in some jam. And the Wimpy Kid. And onward! Yes! Talking cats! *Goosebumps*! Fantasy stories! *Twilight*! The epic of Katniss. I can step to every section of the bookstore and see my child there, serious as a chemist, working those shelves to find the perfect combination of subject, cover art, heft, color. Making magic stairways that lead her upward.

You will forgive me a small tug of melancholy now, as we see her move to the adult shelves and give them tentative scans.

Do you know what we did this week? We went to Anderson's so our daughter could meet R.L. Stine. She was bouncing off the roof—it was like taking her to meet a rock star. She took her ruined, favorite cary monger books with her. And they immediately fell into a discussion about the Tower of London and how creepy it was and how he'd put an element of it into one of her destroyed books and she shouted that she knew it, she just knew it! Then she told R.L. Stine exactly what part of the Tower he'd been thinking of.

I didn't have that when I was a child.

Thank you, Becky.

LUIS ALBERTO URREA is the author of, among other books, *The Devil's Highway*, *The Hummingbird's Daughter*, and *Into the Beautiful North*. Winner of a Lannan Literary Award and Christopher Award, he is also the recipient of an American Book Award, the Kiriyama Prize, the National Hispanic Cultural Center's Literary Award, a Western States Book Award, a Colorado Book Award, an Edgar Award, and a citation of excellence from the American Library Association. He is a member of the Latino Literary Hall of Fame.

Abraham Verghese

Prairie Lights, IOWA CITY, IOWA

I was at the Iowa Writers' Workshop from 1990 to1991. I spent so much time (and money) at Prairie Lights that even now, much of what is on the shelves in my study comes from that period.

And so many volumes I was guided to by the incredible and long-tenured staff who would plop a book into my hands and say, "You must read this." Or they would guide me to a specific author reading.

Jim Harris, who owned it then, and also Jan Weissmiller and Paul Ingram and so many others, were our professors in a way, shaping our sensibilities, but most important, treating us as serious writers, people with great potential even though, at that stage, we did not have that kind of faith in ourselves. What we had was hope and dreams and a love of literature and deep doubts as to whether anything would come of it all.

Prairie Lights was a relative bookstore newbie when I was there, being only about twelve years old. In a town full of bookstores, selling new and used books, it had a special connection with the Writers' Workshop, and a rutted path seemed to lead from one to the other. This was pre-Internet (at least for me). For years, until NPR had to pull the show in 2008 for economic reasons, the store was the location for *Live from Prairie Lights*, weekly readings hosted by Julie Englander of WSUI, broadcast from the bookstore's second floor.

I felt great pride in 2010 when I saw the front-page *New York Times* photograph of Jan Weissmiller—the new owner of Prairie Lights—escorting President Obama around the store. It was an impromptu stop on his health-care tour that year after he mentioned the store in his Iowa City speech, describing how businesses like these struggled to keep employees insured.

I have had the great pleasure of visiting Prairie Lights annually or just about. It is larger, grander now. What is new is its lively online presence (www.writinguniversity.org, where it also streams the readings each week) and a wonderful coffee house on the second floor—a space, Jan said she had learned recently, where the local literary society met throughout the 1930s, pulling in such glorious names as Carl Sandburg, Robert Frost, Sherwood Anderson, and E.E. Cummings, among others.

What has not changed is its mysterious core—a hush, a sense of reverence for the written word. The reading series, still named Live from Prairie Lights and taking place four or five nights a week, is always packed—anywhere from forty or fifty people and often more than a hundred. There is no audience quite like an Iowa City audience. Name an author, and he or she will likely have read there: Susan Sontag, Gloria Steinem, Annie Proulx, J.M. Coetzee, Kathryn Stockett, and poets Mark Strand, Jorie Graham, Galway Kinnell, and many, many more. To my great glee, *USA Today* named Prairie Lights

> *There is no audience quite like an Iowa City audience. Name an author, and he or she will likely have read there.*

a "destination bookstore" in 2008, along with such luminary stores as Powell's in Portland, Washington D.C.'s Politics and Prose, The Strand in New York, and City Lights in San Francisco.

For Iowa City's smallish community of some 70,000, Prairie Lights has an extraordinary and large presence and is thoroughly integrated into its community. This collaborative approach started with Jim Harris's farsightedness when he bought the store in 1978, and it's been a tradition Jan has continued since she and Jane Mead, a Workshop graduate with three published books of poetry, bought the store from Jim in 2008. Not only is Prairie Lights tied in to the Writers' Workshop, but, I am pleased to see, the store is also actively involved with the medical school there: Prairie Lights supports The Examined Life Conference of the University of Iowa Carver College of Medicine.

I always dreamed of one day reading at Prairie Lights, and when that moment eventually came with the success of my first book, *My Own Country*, I choked up—it was hugely significant to me to be reading there, in that space. It was an affirmation that was personal and private, yet one that I think every writer with an adopted store would understand. I read again with my recent novel, *Cutting for Stone*.

Independent bookstores have been crucial to the success of my books, and the word of mouth that a Paul or a Jan can generate—if they like what you have produced—is nothing short of phenomenal. Compared with online reviews, the credibility of someone who has worked in a store like this for ten or even twenty years is very strong. These folks are reading galleys every day and have their pulse on what is truly good. When I visit, I talk with Jan, and to Carol, who always had suggestions for my kids (she is the children's-books buyer), and of course to Paul, who is something of an institution in his own right and should be given a professorship at the Workshop. Paul came to and stayed at Prairie Lights in 1989 after earning a degree in linguistics, working in two university bookstores, and then deciding that the book life was the life for him.

I am honored and humbled to know people like these. Though I may live far away, whenever I need to imagine a place of peace, a place far from the mundane concerns of everyday life, a place where such concerns are transcended and reshaped into art, I picture myself pushing open the front door, seeing Jan's smile, hearing Paul hail me from the back...is this heaven? No, it's Prairie Lights.

ABRAHAM VERGHESE is the author of *My Own Country*, *The Tennis Partner*, and *Cutting for Stone*. A graduate of the Iowa Writers' Workshop, he has published essays and short stories that have appeared in *The New Yorker*, *The New York Times*, *The Atlantic Monthly*, *Esquire*, *Granta*, *The Wall Street Journal*, and elsewhere. He lives in Palo Alto, California.

Audrey Vernick

BookTowne, MANASQUAN, NEW JERSEY

I know I give the settings of my stories short shrift. The *where* never mattered as much to me as the *what* or the *who*. So it came as a surprise, when the time to launch my first novel into the world rolled around, that setting mattered more than anything else.

I readily admit that I have outsized envy for those who live in quaint towns with a charming main street—the pizza place where you're greeted by name, a bookstore whose owner holds behind the counter new releases she knows you'll love, the coffeehouse where they start pouring your cup as you open the door. In my mind's eye, I see the place where I always imagined I would someday raise my family near the beach, so there would likely have been a surf shop, too, and a vast expanse of Crayola blue in the background. Though the picture I see was drawn by a child's hand, the image was one grown-up me longed for.

But the actual real-estate transactions of my life paid no attention to the way my brain and heart had it planned out. We ended up in a suburban town with no main street to speak of. Life has a way of messing with our expectations. As a writer with a history of ill-timed publications, I should have been used to that.

This novel launch was the only time I'd gotten the timing right—a book for preteen girls being published when my daughter was 12—and I wanted to celebrate. And really, it had to happen in a bookstore. So I did what those who are not blessed with a hometown bookstore have to do: I adopted one.

Luckily, BookTowne was not only willing to be adopted by me, but the good people there actually seemed eager! And it was the perfect setting for the launch of my novel *Water Balloon*.

What made this event especially poignant was the fact that

> *Luckily, BookTowne was not only willing to be adopted by me, but the good people there actually seemed eager!*

both of us—writer and bookstore—were newbies, tentatively stepping into the world of bookstore promotions. BookTowne was new and small and just starting to grow its legion of fiercely loyal customers. I was a debut novelist. Our joint venture reminded me of the way my 5-year-old son had reached for his 5-year-old neighbor's hand when boarding the school bus for the first time. Brave—mostly brave—about stepping into this new big-kid world.

Though I had known where Manasquan was and had been there a time or two, I did not recognize it as exactly the child-drawn town I had meant to live in. In fact, it was my now-teenaged son who realized it. When visiting friends there, he felt that deep, contented sigh of a feeling I'd wanted his quirky, familiar hometown to provide.

BookTowne is a brilliant microcosm; it's all that is lovely about Manasquan, New Jersey, shrunken down into a small retail space. The store does not carry vast numbers of each title, which makes browsing there a lot like looking through the well-stocked bookcase of your smartest, funniest friend. It's that same sensation: *Oh! I wanted to read that book! OH! I read that—I loved that book!* Amazingly, the people hired to work there by owner Rita Maggio have the semi-magical ability to appear and offer help only when you actually want it.

This is not accidental good fortune. If Rita were to draw how she viewed Manasquan, her bookstore would be right at its heart. She knows that bookstores can radiate warmth in almost the same way the scent of baking bread can beckon a passerby into a bakery. She believes that every town has the right to a good bookstore.

But BookTowne is so much more than a good bookstore. In the weeks leading up to the launch, we worked together the way family does, building on each other's ideas and creating something we were all excited about.

That evening, we celebrated with a sparkling cider toast and homemade cookies that were intended to look like balloons but may have been mistaken for well-fed fish. My editor sent along a happy bouquet of balloons. There was a girly prize package that was ultimately won by my son's very ungirly 15-year-old friend. A male friend.

My recollections of that evening are bathed in a wistful yellowy light. I've yet to check the photos to confirm, but it hardly matters. It's my story, my setting.

When the time for mingling had ended and my reading was about to begin, Rita introduced me. It was clear she had read my book. This was nothing short of shocking to me. I had read reviews, but the book was still so new I had yet to hear anyone other than my writing friends, agent, and employees of my publishing company talk about it. She made it sound like a book I'd want to read, like one you'd find on the shelves of a store like BookTowne, something you'd find in a cool, well-read girl's backpack. It was a very touching, humbling moment.

While reading from the first chapter, I looked up and took in this beautiful yellow-lit space, filled to capacity with my family, friends, my son's friends, my daughter's friends—my perfect readers—and their teachers. There were these other people there too, adults and preteen girls. The friends of BookTowne. People who didn't know me, didn't know my book, but came to celebrate with us anyway. Because BookTowne is that charming bookstore on Main Street in their funky little town. The warm, welcoming heart of their community. The kind of store where book-loving people support a first-time novelist who adopted this store and loves it as though it were her own.

One of the great delights of **AUDREY VERNICK**'s professional life is that she can have earnest conversations with editors about whether a protagonist should be a pot-bellied pig or a square-lipped rhinoceros. She has written a number of picture books, including *Is Your Buffalo Ready for Kindergarten?* and the nonfiction *Brothers at Bat*, and the middle-grade novel *Water Balloon*. Audrey has also published short fiction for adults. She received an MFA from Sarah Lawrence College and is a two-time recipient of the New Jersey State Council on the Arts fiction fellowship. She lives near the ocean with her husband, son, and daughter. You can visit her online at www.audreyvernick.com.

Matt Weiland

Greenlight Bookstore, BROOKLYN, NEW YORK

"The Light"

With apologies to Edgar Lee Masters, Roger Angell, and the Beastie Boys

Where is the loner, the talker, the rent-controlled?
Where is the loud one, the Brooklynite, the heart of gold?
The boozer, the busker, the beat cop for the night?
All, all, are browsing in Greenlight.

One came on the G train, another on the C.
One took a car service way out in Coney.
One grabbed a cab while another took a bus.
One roared up in a motorcycle covered in rust.
Some found directions on the store's website—
All, all, are browsing in Greenlight.

Where is the shy girl, the fly girl, the boy turning five?
The toddler, the infant, the yet-to-arrive?
The teen with a Wiffle Ball, the kid with a kite—
All, all, are browsing in Greenlight.

One is making tea with Maisy,
while her friend reads to the bear.
One is by the bathroom saying, "Ma! My underwear!"
One is spinning Dr. Seuss books around on a rack.
One is in the hunt for Mo Willems paperbacks.
One gnaws on an everything from Bagel Delight—
All, all, are browsing in Greenlight.

Where is Nathan Englander and Jhumpa Lahiri?
Where's the summer intern whispering to Siri?
Where is Jennifer Egan and Sasha Frere-Jones?
Where o where is the soccer coach, late with the cones?
Where is Dan Zanes and Dan Yaccarino?
Where's the guy from Greene Grape with the jeroboam of Pinot?
Where is Amy Waldman and wide-lapelled Touré?
Where is that skinny designer reading Tina Fey?
Where is Johnny Temple and Meghan O'Rourke?
Where's the sci-fi geek, the unreconstructed dork?
Where is Jennifer Egan and James Hannaham?
Where is Sean Wilsey and Colson Whitehead?
Where is the Manhattanite longing for street cred?

The daydreaming dancer, glinting in limelight—
All, all, are browsing in Greenlight.

One is scanning bookshelves full of new hardcover fiction.
One is pacing round the store to fend off an affliction.
One is talking up the guy she saw the other week in shul.
One is flirting with a girl from 40 Acres and a Mule.
One has snagged a pepperoni slice from block-away Not Ray's.
His girlfriend, blushing red, is buying *Fifty Shades of Grey*.
It's getting very crowded here, the store is quite a sight—
All, all, are browsing in Greenlight.

Where is the grizzled pigeon and the spunky little squirrel?
Where is the guy who made that amazing Biggie mural?
Where's the sidewalk genius who thinks he's Emperor Augustus?
Where are the Black Veterans for Social Justice?
Where are the sous chefs from Pequeña and Habana?
Where are all the tourists from Boston and Atlanta?
The role-playing gamers, elf and monk and knight—
All, all, are browsing in Greenlight.

One is skimming pages of *The Taming of the Shrew*
One walks past the cookbooks and thinks of Smoke Joint barbecue.
One buys early Updikes—including *Rabbit, Run*—
So he can write an essay for a future *n+1*.
It's really filling up in here, it's starting to feel tight—
All, all, are browsing in Greenlight.

Where are Brette and Eleanor, Alexis and young Geo?
Where's the little boy whose first name ends with Z-O?
And where are Jessica and Rebecca—the dreamers and no-moaners,
The ones who made it happen, the partners, the owners?

Here they all are, a panoply of browsers
Ebullient on the shopfloor, like Alice Trillin saying "Wowsers!"
There are books from every publisher and every little press:
Books on baking and bonsai, charity and chess.
Books below the windows, books behind the door
Books up by the ceiling, and way down by the floor.
Books for every care and whim, books to match and mix
Books are what we're browsing in the shop at Fulton, 686.
It's neck by jowl in here, and yet it always just feels *right*—
All, all, are browsing in Greenlight.

MATT WEILAND is a senior editor at W.W. Norton & Company. He has also worked at Ecco, *Granta*, *The Paris Review*, *The Baffler*, and in public radio. He is the coeditor, with Sean Wilsey, of *State by State: A Panoramic Portrait of America* and *The Thinking Fan's Guide to the World Cup*. His essays and reviews have appeared in *The New York Times Book Review*, *The Washington Post*, *Slate*, *New York* magazine, and elsewhere. Originally from Minneapolis, Weiland lives in Brooklyn with his wife and son.

Stephen White

Tattered Cover Book Store, DENVER, COLORADO

Three can keep a secret if two of them are dead.

Or if one is a bookseller that recognizes the value of the unspoken word.

The wisdom in the first line is Benjamin Franklin's. The awkward qualification is mine. Years ago, as I fell in love with Tattered Cover the way thousands of other book lovers in Denver fell in love with Tattered Cover, I had no way to know a day was coming when I would need a great bookstore that could keep a damn secret.

But that day did come, and Tattered didn't disappoint.

I didn't know her then, but the reason that Tattered didn't disappoint was because of Joyce Meskis. Joyce believes that there is a right way to sell books, and to treat customers. She has a set of principles about bookselling that guide her vision, and she has a rock-solid determination to do her best to meet them.

Honestly? As I became a regular in the original store on the north side of Second Avenue in the seventies, the principles and vision of the owner were not on my radar. I just knew I adored the shop she created, a place where I would spend hours sitting on the stairs, looking at books.

Joyce was just one of the people who would ask me to please scooch over a little bit.

. . .

Although there's a good chance my name rings no bell—my first editor told me that I had the misfortune of being born with a pseudonym—I have written almost twenty novels, a few screenplays, a single lonely short story, and some number of essays.

But for most of my adult life, long before my first novel found its way to Tattered's shelves, I was a guy enamored of books. In Denver, loving books means some degree of devotion to Tattered Cover.

Writing had not been a lifelong goal. The aspiration came late. I began to write in secret. My wife knew. My toddler-aged son knew (in his toddler way). But that was it. As pages accumulated and my effort began to look suspiciously like a manuscript, I finally admitted to myself that I was probably writing a book and that I definitely had a dream. But the dream—to publish a novel, and maybe even, *ha*, to write for a living—felt like a fantasy, and often like a vice. As a practicing psychologist, I knew enough about vices to keep evidence of mine to myself.

To shed my ignorance about the steps, creative and practical, necessary to enter the marketplace of writers, I eschewed attending writers conferences and writers groups and creative writing classes. Instead I chose to teach myself about writing the way I had learned almost everything since my father started dragging my brothers and me to used-book stores when I was a kid.

I read.

Long addicted to fiction, I had a comforting history with the wonders of the creative side of what I yearned to do. But the practical side? How to negotiate an introduction to the mostly New York world of publishing houses and literary agents?

If you find yourself with the kind of need I had—or really any urge that requires knowledge or guidance or wisdom or inspiration or reflection or escape, any of the things that literature, little *l*, or Literature, big *L*, can provide—I hope you have the great fortune that I had to live within blocks of a bookstore like Denver's Tattered Cover.

At my fingertips I needed a lovingly curated collection of the best fiction from all the greats who came before, as well as a selection of the most questionable fiction from the not-so-greats who came before. Tattered Cover had all that for me.

On the business side, as I became inclined—and I did—to want to read a dozen *How To's* (...*Get Published*, ...*Write a Novel*, ... *Negotiate a Contract*, ...*Pen a Query Letter*). Or all the *Memoirs of* ..., or the *Biographies of* ....

Tattered had those.

I would also need access to all the advice that had been offered writer-to-writer since, say, Fitzgerald, F. Scott, in addition to the latest wisdom and the freshest counsel published only days or weeks before. Back in 1989 there was no Internet to search; all the books I might need would have to be in stock. Visible and available. On a shelf. So that I could browse them, and peruse them, and choose them, and own them.

Tattered had me covered there, too.

The opium den where I fed my addiction was a tiny elbow of shelves, maybe four feet by four feet, on the top floor between the elevators and the bathrooms, across from the endless titles that comprised the store's collection of non-genre fiction.

A cardboard sign marked my alcove—I felt some ownership; I

was almost always alone up there—as *Writing*.

To me, it might just as well have been called *Dreaming*.

. . .

The Tattered of that phase of my life was the iteration that filled a converted four-story department store from plaster to plaster and from floor to ceiling with books.

The shop was immense, but it never felt as big as it was, though sometimes on weekends and during book signings and always around the holidays it somehow managed to feel not quite large enough.

That edition of Tattered—I consider it the third but others insist that depends on how you count—was a place where I occasionally went to locate a specific title, but where I usually went just to be around books. To discover new books. To be entranced.

Tattered was a great bookstore by then. While no one—certainly not Joyce Meskis—intended for it to be anything more than a great bookstore, it somehow became much more than that to Denver.

For locals, the big Cherry Creek Tattered Cover became an anchor, a destination, even an institution. That Tattered on First Avenue became our city's crossroads, our town square, our community center. For two decades the glorious big Tattered kept the beat of our collective urban heart.

It was a lot to ask from a bookstore. By then, though, we'd been spoiled by Tattered Cover for years. We had come to expect a lot from Joyce's place.

. . .

Other than in size, and perhaps in degree of wonder, the First Avenue store wasn't much different from its predecessors, or from the Tattereds that would follow.

It had been years since Tattered busted out of the pleasantly cramped first home, the one that Joyce bought in the mid-seventies on the north side of Second Avenue. Then too fast, like a teenager outgrowing shoes while they are barely scuffed, Tattered shed its bigger, second location—the expansive, partly subterranean store across

Second Avenue—and moved to the palace less than a block away. Most things stayed constant at Tattered as the locations changed. The bookmarks, for sure. The collections, though growing, always felt right. The carpet. All Tattered Covers have green carpet. The green is a certain hue that is more Celtic than British Racing, more warm than daring. It is not a spring green; when I settle into a chair with a book in Tattered it is always summer transforming into fall.

The bookcases. Tattereds share distinctive, darkly stained knotty pine bookshelves that reach high above the head. Some of the cases line walls, a few stand back-to-back to create islands in the green sea. Most butt end-to-end in short runs, or break into perpendicular turns that lead to alleys. Those lanes might truncate in a wide cul-de-sac, or meander like the rows of a corn maze through book-cluttered spaces.

Another constant? Yes, be careful. You must always watch your step in Tattered.

The unpredictability that is Tattered means that locating a specific section inside any store requires a good memory, an experienced guide, or a well-drawn map. The alternative, getting lost, leads to the joy of discovery. By design, discovery is its own reward.

Long before it was fashionable for booksellers to encourage leisured browsing by customers—or extended reading or occasional napping by customers—Tattered provided ample nooks to hide in, plenty of overstuffed chairs to get lost in, and old sofa after old sofa to snuggle next to your kid and read her a book in.

It was all part of Joyce's vision.

As was the staff that executed that vision. The staff in Tattered Cover became as familiar to me as were the carpet and the shelves. I saw the same helpful faces, store after store, year after year. The staff, I was sure, recognized me as a regular—one of thousands of contented anonymous Tattered regulars. But in the many years before I began dreaming that a book of mine might someday be found on Tattered's shelves, I would have been surprised to learn that any staff member in the store knew my name.

What I knew about the staff wasn't complex. They read more than I did. That meant they read a lot. Intuition seemed to inform them when I was just looking, which was usually. But engage one of them on the floor with a question or a request for guidance and any staff member would talk books with you, patiently. Find books for you, eagerly. Ask what you had liked, recently. Tell you about books they loved, passionately.

. . .

A day arrived that my dream of becoming a writer transformed into my determination to be a writer, and that metamorphosis, too, crystallized at Tattered.

Some book in my hand, I was perched at the edge of a tread on the wide staircase that led from the first floor to the second in the big First Avenue location. A few feet away, through pine spindles, I overheard a woman, a staff member I had seen many times, speaking with a man I didn't know about something about which I knew nothing.

I listened impolitely, captivated.

Their conversation was hardly private. That big staircase in Tattered was no place to keep a secret in Denver. It was Main Street for anyone in town who loved books, or who knew someone else who loved books, or who wanted to raise a child who loved books, or who was interested in having a thing, intellectual or profane, with someone who loved books.

The woman in the conversation was a "buyer" for Tattered. The man was a "rep" for Random House. He was selling titles from his "fall list" of forthcoming books. She was buying new books to fill Tattered's endless shelves. I knew little of book publishing or bookselling then, but my ignorance didn't concern me. I was assembling a fine collection of Tattered-supplied reference volumes at home. I could look up the details.

The impromptu meeting was no hard sell; the buyer seemed to be buying everything the rep was selling. Yes, he took notes about her orders—three of this, two dozen of that—but their interchange did not seem to be about commerce, buying and selling.

> *The consequence of what I heard that day was tucked in the tangents between the affirmations of the buys, in the illuminating back-and-forth between two people whose lives were focused, in that moment, on their mutual love of books.*

It was about books. And authors. His excitement about what was coming. Her joy about what she had just read. And what galleys from other publishers were near the top of the stack beside her bed, the ones she couldn't wait to get to. What he was trying to convince her she had to read next.

The consequence of what I heard that day was tucked in the tangents between the affirmations of the buys, in the illuminating back-and-forth between two people whose lives were focused, in that moment, on their mutual love of books.

That was the day my dream became my determination. The day I knew I had to do whatever I could to become a writer, to earn membership into the world of books, a world that included a place like Tattered Cover, so I could know and work with and be among people who loved books as much as that woman, that buyer, loved books.

But I hadn't earned it. Not yet. I was not ready to reveal my dream about becoming a writer. Until I was a writer. With a contract.

And that truth about my aspiration leads back to the part about why I needed a bookstore that could keep a damn secret.

. . .

Once I, or you, carried a book to any staff member at any cash register for purchase at Tattered, the passionate, opinionated, hyper-knowledgeable, book-loving staff would become mute about the titles that comprised the purchase.

The familiar staff at the register at Tattered never once offered a single comment to me—not of approval, not of wonder or curiosity, not of judgment or disdain—about any book I was buying. If the staff had figured out that that I was busy accumulating the most comprehensive home collection of guides for prospective writers that might exist west of the Mississippi—and I was sure they had—they never breathed a word that they recognized my plans.

"*Are you interested in writing?*" Never asked. Not once.

"*What are you hoping to publish? Fiction? Nonfiction?*" Never asked. Not once.

It was no different for any other customer. If the book you were buying was about baby names, or erectile dysfunction, or the history of lesbian erotica? No comment.

The latest Grisham, or an early Bellow? No comment.

"Romance" as in bodice ripper, or *Romance* as in the Durants, *The Story of Civilization, AD 1100–1300*? Not a word. Ever.

If your desire on any day, or your need on any day, made a difference to the person at the cash register, you would not know it. Not from their words. Not from the look in their eyes. The curiosity that drew you in Tattered's door, or that developed as you browsed—the curiosity of yours that deserved to be sated by a book—is held in trust at Tattered Cover.

In that green-carpeted pine-shelved store full of cushy furniture, the act of buying a book is as privileged as a whisper to a coconspirator, or a secret shared with your priest or your rabbi.

One of Joyce Meskis's principles of selling books the right way is her insistence that no customer should ever feel the *slightest* hesitation about carrying any purchase to a cash register. Any purchase. Not the slightest hesitation.

How sacrosanct are her principles? Once challenged by the government to reveal the specifics of a purchase, Joyce Meskis went to court to protect her customer's right to privacy.

I would guess 99 percent of customers didn't care, or didn't notice, that their transactions were completed without comment at Tattered. But the 1 percent? They cared.

Meeting the needs of everyone who entered her store was part of Joyce's principle about selling books the right way.

. . .

We can argue about whether Tattered is the best bookstore of a generation—based on a dozen metrics, it is certainly part of the conversation—or even which Tattered was, or is, the best of the bunch. (I am prepared to make a case for stores one and three and four and six, but don't make me choose only one. I can't.)

You won't win the arguments. I won't lose. In the end it doesn't matter. There are multiple Tattered Covers now, each with its own charms. The quality of the stores in other locales that book people count as peers of Tattered—it's a short list—only confirm that Tattered's reputation in the world of books is not mere legend.

But any discussion about the bookseller with the most indelible vision about how to sell books the right way, any discussion about the most principled bookseller in an industry full of great role models, or any discussion about the single most influential bookseller of our lifetime?

Those discussions start with Joyce Meskis, and her Tattered Cover.

Stop by when you're in Denver. Browse for a while. Pick up a book, maybe something controversial.

The book will be your secret.

Tattered Cover? It's ours.

New York Times best-selling writer **STEPHEN WHITE** (authorstephen-white.com) is the author of 19 crime novels. Tattered Cover is his neighborhood bookstore. How cool is that?

Joan Wickersham

The Toadstool Bookshop

PETERBOROUGH, NEW HAMPSHIRE

When it comes to bookstores, I'm polygamous. I love the one I'm with. Like Mozart's Don Giovanni, who adores fair ladies and dark ones and the old and the young, I am passionately susceptible to the many different ways in which a bookstore can entice—a basement full of remainders, a fireplace, a window overlooking a river, a table display that opens your eyes to books you've never noticed before, a weird little back room full of used books in which you discover a copy of something you've been craving for years. But I confess to having a special tenderness for The Toadstool Bookshop in Peter-borough, New Hampshire.

The Toadstool is huge and it wanders.

It has a room devoted to new books; another that is a broad, deep, and quirky used-books store; and a third, smaller room filled with CDs and films.

It also has a café, tucked into its own space apart from the books, avoiding that awkward jostling bookstore-café thing where the book browsers feel like they are disturbing the soup eaters and vice versa.

> *When it comes to bookstores, I'm polygamous. I love the one I'm with. …But I confess to having a special tenderness for The Toadstool Bookshop.*

It is welcoming and juicy and inexhaustible. No matter how long you spend there, you leave vowing to stay longer next time.

But admirable as these assets are, I fell in love with The Toadstool because it's right down the road from the MacDowell Colony, and my experience of the store is bound up with the happiness of the time I have spent writing at MacDowell.

A MacDowell residency is a time of intense solitude and utter freedom. You are given a studio, meals, and a place to sleep. Your time is yours to structure in any way you want. During my first residency, in the fall of 2004, I quickly fell into a rhythm of waking early, hiking over to my studio, making tea and listening to music and plunging into my work before the sun was up. My writing took off in a way it never had before. By the middle of the afternoon, I would be excited and exhausted, ready for a break; and I would head down the hill into the town of Peterborough, where I would inevitably find my way into The Toadstool.

It was November, and I remember I bought a lot of books to give as Christmas presents. And I bought a CD by Anonymous 4 called *Wolcum Yule*, an album of serene and austere old carols that I played over and over in my studio. But as tempted as I was by The Toadstool's bulging shelves of fiction and biography, I don't think I bought a single book for myself. I was listening to the voice of my own book telling me what it wanted to be; I couldn't afford to become distracted by another writer's preoccupations and cadences. The store was rich and packed, alluring; I was falling in love with The Toadstool, but we were careful not to become too deeply involved. We exchanged longing glances but acknowledged that the timing was wrong.

The MacDowell residency ended, and I went back home but never quite forgot about The Toadstool. I talked about it in a wistful paradise-lost kind of way, especially to my older son who in his late teens had become an avid comber of bookstores. He would mention a writer he was hooked on—David Goodis, Chester Himes—and I would say, "I bet you could find more of his books in the used section of The Toadstool." Finally one morning we got in the car and drove up to Peterborough. After all that advance praise The Toadstool could have been a disappointment, but my son and I were both enthralled. He came away with a shopping bag full of used noir-ish novels, and I bought a stack of recent fiction to make up for all those books I'd denied myself during my time at MacDowell.

. . .

I have been lucky enough to return for several more MacDowell residencies since 2004. When I am working at MacDowell, I visit The Toadstool almost daily, in that edgy, wistful, look-but-don't-touch way, exhilarated and refreshed by the presence of the books and the bookstore but careful not to let myself become lost in other writers' voices.

And my son and I have continued to make regular pilgrimages up to Peterborough to shop at The Toadstool. He heads straight for the used section, where he amasses an armload of novels, sits in a chair to sift through them, and generally ends by buying them all. I try—and fail—to cover the entire store. Speaking of failure, some of my most vivid Toadstool memories are of books I saw there and failed to buy: the complete poems of Joseph Brodsky, an old edition of Willa Cather's *The Professor's House* (Cather wrote at MacDowell and is buried in nearby Jaffrey, New Hampshire; her books often show up in local bookstores, but you don't often see *The Professor's House*, unlike the strangely ubiquitous *Death Comes for the Archbishop* and *Sapphira and the Slave Girl*). But I've had many more successes: other Willa Cather novels; a boxed set of four volumes in the George Braziller "Great Ages of World Architecture" series for my husband; several old children's hardcovers—*Shadow of a Bull, The Witch of Blackbird Pond*—each of which has caused the staff person at the register to say, "Wow, I wonder if the owner even knew this was here," making me feel that I am getting not only a treasure, but a bargain, a diamond priced as rhinestone.

But although I am happy to enjoy The Toadstool as the sunny book-buyer's banquet it is, I always have a poignant moment at the checkout counter when I catch sight of the nearby shelves devoted to books by MacDowell Colony Fellows. It's an exciting collection of work—poems, novels, short stories, plays, works of history and biography and journalism and criticism. My books are there, the new one I wrote during my last few residencies and the one I was working on in 2004, mingled with other books I first heard about when their authors were still struggling to figure out how to tell the story. "How was your day?" is a frequent question around the dinner table at MacDowell. The answer is "Great" or, sometimes, "Awful," but there we all are, doggedly ready to head back to our studios the next morning. I always find, looking at those shelves in The Toadstool, that I am longing to be back at MacDowell, deeply engaged in the trance of my work.

And that, really, is what I love about The Toadstool. There, more than in any other bookstore, I'm aware of writers and of writing. Those shelves of books by MacDowell writers, some of whom are working just up the road while my son and I are happily buying new things to read, remind me that every book in the store—every book in every bookstore and every library—was once a work in progress.

JOAN WICKERSHAM is the author of *The News from Spain: Seven Variations on a Love Story* and *The Suicide Index*. Her op-ed column appears regularly in *The Boston Globe*.

Terry Tempest Williams

The King's English Bookshop, SALT LAKE CITY, UTAH

In Salt Lake City, Utah, The King's English is more than a phrase about proper speech; it is a place where speech is honored, free speech in particular. Betsy Burton, its proprietor, is more than a bookseller; she is a community advocate.

"Local First" is not just a slogan she uses for supporting local businesses within her hometown, but a philosophy she extends to include local writers. I am fortunate to be one of The King's English Bookshop's local writers. When my husband and I moved into our first home on 1520 Garfield Avenue in 1977, we lived within walking distance of Betsy's store.

> "Local First" is not just a slogan she uses for supporting local businesses within her hometown, but a philosophy she extends to include local writers.

Fourteen years later, I published *Refuge: An Unnatural History of Family and Place*, a book about the historic rise of Great Salt Lake and the corresponding death of my mother from ovarian cancer. Part memoir, part natural history, it is a story of love and loss, women and birds. When it was published in the fall of 1991, Betsy Burton invited me to read from *Refuge* at The King's English. Salt Lake City is a small town where my family is known. The book was personal.

My perspective was on the page. I believed the men in my family deserved to be heard from their point of view. Betsy listened to my concerns and agreed to have a family panel instead of the traditional reading and book signing. The panel would consist of my father, John Tempest, and my brothers, Steve, Dan, and Hank.

This is what I remember:

The King's English was packed. Bookshelves had been moved to the side. Chairs were set and the men in my family were seated behind a table. I introduced my family and stepped to the side.

My father spoke first. Picture him as the Marlboro Man without the cigarette—tall, dark, and direct. "As most of you know, my daughter has written a book about Great Salt Lake and my wife's death. I'm not happy about it." He pauses as his emotion surfaces. "It's easy for her to say what a wonderful experience Diane's death was, but she could leave. I couldn't. Terry was there during the day and went home at night. And she isn't the one who now sleeps alone. It's easy for her to romanticize the situation and turn it into poetry, but I am the one who's left. This isn't some fictional story. It's my life." Another pause. "And as far as Great Salt Lake goes, it's a cesspool covered in flies. We all know that once you've seen it, no one ever goes back if they can help it. Terry's got a flair for exaggeration. Maybe this book will help some people. That's all I have to say."

No one in the chairs moved.

My father sat down. My brother Dan stood up, a graduate student in philosophy at the University of Utah, and for the next twenty minutes read his dissertation on Wittgenstein and the covert uses of language. His abstract language interspersed between mathematical equations went right over my head.

Next was Hank, my youngest brother. He was short and concise. "I don't remember that much because I was…" And as he finished his sentence, I flashed back to our family entering rehab together to support his sobriety.

I looked at Betsy. And she looked down as she covered her mouth.

Steve, ever the peacemaker, and closest to me in age, defused the growing discomfort and simply bore his testimony in the Church of Jesus Christ of Latter-Day Saints as he spoke of his love for Mother and how he believed he would see her again. "Mother died as she lived—with grace."

I could not speak. Betsy did and thanked everyone for coming.

What I remember is that people left quickly. I signed very few books.

Now, Betsy and I can laugh about it. So can my father, who loves Betsy and was in a close relationship with the manager of The King's English for almost twelve years.

This is all to say that we are family. Every Christmas Eve, my father buys each person in our expanding family a book that Betsy recommends. He signs each novel or biography or cookbook and passes them out as the first gifts of Christmas Eve.

And it was Betsy Burton's mother, Fran Minton, the curator of education at the Natural History Museum of Utah, who gave me my first real job as assistant curator of education right before she retired. I worshipped her. She was a woman as blunt and smart as my father. We come from rough-hewn western stock where intelligence is gauged not only by the books you have read, but by the way you have been taught to read the land, the weather, and each other.

Betsy Burton and I have come to read each other. Local first. We have become sisters in our love of words. Literature has shaped us and gathered our voices in the name of community—literature and the sage-brushed landscape buttressed by the Rocky Mountains that we call home.

The King's English is home. The place where I always return. The place where Betsy Burton not only sells my books, but edits them. The place where independence lives and freedom of speech thrives. The King's English is where my family has gathered in grief and celebrated in joy.

TERRY TEMPEST WILLIAMS is the award-winning author of 14 books including *Leap, An Unspoken Hunger, Refuge, Finding Beauty in a Broken World*, and, most recently, *When Women Were Birds*.

Simon Winchester

The Bookloft, GREAT BARRINGTON, MASSACHUSETTS

Nobody likes a strip mall. They are the cheerless inventions of those cheerless creatures known as "developers." Most often they—the strip malls more than the developers, one has to suppose—are diabolically ugly. They are built gimcrack, and they usually sport the cheap varnish of the ephemeral. They alter and usually spoil the internal workings of the towns they so parasitically surround. They were all built in blind fealty to the automobile. Most of us surely wish that strip malls just didn't have to exist.

But they do; and there are the usual swarm of them around the charming old western Massachusetts railroad town of Great

Barrington, near where I live. Great Barrington, which lies in a shallow river valley in the southern Berkshire Hills, is a settlement of some antiquity, and a place that no less than the *Smithsonian* magazine has lately declared to be the Best Small Town in America. It was given the award for being what we locals all know it to be: an eminently habitable and strollable little omnium-gatherum that manages to mix architectural charm, culinary energy, and a sound and lasting commercial success.

So it will surprise no one to learn that it is a town with a cheese-monger, a café run by a couple from Normandy, and a hardware store that sells antique brass tools. It has a toy shop and a candy store, and there is a place run by two men who always wear shorts and who will enlarge old pictures taken on black-and-white film. It has two great diners and a grocery store where you can buy Cooper's Oxford marmalade and baguettes. It has one of the best bagel stores beyond the Lower East Side.

But what Great Barrington does not have in its town center is a proper bookstore. Other than mine, that is, which is a full half-mile away from Main Street and has been set down for all of its existence in a strip mall.

So the first thing to say about The Bookloft (other than that it is one of only three remaining proper bookstores in Berkshire County and is still going strong after more than 35 years in business) is that it is not your imagined small-town bookshop. No mullioned bow windows, no thick carpet and coal fire, no cat on the counter, no sleepy clerk dozing before his opened volume of *Dombey and Son*. It stands instead rather modestly between a hairdresser and a telephone store—there is a GNC store and a nail salon a little farther away, and a dollar store, a Kmart and a supermarket beyond them. And it has an architectural style that, to put it kindly, is entirely consonant with the look and feel of the mall around it.

But once through the door—a positive Aladdin's cave! A sanctuary, a private and never-seething lectorium. It is just packed, with groaning shelves jostling against shelves, with thousands upon thousands of just-what-I-always-wanted and I-really-must-take-a-look-at-that and the-review-said-it-was-brilliant books.

A subset of the ten or so staff, some full-time, some hauled in for duty when there's a rush, greet newcomers from the desk, as if they were the chefs in a Japanese restaurant. You approach, glancing at the stack of bottles of homemade maple syrup on the impulse-purchase side. Have you got? you ask, and almost without demur, and seldom with recourse to the monitor at the desk's far end (beside Biography, across from Classic Fiction), one or all the staff will say something akin to I'm sure we have a copy, back there, around that corner, second shelf up—have you found it yet?

They Know Books at the Bookloft, as the best of the independents do, and as most of the chains never need to. The staff there read; they know; they anticipate. They scan all the trades, the blogs, the Twitter feeds. The handwritten Staff Picks: a fifth of all sales come from such suggestions. Hand selling is the order of the day. They know their customers, they know their tastes, they are ever prepared for demographic quirks they have never imagined. Books on Somali cuisine? On uses for argon? Knitting on Anglesey? Tort reform in Albania? Little seems to faze or escape the jackdaw minds of those whom Eric Wilska has been employing here since he first opened the store, in what was the then-very-new strip mall, in 1974.

He was something of a free-spirited, tie-dye-and-THC kind of youngster back then. He remembers, if cloudily, that he was either

> Have you got? *you ask, and almost without demur, and seldom with recourse to the monitor... one or all the staff will say something akin to* I'm sure we have a copy, back there, around that corner, second shelf up—have you found it yet?

going to open a free school or a bookstore, and that a few lungfuls of chemical magic swiftly decided him on the shop idea.

No bank would lend him a dime, of course; but his grandfather loaned him $3,000, and somehow he managed to get a lease on a small mall space a few yards away from where he runs the business now. He gathered perhaps 4,000 titles to offer, and in those first days had only a salvaged cable spool as the store's central table and gathering spot.

His grandmother made the first sale: *Diet for a Small Planet*, by Frances Moore Lappé. Just as you might expect, though Ms. Lappé's book is still in print today, and one might look at that particular sale as a harbinger, of sorts, a forecast of the kind of book and the kind of customer that this clever little store has been managing to bring together ever since. *The Pentagon Papers* sold well in those first few years; the official report on the Watergate affair; and *Helter Skelter*. "All blockbusters," mused the craggy wraith that Eric Wilska has now become. His manager, a bearded and ever-quietly-smiling-to-himself bear of a man, Mark Ouillette, agrees. "A great help."

These two men, a kind of literary dog-and-pony show, have managed—with the invaluable help of Eric's wife Ev, a fiction writer and reader of formidable perspicacity—to keep this uniquely successful independent store up and running through all the bad times that have been brought serially to them and their kin by the men in black hats, the now-slowly-receding-in-the-mirror Mr. Barnes and Mr. Noble and the now-still-on-all-sides, everywhere, Mr. Bezos. How they have done it is a mystery to all, not least to them, too. "It can't be our management skills," grinned one or other or both of the pair, pleading incompetence. "We wouldn't hire ourselves if we came here looking for a job." All they can suggest is that their success—the first months of this year were the best ever, despite all the other trends elsewhere—is born of a formula compounded of having a huge stock (30,000 titles), a remarkably gifted staff, and a deep and abiding loyalty both to, and of, the customers.

All of that, plus the maple syrup and the maps; their links to their second store, secondhand-only, a few miles away in West Stockbridge; their friendly acceptance of all new technologies; and their ready awareness that theirs is perhaps the most literate and literary corner of the American world. Herman Melville lived up the road. W.E.B. Du Bois just down the street a ways. Roy Blount, Jr., is nearby. Edith Wharton was a few miles away. Edna St. Vincent Millay. Pauline Kael. Ruth Reichl. The names keep on coming—and those of their number who are living and fit enough in these parts come and speak at the Bookloft, as ready recompense for the pleasure that they all admit to savoring in coming here to shop.

That they are all here conjoined—the writers and their bookstore, the book-loving customers and their formidably well-read army of booksellers—underlines the point that Eric Wilska likes to make: that this is a *community* bookstore, providing a much-needed service for a community that, as he believes and which all of us pray is true, simply could not and will not countenance the vanishing of one of the last truly great independent bookstores in the country.

And if this precious place happens to be lacking a mullioned bow front window or two, and has to exist sans a cat napping on the Agatha Christie shelf, but is in fact down from the dollar store and a step away from a Vietnamese nail salon, who truly cares? Just so long as it is here, and stays here until we are all gone, and long after. It is the kind of place that almost makes the notion of strip malls acceptable, provides the very idea with some kind of commercial blessing, and is a literary benison for us all.

SIMON WINCHESTER is the best-selling author of *The Professor and the Madman*, *Atlantic*, *The Map that Changed the World*, *Krakatoa*, *A Crack in the Edge of the World*, *The Man Who Loved China*, *Skulls: An Exploration of Alan Dudley's Curious Collection*, and more than a dozen other books. His work has appeared in *The New York Times*, *The New York Review of Books*, *National Geographic*, *Lapham's Quarterly*, and elsewhere. Mr. Winchester was made Officer of the Order of the British Empire (OBE) by Elizabeth II in 2006. He lives in New York City and Massachusetts

Afterword

1. I've spent a lot of time on tour these past few weeks, moving from bookstore to bookstore across the United States and into Canada. Book tours are wonderful and tiring and lonely. Touring America without a driver's license involves a lot of time in sketchy Greyhound stations and pleasant walks through strange towns in search of the bookstore where I'm supposed to read that night. There are long hours in buses bound for cities I've never seen, taxis between bus stations and hotels, peaceful interludes in airports, the occasional train. It's tiring, but I feel very lucky and there are things that I love about it.

What I love, specifically, are the independent bookstores where most of my events take place, this archipelago of books scattered over the landscape. I grew up surrounded by books, and my apartment in Brooklyn is filled with them. When I was a child I was in love with Laughing Oyster Bookshop, the wonderful independent bookstore that's still my favorite shop on all of Vancouver Island, and to this day stepping into a bookstore feels a bit like coming home.

What I don't love, what I find disorienting and a little flat, is the crushing sameness of the spaces between cities and towns. The highways of South Carolina look startlingly similar to the highways of Vermont. The outskirts of nearly every town look more or less the same. The same big-box stores, the same retailers' names in the interchangeable malls, the same ten or twelve restaurants with the same logos shining out in the twilight.

I don't mean to suggest that this flattening of the contemporary world is a uniquely American problem. Here and in other countries, the story's always the same: We were lured to the outskirts of town by lower prices, but the low prices always came with hidden costs. The old downtown shops that we liked on principle but didn't get around to visiting very often couldn't compete anymore and went out of business. There are concrete reasons why this phenomenon has hurt communities, statistics concerning the greater amount of money that stays in a community when a purchase is made in a locally owned store versus a national chain, differences in contributions to local charities by locally owned versus non–locally owned businesses, a lowering of the tax base when wages in a community are driven down. But there's another, less tangible loss. When every town has exactly the same small handful of businesses, it starts to look exactly like every other town. The things that make a given place uniquely *itself*, the things that made it different from all the other places on earth, begin gradually to erode.

"Amazon isn't bad," a bookseller of my acquaintance said on Twitter, two or three years back. "Monoculture is bad."

2. I'd thought originally to write this as a pure celebration of independent bookstores and not mention Amazon at all, but when there's an elephant in the room it seems only polite to introduce it.

Once we were lured to the edges of town by the big-box stores; now we're lured to the Internet, and if we're buying from a massive corporation, the effect is the same. The thing about Amazon is that it's the opposite of independent bookstores. Independent bookstores tend to reflect the personalities and eccentricities of their owners, managers, and staff—some divide books carefully by genre; some shelve Arthur Conan Doyle in the same section as Ray Bradbury and Charles Dickens *because it's all literature, dammit*; one that I know of makes a distinction between Fiction and Literature, and yes, there may possibly be a moment of fleeting doubt when one arrives in town to discover that one's books have only made the fiction shelf. Some bookstores sell only crime fiction and sci-fi. Some have cats.

All are driven more by a love for books than by a love for money, because let's face it, the margins are low, and most have display space set aside for staff picks, where the store's booksellers get to feature the books they've personally fallen in love with. Get a few of these people in your corner, authors are told, and your book just might succeed, or if not this book then perhaps the next one you write or the one after that. Even if you're published by a small press, even if you're published by a large publisher who's decided to devote all of the season's marketing dollars to someone else, even if none of your books have sold especially well in the past.

There are no staff picks on Amazon, because there are no *people* on Amazon. That is, naturally there's an enormous fulfillment staff to keep the boxes moving, and naturally there's a corporate structure in place, but when was the last time you walked into Amazon and got into a conversation with a bookseller about this new book that you probably hadn't heard of before but that the bookseller thought you might really like?

The closest Amazon can come to this experience is the "You might also like…" algorithm, which is useful to an extent but of course has the terrible weakness of only being able to suggest books that are in some way similar to the books in which you've already indicated an interest. You're not picking up a book on a whim and then buying it because even though it's not your usual thing, the cover caught your attention or a bookseller pressed it into your hands and there's something about it that speaks to you. You're being presented with a preselected menu of books that an algorithm has decided are somewhat similar to books you already like. If at least one of the reasons to read is to expand the mind, a point is being missed here.

But if Amazon has had a largely negative influence on the literary world for publishers and the writers who publish with them, the argument sometimes goes, it's been a boon for readers, a source of cheap books that arrive on one's doorstep the following morning. If it's put scores of bookstores out of business, we're told, it's because Amazon has a better business model than those bookstores ever did.

These arguments tend to ignore a number of uncomfortable realities: Amazon derives a considerable competitive advantage from tax evasion, it undercuts the competition by selling books at a loss, and serious questions have arisen regarding the way it treats the employees in its fulfillment centers. These unpleasant details aside, I wholeheartedly reject the notion that a bookselling monopoly is in any way good for readers. I believe that a healthy and vibrant culture, literary or otherwise, depends on diversity. I don't think it's in anyone's best interest for writers or books to come to our attention from only one source.

In her keynote address at the American Booksellers Association Seventh Annual Winter Institute, held in New Orleans in 2012, Ann Patchett discussed the tour for her first novel. She had two missions, her publisher told her: to sign stock and to make friends with booksellers. The point of the tour wasn't the audience, which for most debut novelists is sparse to nonexistent. She was sent out on the road to meet the booksellers, and specifically, because bookstore owners and managers tend not to be there in the evenings, the girls—there are some guys, but they're outnumbered—who work the cash register. The idea being, she said, that "if I made nice with these girls…after I left, [they] would read my book, and [they] would hand-sell my book."

By the time of her breakout novel, *Bel Canto*, a foundation had been laid. Booksellers all over the country fell in love with the book. They knew who she was because she'd spent hours with them. Independent bookstores are personal. It's clear to me when I read through this collection that things happen in independent bookstores that don't happen in the other places where we buy books.

Every time an independent bookstore closes, the literary and cultural landscape becomes less diverse. I hope there will be a time when Amazon can coexist more easily with the bricks-and-mortar bookstores in this country. There's an argument to be made that Amazon's current business practices are no longer even in Amazon's best interests, since every closed bookstore represents one fewer place that might potentially be persuaded to stock the titles from Amazon's new publishing imprints. For the rest of us, a less diverse literary world means fewer people who read and recommend books for a living, fewer staff picks, fewer possibilities for new writers to be brought to our collective attention.

3. But this is no time for a requiem. This seems a perilous moment in publishing and in bookselling, and yet the American Booksellers Association reports that its membership has been slowly but steadily increasing. A December 2011 press release reported "more than 1,900" current members. Which is bleak in comparison to its membership numbers from the 1990s, but on the other hand, there were only 1,400 members in 2009. The ABA credits a growing Buy Local movement and exceptional entrepreneurship. *The New York Times* reports that Greenlight Bookstore, which opened in Brooklyn in 2009 and instantly became one of my favorite bookstores, reported sales of over $1 million in its first year.

I had the spectacular good fortune of visiting Shakespeare and Company in Paris last week. My French publisher had installed me in a nearby hotel for a week of interviews and receptions and photo sessions. On the second or third day there was a break in the schedule, and my husband and I set out to find the bookstore with the feeling that I imagine very religious people must feel when they leave their hotel, map in hand, in search of a nearby holy site.

Shakespeare and Company doesn't disappoint. It's a labyrinthine place with books crammed into every possible corner, narrow beds among the shelves upstairs, and a sink in a corner with a sliver of dried-out soap for the Tumbleweeds, the itinerant writers and readers who stay for a while in exchange for a couple of hours a day of work in the store. There are books that seem to have been on the shelves for decades. There are notes pinned to a wall, an old typewriter in an alcove. Movement is somewhat complicated by the crowds. There are too many people there, but on the other hand, they all love books.

A white banner over the door memorializes George Whitman, who opened the current iteration of Shakespeare and Company in 1951 and died last year at the age of 98. He considered himself the heir to Sylvia Beach, who opened the original Shakespeare and Company in 1919 and closed it permanently during the Nazi occupation of Paris. Whitman's dates of birth and death are noted, above what might be his most famous quote: "The business of books is the business of life."

Cynics will dismiss him as a hopeless romantic, among the last of his kind, but that quote has a ring of familiarity about it. It makes me think of the other booksellers I've met, my contemporaries in every way, who've welcomed me into their stores. They are intelligent, interesting, and dedicated to books. Theirs isn't an easy business, but it's still possible, and they're still making it work.

I've heard too many times that the demise of bookstores is inevitable. I've lost count of the number of obnoxious Internet comments I've read along the lines of "Bookstores are dead, e-books are the way of the future, accept it."

This raises a number of obvious points: Firstly, there's no reason whatsoever why e-books and independent bookstores can't coexist, and secondly, new bookstores open all the time and some of them are wildly successful. But finally: *Accept* it? Why should we? Why would we passively accept the idea of a less varied and more monocultural literary landscape, why should we accept the idea of losing the Shakespeare and Companies of this world? Or in this country, the McLean & Eakins, the Northshires, the Morris Book Shops, or their equally vibrant counterparts in other cities and towns? I don't think we have to. I don't think we should.

4. There's a bookstore on my street in Brooklyn that's been in operation for forty-one years. When I moved to the neighborhood a few years back, Community Bookstore had an air of neglect about it. I found it a little depressing and rarely went in. It has new co-owners now, Stephanie Valdez and Ezra Goldstein, and watching them revitalize the store has been an immense pleasure. I attended the store's fortieth birthday party last year and understood how the previously neglected little shop had persisted for so long.

They had borrowed the church across the street for an afternoon of readings. I wondered privately beforehand if the choice of venues wasn't a little ambitious—it's an enormous church, one of those massive grey-stone affairs that loom all over Brooklyn—but when I ventured in a few minutes before the afternoon of readings was scheduled to begin, the place was packed. There were hundreds of us, all here because we loved the store and loved the books and wanted to hear some readings. All of the readers were excellent, because if you're Paul Auster or Jonathan Safran Foer or Siri Hustvedt then you've had a certain amount of practice in public speaking by this point, but I was especially struck by something Nicole Krauss said.

She had recently returned from a national tour for *Great House*, and she began telling us about conversations she'd had with a few people along the way who'd told her that they buy only e-books. When asked why, they told her it was because it was more convenient. She found this interesting, she said. When, she asked, did convenience become the most important thing?

I personally have no quarrel with e-books and believe they'll continue to coexist with print, but there's something in Krauss's sentiment that resonates. I think it applies to the decision of how and where we buy our books.

There was a time when we—all of us, the general public—were referred to as citizens. At some point this shifted, and now we're mostly called consumers. I have some real problems with this change, because while citizenship implies rights and responsibilities, to my mind consumerism mostly just implies shopping.

And yet shadows of the original word remain. The word *consumer*, I've come to realize, comes with its own intimations of responsibility, in that it reflects a very basic fact of life in a capitalist society, which is that we get to change the world we live in by means of where we spend our money. This concept is hardly new, but if it happens that you're someone who enjoys having a bookstore in your town, I would argue that it's never been more important.

—Emily St. John Mandel, 2012

Bookstores by Location

Alabama
The Alabama Booksmith, *Birmingham*
Page & Palette, *Fairhope*

Arkansas
That Bookstore in Blytheville, *Blytheville*

Arizona
Changing Hands Bookstore, *Tempe*

California
The Capitola Book Café, *Capitola*
Book Passage, *Corte Madera*
Warwick's, *La Jolla*
Kepler's Books, *Menlo Park*
Books Inc., *Palo Alto*
Vroman's Bookstore, *Pasadena*
Green Apple Books, *San Francisco*
The Booksmith, *San Francisco*
Chaucer's Books, *Santa Barbara*
Bookshop, *Santa Cruz*

Colorado
Explore Booksellers, *Aspen*
Tattered Cover Book Store, *Denver*
Maria's Bookshop, *Durango*

Connecticut
Bank Square Books, *Mystic*
The Hickory Stick Bookshop, *Washington Depot*

District of Columbia
Politics & Prose Bookstore

Florida
Books & Books, *Coral Gables*
The Muse Book Shop, *DeLand*

Georgia
Eagle Eye Book Shop, *Decatur*

Iowa
Prairie Lights, *Iowa City*

Idaho
Chapter One Bookstore, *Ketchum*

Illinois
Anderson's Bookshops, *Naperville*
The Book Stall at Chestnut Court, *Winnetka*

Kansas
Watermark Books and Café, *Wichita*

Kentucky
Carmichael's Bookstore, *Louisville*

Louisiana
Octavia Books, *New Orleans*

Massachusetts
Brookline Booksmith, *Brookline*
Harvard Book Store, *Cambridge*
Porter Square Books, *Cambridge*
The Bookloft, *Great Barrington*
Mitchell's Book Corner, *Nantucket*
Nantucket Bookworks, *Nantucket*
Broadside Bookshop, *Northampton*
The Odyssey Bookshop, *South Hadley*
Bunch of Grapes Bookstore, *Vineyard Haven*

Maine
Longfellow Books, *Portland*

Michigan
Nicola's Books, *Ann Arbor*
Saturn Booksellers, *Gaylord*
McLean & Eakin Booksellers, *Petoskey*

Minnesota
Magers & Quinn Booksellers, *Minneapolis*
Micawber's, *St. Paul*

Missouri
Left Bank Books, *St. Louis*

Mississippi
Lemuria, *Jackson*
Square Books, *Oxford*

North Carolina
Flyleaf Books, *Chapel Hill*
Park Road Books, *Charlotte*
The Regulator Bookshop, *Durham*
Purple Crow Books, *Hillsborough*
Quail Ridge Books & Music, *Raleigh*
City Lights Bookstore, *Sylva*

New Hampshire
The Toadstool Bookshop, *Peterborough*

New Jersey
BookTowne, *Manasquan*
Watchung Booksellers, *Montclair*

New York
Greenlight Bookstore, *Brooklyn*
The Community Bookstore, *Brooklyn*
WORD, *Brooklyn*
Talking Leaves Books, *Buffalo*
McNally Jackson Books, *New York*
St. Mark's Bookshop, *New York*
Strand Bookstore, *New York*

Ohio
The Book Loft of German Village, *Columbus*

Oregon
Powell's City of Books, *Portland*

Pennsylvania
Chester County Book & Music Company, *West Chester*

Rhode Island
Island Books, *Middletown*

South Carolina
Fiction Addiction, *Greenville*

Tennessee
Parnassus Books, *Nashville*

Texas
BookPeople, *Austin*

Utah
The King's English Bookshop, *Salt Lake City*

Vermont
Galaxy Bookshop, *Hardwick*
Northshire Bookstore, *Manchester*

Washington
Eagle Harbor Book Co., *Bainbridge Island*
Village Books, *Bellingham*
Third Place Books, *Lake Forest Park*
The Elliott Bay Book Company, *Seattle*
University Book Store, *Seattle*

Wisconsin
Next Chapter Bookshop, *Mequon*
Boswell Book Company, *Milwaukee*